WHAT DOES THE FUTU
YOU DON'T NEED A CRYSTAL
HERE ARE FOUR EYE-OPENING

BACKLASH...

Women lose their gains and it's back to a man's world—with a vengeance. In this *Handmaiden's Tale* society, women are veiled, oppressed, and sexually exploited.

UTOPIA...

Women rise rapidly up the economic ladder through the help of genderless computer technology and science...and bring creativity, conflict-solving, and world peace along with them.

STATUS QUO...

The more things change, the more they stay the same in a sluggish global economy where wealth stays in the hands of a few and women do double duty at home and in the office.

SEPARATISM...

The loss of individual rights in favor of society's pushes women into becoming the ultimate special interest groups, taking male lovers but setting up businesses, communities, and families by themselves.

"[READING *THE FUTURES OF WOMEN*] IS LIKE HEARING FOOTSTEPS OVER YOUR SHOULDER."
—*St. Louis Post-Dispatch*

11/17

Please turn the page for more critical acclaim...

"McCorduck and Ramsey inform, amuse, and at times disturb with these scenarios of women's possible future condition."

—*Kirkus Reviews*

❖

"Ahead, the best of times; ahead, the worst of times. Only by such a vivid imagining of alternative futures—from the unthinkable to the yearned for—can fear and desire and common sense be harvested for positive change for women and for men."

—Mary Catherine Bateson, author of *Peripheral Visions*

❖

"This book sets out alternative futures so clearly that the value of equality for women leaps off the pages. The insights provided here will help both women and the business community look anew at the future."

—Felice N. Schwartz, president emerita, Catalyst, and author of *Breaking with Tradition*

❖

"This insightful book fills a gaping hole in the literature of the future. No one has ever explored the future for half of humanity in as thoughtful, comprehensive, systematic, and imaginative a way before."

—Peter Schwartz, chairman, *Global Business Network*

❖

"The story of women today is that we are reaching out to all ages and colors and classes, men and women. This is new. This is global. This book takes us beyond today to look at the power of this new movement worldwide and how we can transform our planet into a less scary, more people-friendly environment."

—Bella S. Abzug, co-chair, Women's Environment and Development Organization (WEDO)

PAMELA MCCORDUCK is the author of *Machines Who Think* and the bestselling *The Fifth Generation*, among other books.

NANCY RAMSEY is a former legislative director to Senator John Kerry and coauthor of *Nuclear Weapons Decision-Making*.

———————

THE GLOBAL BUSINESS NETWORK (GBN) is the think tank in Emeryville, California, that predicted both the 1970s oil crisis and the collapse of the Soviet Union. Its scenario-planning methods have helped governments, policymakers, and business leaders create effective strategies for the future.

ALSO BY PAMELA McCORDUCK

Familiar Relations (novel)

Working to the End (novel)

Machines Who Think

The Fifth Generation
(with Edward A. Feigenbaum)

The Universal Machine

The Rise of the Expert Company
(with Edward A. Feigenbaum and H. Penny Nii)

Aaron's Code

ALSO BY NANCY RAMSEY

Nuclear Weapons Decision-Making
(Priscilla McLean, ed.)

THE FUTURES OF WOMEN

SCENARIOS FOR THE 21ST CENTURY

Pamela McCorduck

AND

Nancy Ramsey

WARNER BOOKS

A Time Warner Company

Warner Books Edition
Copyright © 1996 by Pamela McCorduck and Nancy Ramsey
All rights reserved.

This Warner Books edition is published by arrangement with Addison-Wesley Publishing Company, Reading, MA 01867

Warner Books, Inc., 1271 Avenue of the Americas, New York, NY 10020

Visit our Web site at
http://pathfinder.com/twep

 A Time Warner Company

Printed in the United States of America
First Warner Books Printing: May 1997

10 9 8 7 6 5 4 3 2 1

Library of Congress Cataloging-in-Publication Data
McCorduck, Pamela
    The futures of women : scenarios for the 21st century / Pamela McCorduck and Nancy Ramsey.
      p. cm.
    Includes bibliographical references and index.
    ISBN 0-446-67337-4
    1. Women—Social conditions—Forecasting.   2. Twenty-first century—Forecasts.
I. Ramsey, Nancy. II. Title.
HQ1233.M374 1997
305.42'09'05—dc21

96-46351
CIP

To our husbands, Joseph Traub and Russell Schweickart,
who offer existence proofs of the second scenario

CONTENTS

PREFACE

The Futures of Women had its genesis as a project for the clients of Global Business Network, Emeryville, California. The core business of GBN is the production of future scenarios for corporate, government, and nongovernment long-range planners. Though scenarios help GBN's clients to imagine the future, their real purpose is to help planners make decisions in the present.

The principals of GBN are often referred to as members of the celebrated Shell Oil team that in 1968 "foresaw" the steep rise in oil prices when everyone else was assuming price stability and then in the early 1970s "foresaw" the collapse of the Soviet Union. In fact, they didn't foresee either event. In each case, they examined the predetermined elements and identified what they viewed as the driving forces. Then, with remarkable acuity and intuition, they thought through the possible outcomes of interactions between the predetermined elements and driving forces, including the unlikely and unthinkable. Out of this process the team produced a number of scenarios. That oil prices would rise and that the Soviet Union would collapse were just two of these scenarios. Thus they were prepared when, if not the unthinkable, certainly the unexpected came to pass.

Before apartheid was dismantled in South Africa, GBN associates conducted secret meetings to lead very high level representatives of all the main factions through the scenario process. South Africa's future is hardly assured, but without the scenario process, which convinced rigid ideologues on all sides that obstinacy was suicidal, the progress South Africa has already achieved might have been impossible.

We feel lucky to have learned scenario planning from the experts.

• • •

Scenarios begin with those most concrete of entities, numbers. Sometimes the numbers concern people (their ages, the number of children they have, their income, or how many years they have—or will have—spent in school), the painstaking work of census takers and demographers. Sometimes the numbers are dollars, yen, Deutschmarks, or Swiss francs. These numbers are some of the predetermined elements that scenario creators consider (though even these are subject to unforeseeable change: for example, a major war or the outbreak of a virulent disease could wipe out much of a generation). Scenario creation continues with an examination of trends—some long term, some short term—with the scenarist asking which trends might persist and which might be anomalies.

When we look at women, for example, is the international (but not universal) trend toward more women seeking higher education, obtaining professional training, and joining the workforce likely to continue? A century ago, Western women began reducing the number of children they bore, and the first signs that this is occurring elsewhere are showing up. Will what has proved to be a long-term trend in the West also be a long-term one elsewhere in the world? What about the relatively new but significant Western trend toward childbirth without marriage? Will this cross-country, cross-economic-class trend persist in the West? Will it also be taken up elsewhere?

As we point out in the introduction to this book, though scenarios are grounded in current research, the art of scenario creation comes in imagining the different ways that predetermined elements and trends might interact, combined with a sensitivity to possible trends that have not yet announced themselves loudly and to the impact of technological innovations poised to enter and possibly transform our lives. All these factors are embedded in the larger world, which is itself changing.

• • •

In 1993, GBN wanted to present its clients with a provocative window on the future as revealed by the changing status of women over the next twenty years. We began with a private online computer conference hosted by Pamela McCorduck that ran for approximately three months, October through December 1993, followed by a face-to-face meeting in New York City that same December, organized by Nancy Ramsey. Our two gatherings were intended to examine facts and trends, destroy complacency, and provoke thought about the role of women in the next fifteen to twenty years. Both meetings included male and female, straight and gay, and international participants.

Our two conferences, on-line and face-to-face, produced many interesting ideas, foremost among them that most women are years ahead of most men in thinking about changing roles. Most men are just now beginning to say to women (in effect), "You really mean it." Many men are confused; some are resentful. They consider themselves decent and good at heart and are pained to be perceived as obstacles. On the other hand, they also realize that the privileges their sex enjoyed for centuries are threatened with extinction. One of our participants, a social anthropologist doing work with Generation X, reports that confusion about sex roles is just as rife among the twenty-somethings as it is in older generations, though the flavor is somewhat different.

To our frustration, both conferences often got stuck in emotional issues. When, at one point, McCorduck could not move the computer conference participants past such emotions to think about the future, she realized that unfinished emotional business will play a much larger role in how the future shapes itself than anybody now believes.

Our conferences also revealed that some men are much too eager to replace the old myths with new ones. Nobody said these things in so many words; rather, such notions came out in the course of discussions among men and women. We called them "emergent themes and counterthemes." Here are a few:

• • •

SOME MEN: Don't do it the way we did it—do it the way we want you to do it.

SOME WOMEN: The habit of giving orders is hard to break, isn't it?

•

SOME MEN: Things are really a mess. Rescue us.

SOME WOMEN: You bet. Just as soon as we put on our own oxygen masks, we'll turn to those of you who need help putting on yours.

•

SOME MEN: Women do things so much better. So much nicer. Everybody knows women's management style—power sharing, consensus, and consultation—is superior.

SOME WOMEN: Appreciate us, but please don't sentimentalize us. You may be in for a big surprise.

• • •

The on-line conference was daily evidence that men especially are anguished about these impending changes. In all decency and sincerity, most want to see change happen, but at no personal cost to them, please. These highly successful men articulated the words most men barely dare to think. Are men becoming obsolete? Is there any hope for marriage? Who will look after the kids? Who will look after *men?* Won't women do a better job managing the world on the whole? Please? In her five years of experience with on-line conferencing, covering topics that varied from First Amendment rights and pornography to the future of the global economy, McCorduck had never seen so much raw emotion on a computer screen.

Our face-to-face meeting, on the other hand, provided exhilarating evidence that women and men working as respectful partners can envisage a world that meets, even exceeds, our rosiest expectations. Most people left that meeting believing that the coming changes didn't have to be an issue of "your gain, my loss"; instead, it was possible that everybody could benefit in a world that preserved gender differences without preserving gender inequalities.

We consider our two conferences, and now our book, as the first steps in a collaborative learning process where women and men everywhere will enrich themselves by their participation.

ACKNOWLEDGMENTS

We have taken ideas from everywhere, especially from our friends and the people kind enough to sit for interviews. We owe first thanks to Global Business Network in Emeryville, California. It was GBN that introduced us to each other, and GBN also introduced us to scenario techniques for business planning. We especially thank Napier Collyns, who insisted, over our initial doubts, that the futures of women would lend themselves to scenario techniques, and who gave us the opportunity to try things out with GBN's international clients at a two-day GBN meeting in New York City in December 1993. Danica Remy and Nancy Murphy at GBN were colleagues, confidantes, and supportive friends. However, we take full responsibility whenever in this book we have willfully departed from scenario scripture.

We owe special thanks to those who have read versions of this book in whole or in part and given us helpful comments: Russell Schweickart, Myra Stark, and Lael Stegall. John Mathiason at the United Nations not only provided statistics for us, but he helped us interpret them, and in preparation for the meeting that gave birth to this book, Michael Hampden-Turner and Karen Greenwood trolled the Internet for us.

Conferences we attended poured information and suggestions into our ears. Especially useful to us were the Islamic Women's Conference, Washington, D.C. (September 1994); the Global South Conference, Washington, D.C. (May 1995); the First Women in Technology International Meeting, Santa Clara, California (July 1995); and the UN Fourth World Conference on Women, Beijing, China (September 1995). Nancy Ramsey attended the latter in the flesh; while Pamela McCorduck attended virtually on the Internet.

Colleagues at the Santa Fe Institute were ever patient in leading us along new paths of science: special thanks to W. Brian Arthur, Stuart Kauffman, and Chris Langton.

Here, in alphabetical order, are the friends, colleagues, interviewees, and sources who have generously given us their thoughts: Bella Abzug, Mary Catherine Bateson, Maya Berger, Ruth Berkowitz, Nilde Boggia, Raymondo Boggia, Danielle Bridel, Allison Coolbrith, Christine Cooleridge, Edward Feigenbaum, Rachel Fine, Anne Fitzgerald, Ari deGeuse, Judith Greber, Meenakshi Gopinath, Susan Hager, Lina Hamardeh-Banergee, Charles Hampden-Turner, Jonna Harlan, David Harris, Barbara Heinzen, Arlie Hochschild, Miriam Kelber, Anne Kolker, Mia deKuijper, Rachel Kyte, Jaron Lanier, Merle Lefkoff, Michelle LeVille, Frances Loden, Jon McIntyre, Clovis Maksoud, Fatima Mernissi, Don Michael, Joyce Miller, Vicki Otten, Rhona Rapoport, Shahra Razavi, Ivana Ristic, Ninotchka Rosca, Lynn Rosenzweig, Robert Salmon, Adrienne Santa Cruz, Felice Schwartz, Russell Schweickart, Rhonda Roland Shearer, Lawrence Smith, Myra Stark, Lael Stegall, Beverly Talbott, Meredith Tax, Gunnel Thorsten-Ham, Christian Timothy, Joseph Traub, Emily Tucker, Abigail Turin, Jonathan Weiner, the Women on the WELL, Richard Wu, and Carol Yost.

Two personal assistants helped Pamela McCorduck move this

book through all its stages: first, Edie Thurrell, and then Celeste Neland.

Deep thanks are owed to our agent, Katinka Matson, whose own vision helped push ours along, and to our editors at Addison-Wesley, Nancy Miller and Eleanor McCarthy.

We decided early in the writing of this book that footnotes would be more distracting than helpful, but a savvy reader can easily map our ideas to our sources in the bibliography.

The Official Future Will Not Take Place

In September 1995, in the unlikely location of Beijing, China, the largest-ever international meeting of women (more than 30,000 of them) came together—from Haiti and Mongolia, from Papua New Guinea and Finland, from India and Ecuador, from Tunisia and Canada—to plan their own future and the future of women everywhere. In jeans and saris, in veils and dreadlocks, they moved in with everything from baby strollers to Internet uplinks, determined to subordinate the issues that divided them so that they could concentrate on taking action to remedy their common problems: poverty, economic development, education, health, violence against them, and their less-than-fair share of power in everything from families to national governments to the United Nations.

Despite difficult physical circumstances, the meeting became a forum where national presidents and the wives of presidents, vice presidents, prime ministers, and Nobel laureates shared platforms with village weavers, midwives, computer programmers, and environmental activists. Though they had many ideas for action, their touchstone was the United Nations' own Universal

Declaration of Human Rights, adopted by the General Assembly nearly fifty years earlier, subscribed to by every member nation, at least in principle. Women's rights were human rights, the women in Beijing asserted. It was long overdue for the articles of that brave universal declaration to be extended to women and girls—who were "not guests on the planet," as Gertrude Mongella, the Tanzanian secretary-general of the conference, put it. The document that would emerge from this meeting would lay out in detail how this was to be accomplished.

Surely part of the self-confidence that delegates and representatives of the non-governmental organizations exhibited in Beijing rested on the success of a UN meeting held just a year earlier in Cairo. There, at the UN Cairo Third International Conference on Population and Development, for the first time in history, the world's women had seized their future from the hands of those who had always planned and acted for them—the international bureaucrats, the government functionaries, the professional population experts, the religious hierarchies—nearly every one of those bureaucrats, functionaries, experts, and clerics a man. In Cairo, women declared to the international community that change in the relations between men and women was no longer a distant possibility but a present fact.

In well-organized preliminary meetings and at the Cairo conference itself, women argued that none of the past schemes crudely imposed on them by professional planners had worked, and more of the same would not work either. Only comprehensive health care for all women and girls (including reproductive health), preferably offered by other women, sensitive to the local culture—only that, coupled with nutrition and education for girls equal to that given to boys, could hope to stop the catastrophic population wave that threatened to swamp Planet Earth. Anyway, population issues aside, women and girls were entitled to these by virtue of being human.

It was argument from experience; it was argument from common sense; it was argument from ethics by the people who would be, so the women knew, most immediately affected—women themselves. Over the fierce resistance of an alliance of the Vatican, fundamentalist Islamic mullahs, and grumbling world population bureaucrats, the argument prevailed. The final document laid out a mandate for comprehensive health care for all women—the first ever.

A year later in Beijing, the media noted the numbers of women who had gathered (ten times the number of the previous UN World Conference on Women in 1985) and marveled at their technological sophistication. Documents were uploaded to a central electronic site regularly so that anyone could read and comment; a lively electronic salon permitted women from all over the world to log in via the Internet and have their say too (plus have some fun: Australia put its *Geekgirl* 'zine on-line, complete with "broad-band" jokes; Technomama logged in from Austin, Texas, as did cyberpranksters St. Jude from California and Poptart from Bowling Green, Ohio; the Electronic Witches logged in from Zagreb, and so it went). The media, meanwhile, concentrated on the stars and celebrities who arrived to speak.

What most journalists failed to mention—perhaps failed to notice—was the degree of political sophistication that the world's women now possessed. The lofty but toothless declarations on behalf of world peace and brotherhood of man were gone. In their place were concrete, step-by-step plans that would give women access to everything from clean water to loans to start their own businesses; methods for pressuring governments to educate all children, girls and boys alike; strategies for organizing across borders in a globalized economy; workshops on how to weave gender strategies into national and international policies; how to ensure women's property rights; and presentations of examples that worked: education via satellite for women and girls who couldn't travel to schools; women's computer networks to exchange information in Tunisia, Ukraine, Brazil, and the Philippines. Above all, the meeting hammered out a bill of rights for women. Despite its nonbinding nature, expectations were high that the bill of rights would have a strong political and social impact.

No one who watched the meetings at Cairo or Beijing believed for a moment that women would be permitted to claim their own futures without challenge. Self-determination, human rights, equality before the law—the entire pious bouquet of international goodwill has seldom been tossed women's way. All around the world, West and East, North and South, both men and women have been astonished and affronted to think that it might. Nevertheless, this was the message, first from Cairo and then, more firmly yet, from Beijing.

Sure enough, in the following months, all those threatened by the very idea of women's equality and, worse, autonomy (particularly organizations that for centuries had rested on male entitlement), reacted. In the United States, presidential candidates denounced affirmative action as unneeded and unfair (just as they had previously denounced the Beijing meeting as a leftist women's plot), while in Algeria Islamic fundamentalists stepped up their campaign to torture and murder Algerian women simply because they were women.

But for would-be saboteurs, it's surely too late. A vast and unprecedented transformation has already taken place, a change that few institutions, in the West or anywhere else, have begun to assimilate, a change that no one fully understands. That change is inside the heads of women—not only inside the heads of Western women, who have been among the first to feel it, but inside the heads of women elsewhere in the world too. A Bangladeshi peasant has a revolutionary insight: "I am more like my husband than I am like my cattle." An African woman raises her eyes: "I am entitled to this land I farm and I will not accept less." A Hispanic woman in the barrio folds her arms across her chest: "No. Now and forever, no."

All over the world, women recognize this internal change in themselves, and they are preparing to seize—if forced, they will battle for—their own futures. When the full depth of this change is widely understood, even more powerful reactions will come. But should women be temporarily impeded, suppressed, and denied, the world will not revert to its old ways, where women were obsequious and accepted male entitlement without a murmur. It is too late, far too late, for that. Women's transformed view of themselves, combined with other global seismic shifts—the restructuring economy and the rapid spread of information technology—means that this is a very new future we all face.

• • •

This book takes it from there.

It offers four main scenarios of how the future might look. But unlike the Official Future, the one we meet nearly everywhere else, in periodicals and best-sellers, where women are invisible except as the delivery system for the dreaded population bomb, our scenarios focus on the lives of women. Our scenarios even contrast with the version of the Official Future that many women secretly harbor, of gradual but inevitable equality. We ask what might happen if certain trends were followed to their logical ends under various economic and political conditions, and we consider the new technologies that are also poised to transform our lives.

Our scenarios encompass women worldwide because despite their luxuriant differences, the world's women have identified and aim to solve common problems: their poverty, their unequal access to nutrition and health care, the violence against them, unequal opportunities for education, the denial of their reproductive rights, and underrepresentation in their own governments. Politics and economics will profoundly affect how each of these problems is met, and scenarios let us imagine how that might happen.

Nearly everyone understands that change is inevitable. Nearly everyone would like a chance to influence the shape of that change, however. Scenarios permit us to see how the choices each of us makes in the present are linked to outcomes twenty years in the future. Imagining these four possible futures today gives us a means of grasping the consequences of choices and gives us hope of influencing the course of events. As futurists, moreover, we see signs that the connections between people over time and space that we once only sensed will soon become more and more discernible, even provable. Like the famous butterfly in Brazil whose wingbeat causes a storm in Chicago a month later, the woman who slips across a border from a poor country to a rich one, baby slung across her back, carries our destiny to us.

Women in the twentieth century, and perhaps more in the twenty-first, are emblems of change—and now they are agents of it, as well.

THE OFFICIAL FUTURE WILL NOT TAKE PLACE

The Official Future will not take place.

For women this is good news, because they are conspicuously absent from the Official Future. Study the work of such respected futurists as Paul Kennedy (*Preparing for the Twenty-First Century*) or Peter Drucker (*Post-Capitalist Society*) and ask yourself where half the world's population goes after it gives birth to ever more children. Even such popular futurists as Alvin and Heidi Toffler generally subsume women into a homogeneous, unisex future.

Those books that do address the future of women (Naomi Wolf's *Fire with Fire*, or Patricia Aburdene and John Naisbitt's *Megatrends for Women*) confine themselves to American women, and furthermore the authors take a relentlessly upbeat stance. All of us can certainly hope the future will be wonderful, but we'd better be prepared for alternatives.

Finally, most studies that address the future also tend to be cheerily (or gloomily) dogmatic: this *will* take place. But it won't. At least, not the way you think.

WOMEN'S OWN VERSION OF THE OFFICIAL FUTURE

Although women are generally absent from the Official Future, many women harbor their own secret version. It runs something like this: There will be a slow but nevertheless inevitable progression toward gender equality. Did the Equal Rights Amendment die? Was affirmative action strangled in the alley? Never mind, one by one we're achieving equality anyway. Our daughters are better off than we were; their daughters will be better off than they are. We're getting equality because we earned it. We're getting equality because we deserve it. Women's differences from men are valuable, and they are recognized for that.

If women are later than expected in achieving equality, not to worry: we're on the glidepath, and we'll arrive before they know it. We're ALMOST there now. As a respected newspaper columnist declared on February 14, 1995, in the *Washington Post*: "In the case of women, affirmative action has long ceased to make any sense." Anyway, no use being impatient and confrontational about this: it only makes people angry and turns them off—no one wants to hear the W-word. We *did* Women in the 1970s: the Woman Thing is tedious, the last gasp of the academic feminists, a solution looking around for a problem. Behold all the male journalists who write sad little pieces about their *wives*, off covering wars in Bosnia or doing fieldwork in Nigeria, and how it feels to be left at home, male Penelopes, wasted with longing. If that isn't a sign of change, what is?

Of course, not all of us buy into the official dream of equality; some take the attitude "we can do it our own way." We'll start small businesses. They won't be great, maybe, but we ourselves will be independent. There'll be plenty of room for everybody in this expanding global economy. We just need a little bit of personal attention around the edges—the special World Bank expenditures, equal access to international development funds and to bank loans—we'll be fine. In a mid-1990s AT&T ad, a clearly successful young woman sums it up: "I'm not looking to build an empire. I don't want to swim with the sharks. I don't want to be the son my father never had. I just want to keep a ceiling over my head (preferably not glass). It's got to be my way. My gains, my loss, my hours, my dress code, my screwups. My place."

Though there are skirmishes even yet, our rights as women will eventually be honored, including our rights to reproductive autonomy. We welcome the biotech fix, almost here, that turns abortion into a nonissue. Society may not always do the right thing, but in this case, it's a matter of global self-interest that women be well educated and reproductive autonomy be promoted: that's what the Cairo conference was all about, and we won that one.

With the new information technology, women will flourish. This technology means brawn no longer matters. Brains do, and have we got brains! More women are in school everywhere, and they're staying longer. Educators tell us that as girls, we learn better than boys; psychologists tell us that as women we have superior symbolic skills. As hunters and gatherers in the symbolic realm, nobody does it better.

The level playing field seems to stretch out in other ways too: the new technology is already reshaping the old authoritarian vertical hierarchy into loosely coupled connections, relatively autonomous, with power everywhere—and nowhere special. The great pyramid that characterized nearly all past human organizations, from the nation to the family, is dissolving into the multidimensional matrix.

Furthermore, new technology will give us the ability to work in flexible places and flexible times and raise our families while we work. At the very least, it will give us sexual anonymity, which means we'll finally be judged on our work and not our looks. Make no mistake about it, we'll excel. Given our strengths, and the numbers of us pouring out of higher education, especially the professional schools, there's no alternative to treating us as equals. We won't have to be fake men in skirts; we'll be valued, even needed, for who we really are. The glass ceiling will dissolve naturally; it won't need to be shattered.

Anyway, if we don't get justice, we'll just organize and do it all over again.

WHY WON'T THE OFFICIAL FUTURE TAKE PLACE?

In 1970, the top managers of major American corporations were 99 percent male. A young woman joining a corporation then had every right to believe that by the time she'd achieved seniority, that percentage would have changed in her favor. It did. Twenty-five years later, only 95 percent of top managers of major corporations were men. At this rate, it will be the year 2270 before women and men are equally likely to be top managers of major corporations.

In the Congress, women were 6 percent of elected representatives in the mid-1990s, a tripling of the 2 percent they were in 1950. At this rate, the Congress will achieve equality between men and women by the year 2500.

Each of these calculations is a linear extrapolation and, as such, represents only one possibility. The percentage of high-level women may well remain frozen at under 10 percent forever in business and in politics. (In fact, a 1995 study by the Geneva-based Inter-Parliamentary Union finds that the percentage of women elected to national legislatures worldwide has dropped by nearly a quarter since the collapse of communism in Europe and the resurgence of democracy there and in Africa, both places where free elections have replaced party-mandated elections.)

Worse, as the example of Norway shows, legislative bodies

that achieve equality are thought to be "feminized"—a pejorative word—and are effectively pushed to the margins by other powerful national organizations, particularly businesses. The same will happen with professions and businesses that are considered to be "feminized."

What happens when women recognize that their Official Future will not arrive—ever? That they're astride a glacier, not a glider? Women generally avoid thinking about these numbers and the difficulties they represent because nobody has the stomach—much less the time—for confrontation and battle, or for large-scale organizing efforts, the traditional means of achieving what women want and of preserving what they have. To restart the debate in terms of the angry white male and the endangered black male versus the "femiNazis" plays into depleted myths and is simply counterproductive. It's easier by far to take the glidepath for granted. Unfortunately, even the most forward-looking women assume a linear progression toward equality. Their views are the old ones: more of the same will get us there. Eventually.

Genuine equality between the sexes hasn't happened on a large scale anywhere. It hasn't happened in Cuba, which after its revolution tried to reinvent itself in many ways, including equality between the sexes, nor in Norway, which appears to have succeeded, with its nearly integrated government; it hasn't happened in China, nor has it happened in the United States. Women everywhere see that their share of power, proffered only on men's terms, is always less and, above all, is always provisional.

If the genuinely powerful, nearly all of them men, view the world as a zero-sum game, convinced that the gains of others must be their loss, then even those modest but real advances that women have made toward equality in the last few decades of the twentieth century seem to be a startling threat to the powerful. And like all perceived threats, the dangers are inflated.

Those who feel threatened band together. A Norwegian woman says, "Gender conflicts emerge clearly, and the usual opponents, such as labor and capital, become allies against women, the newcomers in the political arena." The threatened declare that affirmative action must be replaced by competition based on genuine merit (as if affirmative action has forced the world to endure a devastating eruption of female and nonwhite mediocrity into high places). Threat or hyperbole, in either case, the result is the same: passionate arguments against any legislation that threatens to upset the status quo.

Already in contrast to women's own version of the Official Future, women all over the world are being forced to step back, literally and figuratively, don the veil, give up whatever rights they've momentarily enjoyed, just as fast as men can take them away. In the United States, for example, the Supreme Court has denatured affirmative action laws, and straight ahead looms the end to legal abortion and equal legal rights. Optimists read those losses, or the fact that some nations (including the United States) will not ratify the UN Convention on the Elimination of all forms of Discrimination Against Women (CEDAW), as signs that the feminist revolution has already succeeded well enough. But these losses and failures can just as plausibly be interpreted as the beginning of a worldwide reversal in the drive toward equal rights for women. The fact is that some real gains, and an equal amount of window dressing, have comforted and distracted women while their rights are slipping away, and sexual equality recedes steadily over the horizon. Consider these points:

• Even without complete official repeal of affirmative action laws, the momentum of change has ended, and accountability is dribbling away. In the United States, working women get a blunt message: raise the issue of women's rights, or sexual harassment, and we may deal with you as the law requires—but you'll pay. The woman whistle-blower of the mid-1990s Tailhook scandal is ousted (Tailhook, an association of naval aviators who meet annually for professional and social reasons, became a code word for sexual harassment and misconduct when a female officer brought formal charges of misconduct against association members), and the generals retire on full pension.

• A generation of women who've taken equality as a given hardly feel impelled to fight for what they believe they already *almost* have. As women reach the diamond-hard glass ceiling, they drop out or move out laterally ("I'll do it on my own"). Little solidarity exists among women who are resuming what they've often done in the past, that is, fight their sisters for the crumbs (except for those who get the cake, of course). Both young women and young men talk equality, but the focus group interviews we conducted suggest that few young men will make any personal or professional sacrifices for equality, and young women already sense that.

• Women assume that because they represent half the students in the professional schools, especially law and medicine, they're about to crash the priesthood—and once there, they'll not only share in the prestige and pay, but ideally, they'll reform those priesthoods more to their liking. But in the West, the need to cut costs will force lower pay in those professions: medical care is already being dramatically restructured, and the other priesthood professions will follow for the same reasons. Financiers and technologists are the new priests, and women are significantly underrepresented among them.

• Despite some progress among younger adults—women moving up in careers as never before, the fulfillment men find in being fathers—the truth is that women are working harder, they're exhausted, and they're skeptical about the returns for all that hard work. Have these gains, these opportunities, really given them a better life? Yes, they make more money than women used to, but they *must*— real wages have dropped in the United States for the last twenty-five years, and few families can flourish on one income. Worldwide, the transition to a cash economy has made this true nearly everywhere. Slightly more child care is available, but it's substandard. Public systems, especially education, are stressed to the point of breakdown. This means that working families, working single women, face increasing expenses that make it impossible to save for their children's higher education or for their own future.

In the 1990s, much of the job expansion in the United States is in part-time work, done mainly by women, without benefits or security. Sixty-two percent of minimum-wage workers are women. What if the promise of the information age is fulfilled by women being tied to their computers the way working women were once tied to their sewing machines? In Europe, general employment is beginning to contract: bad news for women.

In the developing world, women's idea of a big step forward is a loan of $100 to set up a shirt factory in their front room— inchworm economics. The stack of *camisas* mounts, but the development agencies award the shiny new data-processing center in the village to men. Few counsel Third, much less Fourth, World women to step up into the information age. How can they? When such women are in the main illiterate, it's nearly impossible for them to catch the information age express. They continue to live as generations of women have lived before them, uneducated, undernourished, and falling ever further behind.

But these women and their daughters are beginning to press

northward and westward, both in the Americas and Europe, looking for escape from their plight.

. . .

International trends and driving forces suggest that in the near future, social reactionism could well have its way. In the conservative Christian world, the ideal of Mom cradling a babe at the hearth obscures the reality of Mom doing piecework at the computer. In the fundamentalist Islamic world, veiled women have only one purpose: to raise cannon fodder for the wars against the infidels. In Hindu and Buddhist countries, where it's widely believed that some karmic flaw has caused one to be born a woman and not a man (better luck next time), a blind eye is turned to large-scale exploitation of women in sweatshops and the sex trade. In India, Hindu fundamentalism is making a comeback, with grave implications for women.

The political power of social and religious reactionaries and their allies should not be underestimated. Religious reactionism helped reshape the U.S. Republican party and chased the Democrats out of Congress in the early 1990s; similar movements have overthrown the Iranian government and destabilized Algeria, Egypt, Pakistan, Afghanistan, and Bangladesh, spilling over into Europe.

The men who lead these reactionary movements hold a cramped, ungenerous vision of women's future, confining them to the kitchen, the children, and the temple, mosque, or church, all in the service of men. But then, what vision do women themselves hold for their future? Whatever it is, it's certainly not as well defined as the vision that reactionary men and women intend to impose on them.

Here's one unpleasant future prospect: by the time Western women now in their forties and early fifties are at retirement age, they can expect to be abandoned by government pension systems. Private-sector retirement plans are going bankrupt in record numbers, and the demographics and costs make it clear that the guarantees women count on to save them from being bag ladies in their old age are void unless a massive economic explosion takes place.

Indeed, one of the most salient characteristics of the year 2015 will be the dramatic graying of the population in the developed world, in contrast to the youthfulness of the less developed world. What was once a population pyramid everywhere, with the very old representing the pointed tip, is now a population cylinder in the developed world. People over sixty-five will comprise at least 20 percent of the population, up from 5 percent in 1900. Since women in that age category will outnumber men at least 2 to 1, it will be a different world, especially for women.

THE PACIFIC RIM

There are other reasons why the Official Future will not necessarily take place. A big part of the Official Future is *the rise of the Pacific Rim*, predicted to be the predominant economic, perhaps even cultural, force of the coming century. It could be. If so, the world's women can pack it in right now. Asian societies thrive in a social order that subordinates the individual to the group, and all women to all men. Not one of the Pacific Rim Asian states treats women as equals or permits them to excel. Unfortunately, most Pacific Rim women are forced into being decorative office ladies, throwaway factory workers and laborers, whores, or trophies.

Much of the Pacific Rim has leaped forward from its past thanks to cheap manual labor, but any large-scale need for such labor is nearing an end, as one early leaper, Japan, long ago recognized (hence its government's emphasis on information technology and automation), and as others are now recognizing. But as we enter the information age, the performance of Pacific Rim countries is no better than okay. Technology is adapted and refined impressively there, but invention, particularly that suited to the information age, languishes. One reason might be political: many Pacific Rim states thrive because they're authoritarian (or, in the case of Japan's democracy, run by bureaucracies both official and social, whose turf wars have paralyzed development in key areas, such as information infrastructure). Authoritarianism is historically inimical to genuine invention. Can any geographical area really be a leader when it's only a production funnel?

Asian planners recognize their backwardness here relative to the United States and Europe and speak confidently of being in at the beginning of the information age, leapfrogging industrialism. Singapore, for example, is working hard to become the information hub of Asia by 2000.

Obstacles exist, however. Is political, social, and commercial control as practiced in Singapore, in South Korea, in Taiwan, or even in Thailand—never mind the big imponderables of India and China—compatible with a thriving information society? Furthermore, Asian indifference to copyright protection not only hurts foreign creators of intellectual property, such as software makers, but it discourages homegrown creativity too. Such nations will always be second in line, waiting for a copy. Only when a society protects its creators do they flower—as India showed as soon as it tightened its intellectual property laws.

Many Asian planners also express dismay at the Hollywood-ization of the global information infrastructure, and they speak of protecting their own cultures by barring Goofy, Mickey, and Donald. Their fears may be justified, but the penalties of content control are very high.

Nevertheless, suppose the World Bank projections are correct, and that by 2020, the world's seven biggest economies are China, the United States, Japan, India, Indonesia, Germany, and Korea, in that order, followed by France, Taiwan, Brazil, Italy, Russia, Britain, and Mexico. How they get to the top of the

World Bank's heap, and how women fare in each of these cultures, will be problematical at best.

Another assumption of the Official Future is the *precariousness of the nation-state*. Once more, women should be alert. Nation-states have traditionally provided a common standard of law, with enforcement to back it up. Moreover, nation-states belong to the community of nations, whether the United Nations or trading blocs. But the power of nation-states is drifting elsewhere, to multinationals, nongovernmental organizations, and other entities. The Western notion of individual rights, protected by national law and international action, is being ferociously resisted as an international norm; instead, it is disdained as unwelcome cultural hegemony. With no common standard of law, and with nations powerless to enforce that standard if it existed, women go backward.

Historically, women's rights, whether the right to own property and vote, or to be educated, or to have equal access to money (wages or credit), or even to have autonomy over her own body, were only achieved through group effort. But the underlying assumptions of group effort are discredited at every turn: in the failures of communism, the failures of trade unionism, in the excesses of self-interested pressure groups, and above all, in the waning of organized feminism, which is perceived as the prisoner of extremists and academic obscurantists. Under the circumstances, it's hard to see women "organizing" for effective change.

· · ·

Finally, consider the wild cards of history: atomic and biological terrorism; global climate change and other natural disasters; nanotechnology; dramatic new fertility and contraceptive technologies; expanding life expectancy; rapidly spreading super-plagues; or economic meltdown, just to name a few. In this book, we only briefly consider the wild cards. We all know they're potentially there and waiting, ready to change everything overnight.

IS EQUALITY BETWEEN THE SEXES EVEN POSSIBLE BY 2015?

That meticulous planner Ebenezer Scrooge was counting on his official future until one Christmas Eve, Marley's ghost lurched through his nightmares and presented alternatives. Scrooge was the perfect audience: Marley's *scenarios changed his mind*, reformed him, and caused him to repent (literally, to rethink). On Christmas morning, Scrooge awakened and chose his future—at the small price of a Christmas dinner and an overdue raise for his long-suffering clerk, Bob Cratchitt.

To answer the central question of whether equality between the sexes can be achieved over the next twenty years (and the related questions—if so, how? If not, why not? How close can we come?), we must examine alternative scenarios to the Official Future.

· · ·

A word about scenarios. Scenarios don't predict the future so much as they illuminate it, preparing us for the unexpected. Scenarios are multiple approaches to the future, stories of the inevitable and necessary (demographics and technology) recombined with the unpredictable and matters of choice. The best scenarios aren't necessarily those that come true; they're the ones that subvert expectations, providing deep insights into the changes happening all around us. The better scenarios are, the more they penetrate to the deepest possible understanding of the *present*. That's one reason why most futurists refuse to assign probabilities to the scenarios they construct: probabilities distract us from the hard work of imagining and planning for the unimaginable. Scenarios are also a powerful learning device, since they let us envisage both welcome and unwelcome futures. They offer a way to plan positive change.

Scenario construction begins with the identification of *predetermined elements*. For example, between 1996 and 2015, the world population will not only grow, but in the developed countries it will *age*, while in the less developed countries it will remain relatively young. This pattern is predetermined. What difference does this pattern make to women, who, if they survive childhood, generally live longer than men?

In one of our scenarios, women in the developed countries become more numerous, generally richer, and more powerful than men. Between their hold on giant pension funds and their private wealth, they dominate political, economic, and social policy. In another scenario, those same women find themselves in dire old-age poverty, thanks to social decisions they had no say in. In one scenario, young women in the developing world, already moving into the paid workforce, enjoy new independence from traditional roles, and they even immigrate to the developed world to pursue economic opportunity. In another, they are merely expendable sacrifices to national economic development. In what other ways does the relative youth of the developing world play out against the relative aging of the developed world?

Here is another new predetermined element: UN figures show that although girls and young women do not have equal access to education, those who manage to get into schools tend to stay—unlike their male colleagues who drop away as the years go by. Educated women now exist all over the world, in such growing numbers that they amount to a new critical mass, capable of making radical change. In one scenario, women seize that opportunity to make radical change, insert themselves into the professions, government, and business, and transform them. In another, they do not.

Yet another new predetermined element is that women constitute nearly half of the paid workforce in some countries (the

United States and Malaysia, for example). In one scenario, as the numbers of women in the workforce move toward parity with men, opportunities and pay for women do too. In another scenario, the same movement toward parity with men in the workforce only confines women to pink-collar ghettos; and the professions they come to dominate are considered feminized and devalued, even if, when men dominated them, they were once prestigious and highly paid.

Moreover, we can safely assume that information technology and biotechnology will get cheaper, more interesting, and more prevalent. That is predetermined. What will such technology look like? Who will benefit?

• • •

Suppose we then identify *driving forces,* such as the waxing and waning of the global economy, or the tension between individual and group rights (in different ways, Singapore and Japan subordinate the rights of the individual to the rights of the group; in different ways, the Western democracies elevate the rights of the individual over the rights of the group). If we place those driving forces on intersecting axes, as shown in the figure, they reveal the logic behind the different ways the future might emerge:

INDIVIDUAL RIGHTS PREVAIL

A Golden Age of Equality

Two Steps Forward, Two Steps Back

GROWING GLOBAL ECONOMY

DEPRESSED GLOBAL ECONOMY

Separate—and Doing Fine, Thanks!

Backlash

GROUP RIGHTS PREVAIL

Thus in one of our scenarios, individual rights generally prevail and the global economy grows robustly. Result: a Golden Age of Equality. In another scenario, the rights of groups—religious, political, tribal, or national—tend to prevail over individual rights, and the economy grows robustly: Separate—and Doing Fine, Thanks! When individual rights generally prevail over group rights, but the global economy is depressed, the scenario is Two Steps Forward, Two Steps Back. In yet another scenario, group rights prevail over individual rights, but the global economy is depressed, resulting in Backlash.

In each scenario the same predetermined elements play a role—demographics and technology, for example—but they play out differently in each scenario. Electronic money may encourage easy buying and economic development in one scenario, but it could camouflage fraud and crime in another. Money itself might disappear in some places, to be replaced by barter.

These axes, both continuums from mild to extreme, only represent the skeleton of a scenario. Muscle and flesh come from predetermined elements, combined with trends and possibilities. We've listened, and we've sniffed. We've picked up soft voices among the strident ones, and sometimes we've permitted ideas at the margins to take center stage. You'll read the stories of these four scenarios in the pages that follow. The voices of imaginary women who have lived through them help to give realism and texture to our thoughts. These scenarios are a textual form of virtual reality. Our intent is not that you argue the yes or no of their details, at least not at first, but that you suspend your disbelief momentarily and feel what it's like to live there. By getting inside, participating in the process of such imagined futures, you may ask: what can I do now, in the present, that will help bring this scenario about? Or prevent it from happening? Or cope with it if it does happen? This was the essence of Scrooge's conversion after his midnight visitors showed him some possibilities.

Our scenarios are incomplete, no more than works-in-progress, meant to be evocative, not exhaustive. They do not touch every topic, nor every region. However, each scenario touches on work, the economy, education, the arts, governance, religion, and relations between the sexes. Experts in other fields, other regions, other cultures, will imagine the details of their own scenarios slightly differently. Indeed, our scenarios are nothing more than invitations to everyone to write better, more plausible, even more desirable outcomes.

• • •

Change swirls around us as we move into the coming century, the next millennium. Official focus falls on political, economic, and technological change but fails to take into account one of the biggest changes of the waning twentieth century, the changed status of women. We mean not just their legal and economic status—which can be altered with pen strokes—but also their own views of themselves, of their rights and their potential.

If nothing better than linear progress prevails, its glacial—not gliding—pace will subvert hopes for equality for many generations. Young women are already voicing discontent with their lives. If they can't succeed in business or government, often they blame themselves instead of circumstances, a pattern too typical of women. After all, they reason, equal opportunity laws are in place (at least for now) in most Western countries; obviously some women are making it; why not them?

A more sophisticated analysis drives them to step back and ask whether success on these terms is worth it. Do they really want to be one of the boys in an unchanged boys' world, or do they want genuine change? In anger and frustration, they drop out, in the belief (not entirely unfounded) that they can at least change their own lives—be a self-employed entrepreneur, be a full-time mom—without taking on the thankless task of reforming an intractable system.

Everything—again, technology, the global economy, and global political structures—is changing, most of it quickly. Everything, that is, except the creep toward sexual equality. Optimistically, women greet each small incremental change, each "first woman to" event as assurance that they're on the right path, they'll eventually get there. But incremental changes for women, important as they are to individuals, are not structural changes. Sometimes even negative change is interpreted as merely the last gasp of the resistant old order. Women often see what they want to see and force fact to support hope. Two Steps Forward, Two Steps Back.

The facts do not easily lend themselves to hope. The facts are that women do not get equal pay for equal work, though economic and social trends have forced women to become breadwinners all over the world, for some a novelty, for most the same old situation. Those breadwinners still work the "second shift" at home. And now they face a future, including their old age, with no guarantees for their security. Nearly everywhere, women as a group are getting poorer relative to men. We sometimes wonder whether the greatest number of have-nots in the age of information will be women—of all colors, ages, and persuasions. Backlash.

Then again, the portents also suggest that the future could bifurcate wildly: everyone faces the potential for enormous conflict and savage repression, events just as possible as the glacial path to equality. Complex systems can often become chaotic.

• • •

But—reimagine a glacier. Glaciers are deceptive. Beneath their immense, silent frozen stillness, their apparent inertia, rivers of ice secretly recarve, even destroy, the soil, the rocks, the mountains. A glacier's very weight and size feeds on itself and accelerates growth—the immense Kutiah Glacier in northern India is said to have advanced at times by 360 feet a day. When the glacier disappears (and on a geological time scale, that can happen swiftly) the land beneath it emerges unrecognizable, utterly transformed. New flora and fauna find homes here; the weather, even the climate, changes. Sea levels rise and lowlands flood. It's a different planet.

And so in this book we have also boldly imagined the heretofore unimaginable—a Golden Age of Equality. "Equality" does not mean "the same" in this scenario: indeed, everything is different, nothing is the same, not men and women, not the lives they lead. This scenario is neither far-fetched nor implausible. We offer it here as a possibility for positive change. On the other hand, that new postglacial landscape might push women into lives that are distinctly apart from men's, in the scenario we call Separate—and Doing Fine, Thanks!

• • •

No, the issues aren't resolved yet, and they aren't going away. We owe it to ourselves to consider alternative futures, based on what we know and what we can project from that. This exercise will permit us to examine our mental maps, our assumptions, and allows us to revise them and decide the courses of action we want to take.

In this book we've taken a global view, because we believe the destinies of women everywhere are linked. Our scenarios often focus on the United States because, for better or worse, the United States is to the world as California is to the nation: change happens first in California, then in the United States, and other parts of the world tend to follow.

We have wrestled with nomenclature, and we agree with the *Economist* that the labels commonly used to categorize national economies are out of date. The phrase "developed countries" implies that the high-income nations are at this point the best they can be—which is clearly wrong. It's more accurate to call them the "knowledge economies," especially when their primary source of growth is expected to be the production, storage, processing, and distribution of knowledge, whether as a good or as a service. The knowledge sector already accounts for at least half of all jobs in knowledge economies. Meanwhile, what does a developing country look like? Is it Singapore, with a per capita income higher than that of Britain or France? Or Brazil? The *Economist* wants to call these the "progressing" countries since they are moving forward in a sustainable way. Finally, what to call those economies that are standing still or devolving, as so many are in, say, central Africa? Shorthand labels such as the "West" and the "North" can be equally misleading. In this book, we use these old labels, understanding how awkwardly they fit, but knowing they are the most widely recognized.

If economic labels are awkward, social labels are worse. We use the term "fundamentalist" to mean religious people who adhere to rigid, inflexible interpretations of scripture that may have been codified a thousand years ago, or only yesterday. On the other hand, Western individualism does not mean anarchy. It has long been understood in the West that individual duties to the community are what ensure individual rights.

Finally, we are not ideologues. We simply hold the straightforward Universal Declaration of Human Rights, adopted in 1948 by the United Nations, as the mark against which women everywhere can measure their achievements.

Backlash

In 1984 and again after the election, focus groups were used to determine how women felt about my candidacy for Vice President. Women in the traditional role of wife and mother hated it. They felt that if I was elected to do the ultimate "man's job," that would make the job they were doing less important. If I could be a wife and mother and run a country, what did that say about them? We repeated the focus groups in 1991 when I ran for the Senate and got the same results. The issue for those women and others who believe that a woman's place is in the home is not how a woman gets the job, whether by election or appointment. The issue is the job itself. The anger I saw in those focus groups bubbles up whenever the changing role of women in society is spotlighted.

—*Geraldine Ferraro, losing Democratic candidate for Vice President of the United States, 1984, and losing candidate for Senate, 1991*

In this scenario of Backlash, the priorities, mores, and values of religious, tribal, political, or national groups tend to dominate over individual rights in a depressed, no-growth, regionally oriented economy. This economy is characterized by temporary economic alliances that continuously underbid each other in hopes of capturing what business exists. The bidding wars lead to abrupt discontinuities in employment and wide-swinging currency fluctuations (including the ever-present threat of destabilization on a regional or global level by the new black market—the so-called black economy, far larger and more sophisticated than local black markets, itself fueled largely by the international narcotics trade). The nation-state holds, but nationalist mentalities are a constant threat to regional economic and political stability. Battles over access to shipping lanes and trade routes are commonplace, and piracy returns in modern trappings. All this drives the young and able-bodied from region to region, often country to country, in search of jobs. These migratory workers leave behind large numbers of the very young and the elderly, who suffer from poor health with little prevention, less cure, and marginal nutrition. Unsurprisingly, families are severely stressed, as evidenced by low birth rates and high death rates. Violence, organized and disorganized, prevails, as well-armed groups move in from the margins to impose their will on unprotected citizens. Communications among individuals are often blocked legally by governments and illegally by enterprises to protect competitive advantages. Emphasis everywhere is on the quick fix rather than the long view; the temporary patch rather than rethinking and redesign. For women, things have seldom been so grim: they rediscover that in bad economic times, societies East and West, North and South, consider them expendable. If they work for pay, they are the last hired and first fired; they get the worst jobs and differential wages. If Western women remember how they once approached equality, they remember it as an evanescent dream that died unborn. The international network of politically experienced women is ineffective, exhausted, and has all but disappeared.

MAJOR TRENDS

When a series of events in the 1980s and 1990s (some political, some economic, some social) came to be widely perceived as "victories for women," many women and men worldwide began to express fear and anger that things had gone too far.

For at least these two decades, Christian and Islamic fundamentalist religious leaders in the West and the Middle East alike had already found a fascinated following when, disguised in various code words, such as "family values" or "true faith," they implied that most of the troubles people were suffering—crime, poverty (especially as a result of a restructuring economy that promoted not jobs but the growth of joblessness), political corruption, rampant disease, failing schools, adolescent anomie, tribal violence—could be laid squarely at the feet of women. It was women's unseemly, even unnatural, ambitions for themselves that had caused them to neglect their duty to their husbands and children and upset the old, peaceful, natural, and God-ordained order. As the global economy became even more unpredictable, as wealth increasingly shifted from the few to the fewer, and frustration replaced hope, men and women both sought to cast blame. The assertion of the fundamentalists—that it was women's fault—now swept into the wider world, with devastating results for women.

All these circumstances incubated high violence, not only between nations, but also among tribal groups, international organized crime syndicates, informal gangs, and of course, generations. Violent images dominated popular music, movies, and all other forms of mass entertainment, flowing ceaselessly from the satellites that circled above. These images penetrated every hut in the world's villages and every apartment warren in the world's megacities, inciting even more fury.

Whatever their grievance, all combatants found a common scapegoat in women, and fundamentalist-style repression became the rule, not the exception. Scapegoating women led to a pattern that recurred across many religions and in many countries: secular politicians, needing the support of fundamentalists, would enter into compacts with them that effectively traded women's rights for political support. The signs were indisputable by 2005, when Algerian-style violence had spilled far beyond the borders of Algeria and forced Islamic women everywhere to return to the chador, the long black robe and veil that covered them head to toe, all but their eyes. The truly pious—or truly frightened—added a translucent veil that concealed even their eyes.

Mullahs strove to outdo each other in new rules: women not only were removed from all social and political activity and forced to veil, but were denied the right to divorce and the guardianship of their children. They lost their right to inherit property. Then they were warned against smiling in public, or attending soccer matches, or watching television. Polygamy and arranged and forced marriages became the rule. Honor killings—where a man could kill with impunity a woman or girl in his family who he claimed had dishonored the family—rose dramatically. Even female genital mutilation, nowhere advocated in the Koran, was adopted by Muslims who needed to prove their piety. New figures appeared in the Muslim sections of the cities of the West: for a bounty, these men hunted down runaway wives and daughters and returned them to their husbands and fathers. Copying Iranian postrevolutionary edicts of the 1980s, mullahs in Jordan, Saudi Arabia, and many parts of North Africa and Pakistan drove thousands of women to suicide. They condoned the murder of as many more.

Before she disappeared underground in 2002, the leader of the Iranian resistance group, the Mojahedin Organization, declared: "Islam, according to its great Prophet, is a religion of mercy, peace and equality. Islam is compatible with the principles of human rights and women's liberties. It is, further, the beacon and inspiration to women in their quest for emancipation." She was not heard from again.

Muslim women in the streets of Western Europe and North America were not exempt from the mullahs, and Christian fundamentalists took to their telepulpits to extol the purity and virtue of women in their midst who dressed so modestly, strongly recommending that good Christian women do likewise.

The Guardians, a quasi-religious, quasi-political movement of Christian fundamentalist American men, begun in the mid-1990s by a football coach, pledged to purge America of secularism. The Guardians doubled, tripled, then quadrupled their membership by 2005. The Guardians pledged to "guard" their families, but this involved submitting to a cell group, which was in turn closely controlled by a national hierarchy. Women were bound to absolute obedience to their Guardian husbands and fathers. In 2006, the 2.5 million American Guardians forced their wives and daughters to adopt the chador.

Though the chador was utterly impractical for a Western lifestyle, significant numbers of women who weren't attached to cults felt frightened enough to adopt the chador as a kind of symbolic shield against the violence around them, much as Catholic nuns had once walked twentieth-century streets in fifteenth-century costumes. When violence against women was reported in the media, it was carefully noted whether the victim was wearing such a garment. A victim who had not, the implication seemed to be, probably invited the beating, rape, or murder she suffered. Thus women who would never have considered donning this cumbersome apparel quickly saw that the chador conferred a kind of protection. When the 2007 fall fashion shows in New York, Milan, and Paris frivolously featured Western-style chadors (different from Middle Eastern chadors only in the sumptuousness of their fabrics) the costume became international fashion.

Women who had once been fearful only of going out after dark now needed to fear the daylight too. Thus many consented to having homing devices placed under their skin, which certainly permitted them to be found in case of emergency, but which also offered them up as easy victims of spying. The social water torture women had once suffered as they'd crossed barriers at work, in the arts, and in politics looked benign in retrospect.

The adoption of the chador by North American women was a bleak symbol of the finality of their stunning legal, political, and social losses and reversals, all part of the pattern of political trading that went on openly between ambitious politicians and determined fundamentalists.

Even so-called liberation movements nearly always resulted in net losses for women. In Palestine, women who had fought alongside men for self-determination watched as rights were eagerly exchanged for political support from extremists, an old story from Algeria and Iran. The great imbalance of men to women in China, a result of the one-child policy of the last decades of the twentieth century, didn't make Chinese women more precious; it turned them into victims, subject to state-mandated surgery on their reproductive systems and random surgery to harvest other organs, and it kept them in perpetual danger of kidnap, rape, and slavery.

The international sex trade, operating with the complicit approval of many national governments and police agencies, had become the employer of last resort for larger and larger numbers of women, who were exploited, brutalized, infected with disease, and eventually murdered. Women not in immediate physical danger were considered privileged enough and therefore not entitled to aspire to or expect equality.

The Internet had grown exponentially since the mid-1990s, and searching it for information was impossible without using a search engine or intelligent agent. But these agents—computer codes written by humans, after all—were riddled with social assumptions and legal constraints. The International Telecommunications Protocol of 2004, promulgated by an alliance of

Singapore, Myanmar, China, Indonesia, and Japan, and meant to protect citizens of certain countries from seditious, unsavory, unpatriotic, or "inappropriate" information, required that users declare their citizenship and their sex. Along with automated verification, there were stringent penalties for lying.

When women in the developed world lucky enough to have access to the information networks logged on, they were forced to use an agent designed especially for women, which not only prohibited them access to political information deemed unpatriotic or inappropriate, but also barred them from whole areas of research "for their own protection," a protection that effectively prevented them from holding important jobs.

Already by 2000, the mergers between entertainment, publishing, and telecommunications conglomerates had resulted in communications systems that appeared competitive but which were strictly controlled. These merged trusts and monopolies existed on the condition that they acquiesce to government control of their content, a condition they acquiesced to eagerly, sacrificing editorial independence to profit. Their content imitated what had prevailed on network TV years before: it was sensational, violent, and shallow entertainment, content that bred passivity, crassness, and mediocrity.

Thus stereotypes that had confidently been buried with stakes through their hearts rose up to stalk women once more. It made no difference that the media were new, flashy, state of the art. The content was the same, and it denigrated women with impunity.

Even open-minded men and women suspected—and many felt compelled to assert—that something about women themselves (maybe it *was* their natural inferiority) had contributed mightily to this tragic but inevitable situation. The liberal remedies of the second half of the twentieth century (affirmative action and equal opportunity) had not only shown themselves to be misguided and hopeless, but women's unnatural move into men's spheres at the price of neglecting their own was surely one main cause of the terrible social stresses that plagued the globe. At some level women themselves must have believed this. In the West, at least, they had the ballot, and it was their votes as well as men's that had elected the politicians who now pushed them backward.

Therefore, though the world economy was heterogeneous in the first fifteen years of the new century—despite a general depression, some countries managed to prosper relative to their neighbors—women came out short whether they lived in a prosperous or a poor region. In a relatively prosperous economy, women's personal ambitions were scorned, their training discounted: the professions they dominated were deemed feminized and were measurably lower in pay and lower in status, even when those professions had formerly been the opposite, such as medicine and law. Women noted ruefully that science as a profession was finally open to them in a way it had never been—but science no longer had secure funding anywhere and had become the toy of politicians. Politicians declared which research would be funded, depending on the moment's vote-getting fad.

Though two incomes were usually necessary to maintain a family, the myth that women's work was optional was sanctimoniously revitalized to justify confining women to the lowest-paid, dead-end jobs. In a strange replay of the 1950s (when men were back from the war), working women of all ages were often shunted home (their pay was cut, they were shut out of responsible jobs, or they were discharged), where they were instructed they belonged, and were presumed to be the responsibility of a male breadwinner. Even in the relatively prosperous regional economies, male breadwinners were often on the road, looking for work or taking temporary jobs elsewhere. Women were forced to work at their home terminals while they looked after their children, their aging parents, their ailing grandparents (who lived ever longer), or even just themselves. All this reinforced a belief widespread among men that women had always gotten a free ride; that they were basically trivial (after all, if they did important work, they'd be paid better); that in fact every woman was at heart a welfare queen.

Cold comfort though it was, women in the developed world of 2015 certainly had less to complain about by most measures than did women elsewhere. Compared to the grinding hardship, malnutrition, violence, and general exploitation that women elsewhere endured, First World women's frustration with their intractable second-class citizenship paled.

In the former Soviet Union, and in many parts of China, environmental degradation was irreversible, and whole populations had to relocate. Few postcommunist governments could afford even token payments toward relocation, and when families moved, they found little work and no welcome anywhere. Even well-trained women were forced into menial labor. Former physicians—elderly now, since no medical training had existed in these places for years—were much in demand as nannies, but elderly mathematicians and physicists considered themselves lucky if they could find work cleaning other people's houses. These particular servants knew very well that in the developed world, machines did much the same work, and it was demoralizing to know that as soon as you cost more than a machine, you would be replaced.

As the impact of the same kind of environmental degradation began to be felt in exhausted and poisoned fields and depleted forests of the developing world, women there were on the road looking for work as much as men. Excluded from the formal economy by any number of means—laws, cultural tradition, discrimination—they were bluntly forbidden to take whatever jobs did exist from men, the proper breadwinners. The term "breadwinner" persisted in the face of reality: since the 1990s, the fastest growing segment of households in both the industrial and the developing worlds was headed by women, and by 2005, more than 50 percent of women were in fact their own and their children's sole breadwinners.

Third World women by the tens of thousands were encouraged to emigrate from their villages and megacity slums to industrial countries to be domestic workers, but significant numbers of them were tricked or coerced into sexual slavery with no protection and no escape. As early as 1992, one Dutch study of the international sex trade had warned that "European merchants have begun to exploit the last natural resource of the Third World: its women." By 2015, that exploitation was at its peak.

But sex was perceived as a weapon in more benign businesses too. Men accused women of using sex to exert power in business, to get extra business, to get promotions, whatever they wanted. Conversely, many women argued on behalf of asexuality (dressing modestly, even wearing the chador; avoiding anything but electronic communications with men; refusing to talk—or even think—about sex). They seemed to believe that if only women denied their sexuality, they would be "safe."

In truth, there was no safe place for women. For example, in 1980, approximately seventy women had been in jail or set for trial in Pakistan. Ten years later, that number was three thousand—the result of laws promulgated by fundamentalists that made it a criminal act for women to file for divorce or report a rape. If such laws could not be repealed while the prime minister was a Western-educated woman, Benazir Bhutto, it was all the worse for Pakistani women when her successor, a man, took office. Violence against women in Pakistan and many other countries was widely tolerated: a woman had a choice of enduring it or going to jail if she protested.

The series of fundamentalist coups against the secular Turkish government in 2005 and 2006, which took advantage of the turmoil created by the Kurdish conflict, had not completely succeeded in overthrowing secularism and installing a religious state. But to calm dissension, the government was forced to enact more rigid laws, revoking many of the secular safeguards that had existed since the time of Kemal Ataturk in 1919. Women were the first, the most expendable, the most pliant, and the easiest victims.

Laws changed in the West too, including the United States. Affirmative action laws had been dismantled piecemeal between 1995 and 2000, and then in 2005, a Supreme Court whose justices had, after all, been largely appointed on the basis of their opposition to abortion, finally repealed the right to abortion under any circumstances. This meant that the abortifacients women had been taking under the supervision of their physicians in the privacy of medical offices were now illegal, and police intrusion into gynecologists' offices was commonplace.

If it wasn't the police, it was terrorists. Since terrorism against women's clinics had seldom been prosecuted in the United States, reactionaries moved confidently on to other women's organizations that offended them. Political offices that belonged to women were mysteriously firebombed; women activists were assassinated by parcel bombs; woman-owned businesses were vandalized and torched. Even women's worship groups were attacked if they were perceived as feminist.

What religious fundamentalists all over the world codified in plain language was the sexual bias that prevailed in many places under other names. In the name of resisting imperialism, for example, Uganda's postcolonial constitution still legitimized discrimination on the grounds of sex, as part of "customary" and "personal" law. In the name of "family harmony," women were informally—and in some places legally—barred from any job that might pay them better wages than their husbands earned. If they were unmarried, it was all the worse: they were considered to be taking jobs from "breadwinners," though by 2015, a majority of women in the developing world were in fact the main or sole support of their families.

· · ·

As the new millennium opened, money talked. Women in developing countries looked to international agencies such as the World Bank, which in the early 1990s had pledged to help them, but often they found themselves at a legalistic dead end. Well-meant efforts to modernize agriculture in many African and Asian countries had also introduced the concept of legal ownership, along with the documents, codes, and deeds that legal ownership required. Most African and Asian parliaments already had (or now quickly wrote) laws ensuring that only men could legally own, sell, buy, or inherit property. Thus by 2010, what had once been communal land, belonging to everyone in a tribe or village, had new legal owners—men. Women still farmed the land as they traditionally had, but instead of feeding themselves and their families, they suddenly found themselves sharecroppers for absentee men. Since they were not legal landowners, the World Bank and other agencies would not extend them credit.

Even in the remotest parts of the world, a money economy was taking hold. Though the poorest peasant understood that education was essential in an information age, raising the cash for tuition, for school uniforms, for the simplest information tools, was a monumental task for a subsistence farmer. She did what she could and put her hopes in her sons.

With women an economic and social liability, female infanticide, which had already been notorious in China and India, increased and spread to other lands. That is, a global preference for boy babies became overt and unapologetic. Daughters—"water spilled on the ground," as they were traditionally called in Taiwan, "prostitutes to be exchanged for cattle" in Uganda, "only weeds" among the Zulu—got even less of everything: education, nutrition, health care, employment training, protection from violence. Death rates increased, so that by 2015, female mortality had risen above even the shocking rates of the turn of the century. The UN demographers calculated that in the less developed world, a female's life expectancy was no greater than thirty-five years. This put unbearable pressure on surviving women to continue to provide sustenance (water, food, and firewood) for men, to bear their sons, and to look after the aged and sick until they themselves dropped like overworked animals. Because of all this, birth rates too were falling all over the Third World, a cause for celebration if the numbers alone were considered, a cause for grief if conditions were examined.

Not surprisingly women began to flee. Along cart tracks and dirt paths, across rivers, across borders, malnourished and weak, hiding by day and running by night, undeterred by jail (often an improvement over what they had), undeterred by threats to life and limb, they fled in utter desperation and helped to swell an enormous wave of worldwide immigration that rolled from South to North, from East to West.

This wave of immigrant women, which had barely been noticeable at the end of the twentieth century, rose to dramatic visibility in the early years of the twenty-first century. Yet even as women fled unsupportable conditions at home, they inevitably brought into the center of the developed world traditional beliefs about women's proper subordinate role. Western men held up these traditional women as models for "the way women should be"—in any case, the way they wanted *their* women to be—and intercultural marriages between Western men and women from traditional cultures were a persistent reproach to more emancipated Western women.

· · ·

A silence fell over women's role in history. The political and social gains women had made throughout the twentieth century were omitted from official histories except as side issues, even comical curiosities, like nineteenth-century American utopian colonies. One generation of women had fought on the barricades;

a second generation had taken their victories for granted; a third and fourth generation now forgot them completely. Contributing to this official amnesia were complaints by men that curriculum reforms of the 1990s, so-called multiculturalism, had slighted white males, who after all, had really made all the history, as everybody knew. Indeed, few men had reason to believe that feminism had anything to offer them. Without the support of men, international feminism repeated the story of space exploration: a glorious beginning, pregnant with promise and inevitability; some important achievements; only to lose its grip on the public imagination, its momentum, and finally its support, until feminism was no more than a set of sad exercises in nostalgia and what might have been. A last attempt to institutionalize equality for women had failed.

• • •

In all this, women were complicit. It was women as well as men who enforced the draconian laws and betrayed the runaways—out of fright, out of envy, out of viciousness. Fright, because the penalties for concealing runaways were so severe; envy, because everyone wanted to run away from hunger, from poverty, from disease, from violence—though there were few places to run to; and viciousness because prolonged suffering seldom ennobles the human spirit. In the developed West, women who chose not to battle for equality, who willingly traded inequality for temporary security, joined with their sisters from the less developed South in folding their arms and mocking all the women who had over-reached, especially achieving women, who seemed to have re-treated, exhausted, to lick their wounds. In the developed West and developing East alike, male politicians saw that a nontraditional wife was a liability at the polls, and the small numbers of women who had themselves won national office diminished further. Only grandmotherly women who smiled sweetly as they campaigned, or who had an important family name, had a chance at election. In the East, no political party would support a woman, even one who came from a distinguished family, unless she was reliably under male control.

In a peculiar twist, large numbers of Western women mimicked Eastern women in low calorie intake. With Eastern women, it was traditional and forced upon them—they had always been the last to eat, and they had been fed the least. With Western women, it was a psychological disorder, a pathetic response to the charge of never being good enough. Moreover, what had seemed like a harmless new interest in regional costumes, a gesture to affirm what was different about you in a world where most people had ceded their economic sovereignty to international economic cartels, and their political sovereignty to local security forces, had become something much worse for women. In many places, traditional regional costumes—the kimono, the cheongsam, the dirndl, the starched lace—not only hampered their physical movement (just as the originals had) but absorbed enormous time, as authenticity demanded old skills of hand embroidery, starching, and ironing.

The backlash also saw a rise in explicit bigotry and crimes against homosexuals, who violated the canons of traditional roles as feminists did. Psychologists were left to speculate why uneasy heterosexual males felt increasingly impelled to beat up, often kill, other males they perceived as gay. Lesbians, being women, were more or less ignored as inconsequential so long as they were quiet about their sexuality.

TEACHING HER A LESSON

"It was time she learned a lesson." These words were heard in many languages, many places: from courtroom testimony to pulpits, from editorial pages to political speeches, from therapists to media messages. The lesson to be learned—to be relearned—was male entitlement, and the backlash against women was fueled by an outrage that the fundamental assumptions of thousands of years past were not just under question but might be in genuine peril. In most cultures, women had indeed catered to and deferred to men, a state of affairs blessed by scriptures in every major faith, and, when it wasn't actually encoded in secular law, it was certainly part of cultural practice. Both men and women might intone the phrase, but it was women who took it upon themselves to teach the lesson daily.

For none of this could have happened without the complicity of women who also believed in male entitlement: It was African women, for instance, who, despite futile outcries against the practice in the 1990s, continued to hold down 2 million of their daughters each year so that their tiny genitalia could be mutilated in the name of sexual attractiveness and chastity. It was Palestinian women who, when the new government took over, stoned their sisters who refused to don the *hijab*, a traditional head-to-toe garment that covers everything but the eyes. As the century turned and the Palestinian government foundered, rent by factionalism and unable to find a national patron to prop up its economy, it turned its citizens' disappointment and rage with their squalor into rage against the minority of Palestinian women who still refused to don the *hijab*. Targets of inflammatory official attacks, targets of religiously inspired assassination, these women were appalled to see a version of the garments they scorned adopted voluntarily by women in the West as a high-fashion statement: their sense of betrayal was complete.

In the United States, it was Hispanic women, by 2015 members of the biggest U.S. minority, who disdained education, especially for their daughters, and did nothing to discourage them from dropping out of school in overwhelming numbers. Ironically, by 2015 these mothers were part of the first Hispanic generation that had suffered sharply from unfinished educations, and as a practical matter, many of them had been forced back to school in their thirties for vocational training, having to juggle their families and their studies. But instead of drawing the lesson that high school and college are more easily accomplished without family responsibilities, they saw their perpetual struggle, their perpetual lag, as a sign that education didn't really get you anywhere.

Irony dwelled elsewhere in the United States too. It was well-educated and well-paid white women of privilege, themselves former beneficiaries of affirmative action, who in the 1990s had attacked its principle as unfair to white men and patronizing to women. As they looked behind them now in 2015 and saw fewer younger women following them up the ladder, they attributed it to a generational flaw: if young women were slackers, too lazy to work for their achievements, that was young women's fault. These privileged women had strange allies in reactionary religious women, who bridled at the once-successful American effort called "Take Your Daughter to Work Day" and paralleled it with an increasingly successful "Take Your Daughter Home Day" during which the fine points of homemaking were celebrated.

All these complicit women had much invested in the status quo, or even in male superiority itself, and they were as determined as any man that things would not change except to return to a paradise lost.

THE LESSON OF SELF-RELIANCE

What had been touted in the United States as overdue welfare reform in the late 1990s was the opening for an easy attack on poor women and children, an attack that intensified in the opening years of the new century. As welfare payments diminished, single mothers were instructed to find work instead. Presuming a job could be found, the problems of child care loomed. If child care could be found, it ate up at least half of a minimum-wage earner's income. The other half might be taken by shelter. Self-reliance was the lesson, but it was intended for those too young to understand it. The children of these stressed-out mothers and invisible fathers were left to shift for themselves, children of seven or eight in charge of younger children, circumstances that produced problems immediately and, for them and their society, forever after.

This domestic indifference to the poor was repeated, even magnified at the international level. For years, the United States had sent aid to poor Asian and African nations in the name of supporting democracy, while in fact supporting corrupt one-party regimes for cold-war strategic considerations. When the cold war ended, Americans and other industrial nations informed their Asian and African clients that, disappointed by the return on investments, they would cut back aid and insist that emerging nations be more self-reliant.

But cold-war dictators had invariably pocketed the early aid with impunity and had run up national debts that now crippled the new democracies, especially in sub-Saharan Africa. The misery that this enforced self-reliance imposed on newly democratized, desperately debt-ridden countries made them ripe for takeover not by communists, but by militant Islamics, whose first targets were always women.

THE LESSON OF VIOLENCE

· · ·

Roni's last moments were clawing the ground, trying to escape her attackers. The ends of every one of Roni's fingers were shredded raw, with dirt jammed under her fingernails. Give us our day in court and *then* we can take back the night.

> —Karlie Row, whose sister, Roni
> Braunlich, was raped and then
> bludgeoned to death in Taos,
> New Mexico, October 1994; the
> crime was never solved

• • •

Watchdog groups had noted that worldwide violence against women spiked at the beginning of the century, up from already rising rates during the 1990s. Rates then plateaued just below the spike. The sustained rate of violence was real, not merely a reflection of a new awareness or better record keeping. This reign of terror against women was worse in some places than in others, but it was unprecedented everywhere: men were determined to put—or pummel—women back into their traditional place.

Violence against women not only had been commonplace but was institutionalized in many tribal cultures, cultures that the ignorant had sentimentalized as truer, more human, traditional, or earth-friendly. The sentimentalists now made a logical leap: *if beating women is traditional, then beating women is good*. Thus men in many cultures used their sheer brute strength to terrorize and keep women subordinate; in other cultures, they used firearms. Men everywhere acted on a kind of psychological belief that many women also shared—namely, whatever women got, they deserved.

As global change, especially universal access to TV and, to a lesser extent, electronic (fax and computer) networks, began to change human expectations, traditional men experienced intolerable stress. On the one hand, the new world required of them skills and a point of view they didn't have and couldn't seem to acquire. On the other, women's new resistance to traditional female deprivation, a resistance egged on by images and ideas from abroad, enraged them.

For example, in Palestine, the level of domestic violence had never been acknowledged: women considered it more important to present a united front to the Israeli enemies. But once Arab-Israeli relations began to normalize in the mid-1990s, Palestinian women, who had stood in solidarity with their men during the troubles with Israel, courageously began to speak up to protest the systematic violence they had secretly endured for generations. Their efforts to make a normal life for themselves and their children, which might imply some economic independence, only inflamed the men in their lives who were frustrated by the disappointingly slow rate of change in personal fortunes and by the stagnant Palestinian economy in general. Palestinian women soon learned to live in fear of daring to open their mouths. This pattern repeated itself in many places—in Latin America, in the former states of the Soviet Union, in Southeast Asia.

In the developed countries, men with meager educations had found the workplace shifting out from under them for more than two decades, leaving them humiliated and underemployed, even jobless. Sometimes they found an employer who would train them for certain tasks, but that training was usually related to a specific job, with skills that weren't transferable.

Once they had been able to blame "The Man," that boss who glided in serene privilege, just out of reach. Now, however, The Man was faceless, somewhere at an unknown distance, protected by an electronic camouflage of "know-bots" and "pseuds," computer code that stood in for him, that issued orders, instructions, pay, and then dissolved. Unable to blame The Man, mere lower-case men turned their rage, their frustration at being unemployable, and made scapegoats of the women closest to them. No woman in the developed world had been able to count on legal protection, but now the courts shook off their indifference and took sides, handing down verdicts that effectively punished the victim. Funds for battered women's shelters steadily diminished until shelters began to close, forcing women to stay with the men who menaced them.

In the mid-1990s, Canada's was the first, but only the first, judicial system to accept drunkenness as an exculpation for battery—a law that primarily benefited men since very few women got tanked and beat up men. In the dozens of tribal wars that flared up persistently across the planet, women were victims of systematic rape and murder as weapons of war. When peacekeepers succeeded in calming the sides in such a war, they never even tried to prosecute for war crimes against women. As they explained, if combatants thought they were going to be prosecuted for something so commonplace, they'd never agree to any peace terms at all.

There was economic violence too. At the macrolevel, organized crime had gone global and electronic, with associates in all the nations of Latin America, Asia, and the former socialist bloc. The black economy—more sophisticated than the old black market—ran in parallel to the legitimate economy, scoffing at taxes, extorting payoffs from an ever-growing number of legitimate businesses, and slowly buying its way into governments.

At the microlevel, women found themselves exploited, hounded, and vulnerable, with equal-protection laws dismantled as affirmative action laws had been. For example, according to Orthodox Jewish law, a woman was not permitted to get a religious divorce unless her husband granted her one (no such law for men). The rabbinical courts had come to permit husbands in dead marriages to extort every bit of family property from their departing wives as the price for freedom. In the mid-1990s, the New York State courts stepped in to stop this exploitative practice. But a few years later, judges agreed that this was a clear violation of the constitutional principle of the separation of church and state, and threw Orthodox women back onto the mercies of the misogynist rabbinical courts.

Again, throughout southern Africa at the end of the century, women had begun a modest campaign for inheritance rights, asking to inherit family property from their husbands. Widows had all too often found themselves disinherited, their husbands' families seizing property, leaving them and their remaining children paupers, without any social welfare or employment skills.

A Zimbabwean president was aghast: "If these are ideas being brought by whites amongst you as they came from Europe, they are bringing terrible ideas. I cannot have it that property that is family property should be registered in two names. If the woman wants property in her own right, why did she get married in the first place?" He conveniently overlooked the fact that most women had no choice but to marry, effectively sold into wedlock as their families collected traditional bride-prices; they themselves were no more than property. Between men's resistance to change and women's ignorance of the possibility of change, southern African women were roughly thrust backward from the humble hopes they had entertained for themselves and their daughters at the end of the twentieth century.

WOMEN IN BUSINESS

Western observers in the late 1990s had begun to see a small but significant number of top-level career women leave high-paying jobs—in law, medicine, and business—and return home. These leave-takings weren't for the usual child care or sabbatical reasons (so-called workpausals). They weren't even part of the career hopscotching practiced by successful men. Women simply left their jobs and went home, as if they were in retreat. That small but significant number had grown to a large and significant number by 2015, so that employers would routinely ask a woman job candidate the question they had been forbidden to ask a few years earlier: how long do you plan to work?

Why were so many women who had once expected to be at the top now asked how long they planned to work? As the new millennium dawned and women came steadily closer to the top, executives at the summit began to grow uneasy. If genuine sexual equality occurred, they thought, it could only be a zero-sum game: what women gained could only come at men's expense. The temperature of the ever-present hazing process was turned up: women were made examples of, humiliated, and sabotaged, until they quit or were dismissed.

The business world of the new century had gradually and effectively become a man's world once more. While it was true that in the United States and several European countries consumers were changing drastically, along with the labor force, the composition of corporate employees remained about the same. Women, minorities, the disabled, and other nonwhite male workers were hired in slightly larger numbers than they had been thirty years earlier, but businesses were at a loss to know how to use this diversity. A corporate diversity program was considered successful if it made these workers over into reasonable facsimiles of white males, what was naively called "treating people as just *people*, not special categories." But when employees, women especially, diverged from the white male model (when they had children they worried about more than their jobs; when they were perceived as emotional rather than rational; when they emphasized cooperation instead of competition), they were regarded as failures, poor hires, and they suffered accordingly at raise and promotion time. As companies had to switch from hierarchical to more horizontal models, they were stymied by the lack of adaptability among their diverse employees who could not form teams whose members trusted each other and communicated easily with each other.

The all-male businesses of Japan and southeast Asia watched all this with the inestimable satisfaction of having been proved right. The idea that a diverse workforce might open new opportunities was patently silly compared to the difficulties it raised; and anyway, a successful businessman ought to be able to do any kind of business. A diverse workforce had been touted as a way of acquiring consumer information and of creating new markets, but in fact point-of-sale and point-of-service computers gave businessmen the fast feedback they needed with regard to customer satisfaction with at least as much efficiency and with far less bother than accommodating a diverse workforce would have.

I was one of those famous women lured into engineering back in the 1980s when engineering schools began to make serious efforts to recruit more women students. Maybe nothing could've stopped me from being an engineer. I grew up on a farm in eastern Pennsylvania, and when something goes wrong on a farm, you don't call 911. You *are* 911. By the time I was six or seven, I could fix any machine on the farm. Really. I loved—I still love—the logic of machines.

Anyway, we thought we were the wave of the future: we were the first, but we were sure that scads of women would flood in after us. In fact the percentage of women engineering students never got past 10 percent, and in the 1990s, five years after I got my master's, the numbers began to drop. By 2015 women in engineering are as rare as they've ever been, maybe rarer. I mean *nada*, zilch, noise level, off the screen, under the radar. In retrospect you can see why. My own story is absolutely typical.

My first job out of school, I went to work in a firm where all the project managers were *Father Knows Best* meets *Jurassic Park*. They'd still be wearing flattops if they hadn't been bald. Engineers are notoriously conservative, but old engineers—oh man! I felt as if I'd suddenly moved to a different country. No guidebook, no traveling companions. It was weird, because it sure *sounded* like my native tongue. But it wasn't. And my working assumptions weren't theirs. In a nutshell, I spent more time battling stereotypes, more time proving myself, reestablishing my credentials every time I started on a new project than I did actually engineering. The sheer effort involved in all that made me hesitate to move, even though this particular firm wasn't any great shakes,

I now see. I saw it pretty soon, actually. But you know, I just couldn't go through all that station-identification stuff again.

If I'd had a good mentor, she'd have explained what I didn't then realize, that moving—changing projects, especially changing companies—is the time-honored path to advancement in engineering, as I guess it is in many fields. Ten years out of school—we're talking 2002, 2003, and it dawns on me that my career is in a holding pattern. Even I can see I'm an underachiever, and I'm clueless about how to change that. Plus, I was going through a divorce, so I morph into a single mom (not that my ex was such a great help when we were together) and if there's an engineering company with a fund to pay the babysitter past 6:00 P.M., I don't know about it. In real life, engineering projects are 9 to 5 for maybe the first 80 percent of their lifespan; the next 15 percent is overtime big-time; and it goes on round-the-clock shifts for the last 5 percent. Forget your kids. Forget your life.

But this kept me back too. Rushing out to get my son at nursery school in the middle of a crash session. Clearly, I'm not a serious engineer. Or maybe I'm just not as good as the boys. Back of the class, back of the bus, back of the promotions line.

I actually thought that once the *Father Knows Best* boys retired, my career would pick up. Guys my own age seem to have worked these things through. What I didn't see—hey, maybe I'm as dumb as I look—is who's been coming through engineering schools for the past couple of decades. Not Americans. I don't know what the numbers are—85 percent? 90 percent? Make no mistake, American engineering schools are the first stop off the jumbo jet for every Third World guy who doesn't want to drive a taxi. Good for them, you say. Self-improvement, the American way. I'd say so too. Until I realize that inside the head of every Pandit and Pasqual and Pyong-Lee who steps into my office clutching his personal digital assistant, women are slightly lower and slightly less useful than the stuff the water buffalo drops outside the front door back home.

Maybe if I'd had other women to talk to, more of this would've come clear sooner. But I was—I still am—almost always the only woman around. When there have been others, we weren't terribly supportive of each other. Do well and you make me, the only other woman around, look bad. Do badly and you reflect badly on all women. Sure, there are affinity groups, Women in Process Engineering, but my time is already 125 percent subscribed, and any spare time I have, I'm learning what's new in process engineering. The professional caste system says I can't talk to the female support staff, though I now see that these babes are pretty smart. They see the big picture. So many of them, it turns out, got sidetracked by circumstances into being support staff when they could've been much more.

So I got over blaming a particular boss, a particular work situation, or even myself for a stunted career that's been long on heartache and short on satisfaction. When my youngest is through college, I'm outta here. I'm going back to the farm.

WORLDWIDE IMMIGRATION

The immigrants began coming in the 1980s and 1990s, but as the century turned, their numbers turned a trickle into a series of tidal waves. From the South they moved North, from the East they moved West (except for Australia, which received continuing waves of southbound immigrants, legal and illegal). For the first time in memory, the relatively homogeneous cultures of Europe received large numbers of people of other colors and appearances obviously settling in for the long haul, but stubbornly refusing to adapt to the ways and appearances of their host nations.

By 2015, hidden animosity had given way to open hostility. Though no developed country in Europe had permitted the death penalty for criminals since World War II, France and England both reinstituted it in 2005, giving some satisfaction to one set of Americans, those who believed that Europeans in their self-righteousness about the death penalty just didn't understand how obstreperous a minority could be; and to another set of Americans, who now had confirmation of their belief that the death penalty was a racist gesture.

Immigrant women especially were subject to searches and seizures. Authorities justified this by saying that the women, with no other source of income, were inclined to slip into prostitution, and it was their promiscuity that spread AIDS. Predatory crime syndicates saw these same women as easy candidates to force into the sex trade and turned the fears of authorities into reality.

THE WOMAN-HEADED HOUSEHOLD

All across the industrialized world, demographers had noted the steady rise in single-person and single-parent households for the last three decades of the twentieth century. Women predominated in both these categories: if they were young, they were divorced or had never married; if they were aged, they had outlived their spouses. It wasn't only the industrialized world: in India, 30 percent of rural households were woman-headed by the 1990s, and the same pattern prevailed in other parts of Southeast Asia and Latin America.

But few societies made provisions for this large group of

women-headed households, and none was adequate. Single mothers still struggled to find affordable child care while they worked, and they were burdened with household responsibilities they could barely meet. Governments relentlessly added to women's feelings of guilt and inadequacy. *"Kinder brauchen mehr Liebe als Haustier"* ("Children need more love than housepets") one famous German billboard had admonished with more than a touch of self-righteousness, and another preached, *"Mehr Zeit für Kinder"* ("More time for children"), even though Germany continued to be notoriously backward among industrial nations in providing child care. France, which had provided universal child care for decades, nevertheless adapted the German campaign to French sensibilities and scattered billboards that pictured enormous-eyed waifs, lamenting *"Les enfants abandonnés"* ("The abandoned children") as if abandonment were a great national problem, the result of self-absorbed mothers.

To add insult to injury, an idea that had its genesis in the state of Oregon, that parents were responsible not only for the civil and property damages their children might cause (as they always had been) but were now liable for criminal action, took hold across the United States and was upheld by the conservative courts. This put extra burdens on single mothers, who were already harried with the sheer task of making a living and now were blamed for their children's delinquency and forced to face criminal charges too.

THE NORTH GETS FROSTIER

One dramatic change in 2015 that had been anticipated, but not prepared for, was the proportion of the elderly in industrialized countries. A hundred years earlier, people over sixty had comprised between 8 and 9 percent of the population; now they were nearly 25 percent. Many of these elderly lived alone, though women were twice as likely to be living alone as men. By the second decade of the new century, large numbers of women were entering old age without any organized outside help to speak of. Governmental agencies lacked the funds and expertise to offer the kind of help needed, and daughters, those standbys of the elderly, were no longer available to offer care. It was common to see frail great-grandmothers looking in futility for help to grandmothers, who in turn looked for help to mothers, a generation of women run ragged by their multiple obligations to husband, children, and their own jobs.

Though a wave of immigrant women from Latin America and Asia rushed in to fill the caregiving vacuum, they brought with them quite different cultural norms. Some of these relationships worked well enough, but some did not, with disappointment, sadness, and sometimes lurid results—stories of old people bilked, tortured, and even murdered were commonplace. With many immigrants arriving illegally, the issue of undocumented private nurses in the opening years of the new century had replaced the issue of illegal nannies in the waning years of the old century. The elderly knew they were vulnerable to blackmail by their illegal immigrant caregivers, or by others who knew of these illicit arrangements, and this added to their stress.

Yet if younger women were run ragged, older women felt besieged. Attack came from every direction. Since the proportion of young workers had shrunk compared to the proportion of pensioners, national pension schemes such as Social Security paid less and less.

What was paid out was begrudged. A campaign slogan arose during the United States elections of 2012: "You cheated our schools; Now who are the fools?" It alluded to the fact that taxpayers had indeed starved American schools in the last part of the twentieth century. As a consequence, workers who were expected to support the social security funds now felt woefully unprepared for the changing demands of the workplace. They blamed their low wages and inability to compete in the global economy on the substandard schooling they'd received in the 1990s and beyond. Rebelling against paying out for the very people who, they believed, had cheated them when they were children, many evaded payments into the social security system. Though they were breaking the law, the popular sentiment was such that they were seldom prosecuted. The young and the middle-aged turned viciously on the old, blaming them for past selfishness.

Older women, who had never been much valued in a patriarchal society, were especially singled out for blame. Whether they lived in suburbs or cities, when elderly women ventured out, they were the overwhelming victims of street violence. By 2015, they represented 38 percent of victims, though they were only 17 percent of the population. Sometimes it was only verbal, as when youngsters followed them, chanting, "K yourself, K yourself," which did not precisely stand for "kill yourself" so much as it was a reference to a notorious and old-time American advocate of euthanasia, Dr. Jack Kevorkian. Often it was worse. Older women were routinely pushed, even mugged, sometimes murdered, but public sentiment was harsh: why were these old women living so long, anyway, sucking up far more than their fair share of resources, resources that could go to the young, who really needed them? Western society, never kind to old women, now made them objects of vicious mockery. Comedians mimicked the problems of old age, from incontinence, to the facial distortions of stroke, to the absent-mindedness of senescence, and found a richly responsive audience.

Older women in the developed countries suffered unnecessarily from diseases that could have been ameliorated, cured, or even prevented. High-tech medical solutions, including customized drugs, genetic therapies, and artificial organ replacement, were withheld from them on the theory that these expensive therapies were wasted on the old—not cost-effective

in formal terms. Older women in the developing countries suffered too, but medical care for them was unthinkable.

What was touted in the developed world as lifelong usefulness thrust old women into lifelong labor, sweeping and cleaning
up, especially public places like parks and highway medians. They
monitored public toilets, they sorted goods to be recycled, and
otherwise made themselves useful to a society that barely tolerated them.

THE SOUTH GETS—AND GIVES—DISEASES

In the Southern Hemisphere and in large parts of Asia, a combination of public denial, religious resistance to condom distribution,
and above all poverty, permitted AIDS and other, far more
tractable, diseases to take hold at rates unprecedented since the ad-
vent of modern medicine. With cities and states of the Southern
Hemisphere unable to provide even minimal sanitary conditions,
with jobs nearly nonexistent in the sprawling megacities of the
south, prostitution—in the form of sex tourism—became, with
drugs, one of the largest sources of income for many southern countries, especially the Philippines, Peru, and Mexico, and, strangely
enough, some of the Islamic states of the former Soviet Union,
which had exhausted themselves in decade-long tribal wars. Without other resources, these countries turned the world's new wave of
puritanism into an economic opportunity, forcing great numbers of
young women into the sex trade for foreign visitors.

Inside the trade itself, fear of disease gave an edge to child
and adolescent prostitution, though statistically, children were
just as likely to be diseased as adult prostitutes. Nevertheless,
children were perceived as healthier and more desirable workers,
and many of the uncounted or missing female children in Asia
were actually conscripts into the voracious sex industry.

Diseases of all kinds were spread not only by scandalous
public health conditions—polluted water, trash mountains,

unchecked raw sewage—but also by pervasive malnutrition. By 2008, agricultural production had dropped precipitously in many southern countries, partly because poor farming methods had poisoned and depleted the land, and partly because in some places, up to 80 percent of the men had fled to the cities, leaving women to farm at a subsistence level, but with no surplus crops to send to the cities. Even small truck gardens that had once supplied essential fresh vegetables were carelessly paved over as the megacities spread, in essence devouring themselves.

THE CALIFORNIA MICROCOSM

In California, many of the conflicts that raged around the world could be seen played out on a smaller scale. The same sense of siege that French colonials once felt at Dien Bien Phu seemed to enervate the state. By 2015, two populations, composed of very different ethnic groups, faced each other as adversaries across a great divide.

One of these populations, representing less than half the state's people, were the Traditionalists. They were relatively older, better off, and white. Traditionalists spoke mainstream English, had higher than average formal education, and as a consequence, higher than average incomes, particularly in the largest segment of their population, which was the 45–54 age group, wealthy, mobile, and energetic: enjoying peak earning years and two incomes often combined with young children still at home. The next largest group, between age 55 and 64, had even more disposable income, with children no longer at home. In this latter group, women slightly outnumbered men.

The Traditionalists had always enjoyed unassailable dominance in politics and business. They had assumed themselves, their values, and their language to be the embodiment of the American way of life. But as the 1990s gave way to the first decade of the twenty-first century, they felt increasingly beset by the clamorous Alien Other Half. Traditionalist women, especially older ones, felt particularly besieged, since fear of crime confined them at home, and when they did go out, they fearfully "dressed down" and drove modest (though well-armored) cars so as not to become targets of criminals.

The Alien Other Half of the state's population, which was numerically nearly the Alien Other Sixty Percent by 2015 (and still growing) was a mixture, with its own internal antagonisms. Hispanics were 35 percent of the general population, more than twice as large as the next largest group, the Asians at 17 percent. Because of shifting proportions, blacks represented only 5 percent of the general population, and their interests had almost disappeared from the public agenda.

The Alien Other Half of the year 2015 was not only much younger, but also less well-off, less educated, with many more children and collateral relatives under their burgeoning household roofs. Most hardly spoke English, thanks to the inability of the exhausted public school system to impart even rudimentary language skills. Like older Traditionalist women, women of all ages among the Alien Other Half were fearful of street violence and stayed at home as much as possible. Their virtual imprisonment left them vulnerable to manipulation and exploitation of every kind.

Even the few Traditionalists inclined to listen to pleas for better schools were shocked to learn that their taxes would be used to redesign schools to meet the needs of the Alien Other Half. Traditionalists retorted that, on the one hand, Hispanics couldn't even stay in the schools that existed, let alone in the intellectually flabby new schools proposed. On the other hand, the Asian minorities had certainly managed well enough in the old school system, so that they were overrepresented in the professions. Why couldn't the Alien Others do as the model Asians had done?

Thus Hispanics, whose school dropout rates were historically the highest, were often unable to find work. Even employers—

educators of last resort, forced by the failure of the schools to take on much of the burden of public education—could not reclaim these lost souls for job-specific training. Women of the Alien Other Half competed ferociously with each other for the low-skill jobs that existed—housekeeping, babysitting.

By 2015, bitter enmities played themselves out in gang warfare, narcotics traffic, and addiction. If the "model minority" Asians sent record numbers of their young people on to higher education, a significant number of them stayed behind, banded together in ethnic gangs, transferring ancient feuds to their new homeland even as they engaged in interethnic gang rivalries with the blacks and Hispanics. In the name of public safety, in 2009, San Marino became the first American city to require its residents to use voice IDs to get inside the electronic barrier surrounding the city.

Women had good reason to stay at home. City streets were battle zones, dominated by a lost generation that neither shared the values of the previous generation, nor had any sustaining values of its own.

California's highway system, its nerve net for half a century, began to fall into disrepair at the beginning of the new century, and neither the funds nor the will could be found to make repairs, much less upgrade the system into smart highways. Thanks to telecommuting, telemedicine, elaborate home entertainment systems, even teleworshipping, and thanks also to pervasive fearfulness, highway usage had begun to drop at century's end anyway—at first slowly, and then faster, as the highways grew more isolated and more dangerous.

So human capital was squandered, with the ethnic groups shrieking past each other, fearful and antagonistic, suspecting and evoking from each other the very worst. The rancor affected women first: poor women of the Alien Other Half, who feared for their lives as they scrambled for unskilled jobs; and older Traditionalist wealthy women who were frightened to leave home. It would eventually affect everyone.

CAROL DEAN, 43, DANCER AND FOUNDER OF THE CAROL DEAN DANCE ENSEMBLE, NEW YORK CITY

This new century is the golden age of dance, no question. We have more wonderful young women dancing now than at any time in the past, and we have more performance spaces in which they can dance. We know more. The science once applied to athletes' bodies has been adapted for dancers. No more yogurt and two packs a day. Now, thanks to modern medicine and techniques, we can sculpt the body into any shape it needs to be, staying healthy enough to dance all the while. You won't see dancers of my generation, or even the generation of young women who are the prime dancers now, suffering from the nutritional deficiencies and then the bone and muscular problems that dancers had in the old days.

It would be naive to say that dance is thriving by chance; of course it isn't. Dance as abstract as ours is only meant to be aesthetically provoking, frankly, not full of meaning. It is sheer pattern—very beautiful pattern, to be sure—that makes no statements, political or otherwise. You could even argue that this, along with the most significant painting of the day too, are only a revisit of the 1950s, when abstract expressionism had its first great heyday, but our abstraction is quite different, I think. What we do share with the fifties sensibility is that we value pattern and form above anything else. Content—content is too old-fashioned.

There are artists who make a fetish of their alienation and protest, but you don't see them performing in public. You can't get hold of their tapes anywhere. You have to know when they're performing and go there; and you run the risk of arrest. Most people aren't willing to run those risks, I mean, not for an evening's entertainment, for heaven's sake.

CAN WE AFFORD KINDNESS TO WOMEN?

Economists since the 1990s had been asking whether the Nordic and Germanic countries could continue to "afford to be so kind to women." The argument ran that Scandinavia's notoriously high taxes, for instance, were mainly the result of the state supplying the services that women had traditionally provided for nothing. By cutting out many of these services—child care (which in the 1990s, absorbed a whopping 6 percent of Sweden's Gross Domestic Product or GDP), sick child care, maternity leave, and care for the elderly—taxes could be cut dramatically, especially since most people employed in these tasks were women. Dismissed from jobs that no longer existed, the argument continued, women would have to go home and do the work for nothing.

European Community women resisted fiercely, pointing out that children belonged to everybody, not just women, and paying their caregivers was hardly "kindness." But chronic unemployment among Scandinavian men beginning in the late 1990s gave weight to the economists' arguments, and in the first decade of the new century, the creches, nurseries, and kindergartens, the senior centers and home help agencies, were unceremoniously dismantled and dismissed within a three-month period in 1999, and women were sent home to do it all once more for nothing. Which, of course, they did.

In the United States, workers without child-care responsibilities (half of all married couples by 2015) began bringing suit against employers for privileges they perceived that parents working alongside them enjoyed. These ranged from extra time off at holidays (when childless workers had to continue working) to family discounts to time off for emergencies. The courts held that these privileges were indeed unfair to the childless, and employers were forbidden to extend these unless they offered comparable extras to nonparents. Most employers withdrew them.

GERMANY GOES BACKWARD

The reunification of the two Germanies in the 1990s seemed inevitable in retrospect. What wasn't inevitable for German women, especially those in the east, was the giant step backward forced upon them by unification. Nobody would argue that under communism sexual equality had arrived. But under the new German capitalism, sexual equality was distinctly rejected. It was widely said: "The Berlin Wall fell on women."

Most obviously, state-supported child care and kindergartens disappeared at once ("a job only a mother can do properly," said a complacent German politician who was later elected chancellor in 2005). Jobs had immediately disappeared, as inefficient eastern industries and bureaucracies were shut down. Federal development was slow to stimulate the creation of new jobs for men or women, but when at last jobs did appear, men got priority. Housing in the east was as bad as ever, made worse, if possible, by the disputes over ownership. As long as titles were unclear (and legal squabbles continued well into the new century, with old deeds floating out of attics and cellars) current residents refused to make even ordinary repairs. Little commercial property was developed for the same reason, which meant that twenty years later many women were shopping for groceries in the same dismal socialist barns their mothers and grandmothers had shopped.

Then in late 1995, after a bitter legislative and court battle, a new federal law rescinded the right to legal abortion that women in former East Germany had long held, bringing the eastern states in compliance with West German law. (In a peculiar [and self-contradictory] compromise, abortion would be illegal but unpunishable if it were undertaken in the first trimester; the woman underwent mandatory counseling, which included persuading her to keep the child, and then got a permission slip. Of course, illegal abortions were always available, with their attendant risks.)

Women of the former East Germany saw the abortion decision as one more humiliating, forced sacrifice to the hypocrites of the west on behalf of unification. They knew very well that wealthy German women in the west who needed abortions simply went abroad. They spoke sardonically of the autonomy they'd once had over their own bodies under "godless communism" and the paternalistic red tape they now had to cut, the doctors they would have to toady to for permission, to carry out what they felt was a deeply private decision.

In real numbers, it almost didn't matter. The eastern birth rate had already dropped after unification to less than half of what it had been before unification, and it did not regain its old rate at any time in the next twenty years. The marriage rate dropped more than 60 percent. Sterilizations shot up. (Divorce was down, but this only indicated how economically dependent German women were upon their husbands.) By 2015, eastern Germany had lost a quarter of its population.

Though the big differential between eastern and western salaries gradually disappeared, so that by 2015 they were indistinguishable, women's wages stayed where they were. It had been shocking, something the Federal Republic worked hard to remedy, when eastern salaries were 65 percent of western salaries. But women's salaries remained at 65 percent of men's, and nobody gave it a second official thought.

"What good is freedom to me if I cannot use it?" The question had been asked by every eastern German woman after reunification. She was grieving the loss of her good job, her good apartment, her child care, the autonomy over her own body she once took for granted. Five years after reunification, twice as many women as men were unemployed in the five eastern states. Ten years later, in 1999, when men's employment had improved slightly, thanks to federal development efforts, women's rates were just as intractably low. The Federal Republic did not deny that its policies favored men over women: that was the way of the world, it was only natural.

By 2015, the generation of women who had known some measure of sexual equality under communism was long gone from the workforce, their stories discredited as the foolish nostalgia of the old. Younger women had never known anything else. Willingly or not, they shrugged and accepted the general German view that women's domain was Kinder, Küche, und Kirche.

RUSSIA AND EASTERN EUROPE

One of the few positive aspects of communism, its social services, came under a double-barreled attack beginning in the 1990s, an attack that was victorious as the new century opened. In the economic chaos of the postcommunist period, social services were deemed unaffordable to economies trying desperately to catch up with free market economies. The rise of orthodox religions, Christian and Muslim, held that women must be at home, having and taking care of babies, and anything that permitted them to deviate from this God-given path was wicked. Both attacks shared a fundamental if unspoken assumption, that social services benefited only women, and not society in general, and women did not deserve benefits.

Each former member of the Warsaw Pact reacted in its own way. In Poland, for example, up against the same double-barreled attack, astonished women invoked a long tradition of equality in protest and fought back: women had always participated in uprisings, in conspiracies, in the resistance against the Nazis, and in the anticommunist underground. But this time they failed. Beginning with a Catholic Church–engineered anti-abortion law passed in 1993, women's rights were gradually revoked. Birth control devices and information had never been widely available, and now they all but disappeared. Women were discouraged and then prevented from attending the universities; the professions instituted informal quotas that permitted only token women members; a division of labor was promoted as more "Western."

The Polish abortion underground was dangerous for its practitioners and dangerous for its clients—not only because illegal medical procedures were always dangerous, but also because men were so often tempted to seek retribution against women (out of jealousy, or unrequited love, or just because they could) by denouncing, old communist-style, those who'd had abortions. But out of necessity, the underground continued to flourish. The term "feminism" had long been associated with party ideology, and though some Polish women tried to recapture and cleanse the term, that proved impossible. Polish women realized that not only were they systematically being cut out of all the prosperity capitalism might bring, but the Polish tradition of equality was also being jettisoned.

In Hungary, however, partly because to do otherwise was so difficult, partly because it was such a novelty, a rise in the Kinder, Küche, Kirche ethos among younger women was already detectable at the beginning of the 1990s and grew in strength for fifteen years or more. But Hungary's economy wasn't robust enough to permit women to stay home and look after the children, the kitchen, and the church. Instead, women, obliged to work, were kept in the lowest-paying jobs on the theory that they were soon "going back home where they belonged."

In Russia, the failed transition from communism to capitalism had eventually brought the return of a repressive, hierarchical regime, almost as harsh as anything the country had seen in the 1930s. General Vladimir Fyodorov led an ultranationalist government to power in 2002 on a platform pledged to eliminating organized crime at any cost. But the political extremism only masked the real power, held by an international cartel whose business was drugs, sex, and organized crime. Women were almost incidental to this society, except as commodities in the sex trade. But they were systematically terrorized and suffered disproportionately from it.

Despite the difficulties of acquiring contraceptives, Eastern Europe and Russia exhibited a dramatic decline in births beginning with the dissolution of the former Soviet Empire and its satellite nations. Over the next five years, in Poland the birth rate fell 20 percent; in Bulgaria 25 percent; in Estonia and Romania, 30 percent; in Russia 35 percent, and in eastern Germany more than 60 percent. These low birth rates were sustained for twenty years.

This sudden decline was initially blamed on uncertainty about the future, but as the decline continued, government and church officials began to blame women's selfishness. A number of pro-natalist laws were passed, though they could fairly be characterized as antiwoman rather than pro-child, prohibiting women from seeking out higher education and explicitly barring them from high-paying jobs. But owing to widespread poverty, women still had to work. Wage disparities were explained away by the excuse that "women aren't so good after all," or "it would offend our more important male employees if they thought women were getting equal wages." Most Eastern European countries had also dismantled their admirable child-care systems, on the theory that professional child care was an unaffordable luxury, and however unrealistic, it would be most desirable if mothers were at home looking after their own children.

Poverty had destroyed the health-care system, so that ordinary, preventable disease was rampant and severe diseases claimed victims almost immediately. Poverty made mere housing a luxury; and poverty forced families to forgo kindergartens and higher education for their children. Even if their families could pay, many women found themselves prevented from taking places in the universities that were allocated to men.

In the decade following the dissolution of the Soviet Union, an entire generation buckled under infectious diseases, stress, malnutrition, and alcoholism. In Russia, there was a tenfold increase in families living below the poverty line, and mortality went up by 35 percent compared to pre-1989 times. The homicide rate continued to rise until it was triple even that of the United States. For the first time, hard drug use became a serious and widespread problem in Russia, and when the inevitable AIDS epidemic followed, Russia's already enfeebled medical system simply disappeared. By 2015, the former Soviet Union's population had stabilized at approximately two thirds of its pre-1989 numbers, with demographics skewed toward the elderly.

Into the power vacuum created by the collapse of the former Soviet Union rushed environmental rapacity and regressive social organizations: the Orthodox Church successfully lobbied to deprive women of even the paper rights they had had under communism. As the population fell, the church's push for procreation was more and more welcomed by social planners and politicians, who joined others in pressuring women to produce babies by edict and then by legislation.

Brute-force crime organizations also rushed into the vacuum and took up permanent residence in Russia. Even before the Berlin Wall fell, the Russian Mafia had been among the boldest and most ruthless in the world. Organized crime had existed in the Soviet Union long before the fall of communism, but post-communist chaos had permitted it to thrive, its members practicing extortion, fraud, and murder. Unlike the Mob in the West, which mainly controlled criminal activities, the Mafia operated quasi-legitimate and legitimate businesses too, such as banks. Well armed with automatic weapons, bombs, and rocket-launched grenades, they brought such carnage to the streets—not only of Russia, but of other Eastern European nations—that Russians gladly voted in a repressive regime that promised to suppress crime. Since many of the politicians associated with the extremists were also part of the criminal syndicates, the new government only moved crime off the streets. Legitimate businesses, from multinational oil companies to vegetable stalls in local markets, were resigned to paying protection and bribing suppliers, haulers, and government officials, who continued to license and regulate nearly every activity. But part of the new government's scheme to lend authority to its power was a guise of unusual puritanism, which fell hardest on women who were now subject to curfews and forbidden to dress "provocatively," to read "unsuitable material," or to "be seen in unsuitable places." The definition of unsuitable was left to local authorities, who used it as one more opportunity to extort money and sex from women.

THE ISLAMIC WORLD: THE SLAUGHTER OF THE INNOCENTS

At the end of the twentieth century and the beginning of the twenty-first, women in the Islamic world went through a protracted and contentious period of sorting out the differences between what they considered Western imperialism and the homegrown misogyny represented by the fundamentalist Islamic mullahs. Activists engaged in bitter debates about what constituted human rights versus what constituted women's rights, some arguing that women needed the special protection of the veil, even a return to the harem (a significant minority arguing from what they understood to be theology, that Allah had spoken: women were in fact inferior); and others arguing that all women shared concerns about equity and education; about child spacing and their children's health, and that these issues could be the building blocks of an international women's consensus.

Women had been killed in chilling numbers for crimes

against Islam as part of the guerrilla war in Algeria during the last part of the twentieth century. But the fall of the secular Egyptian government in 2004 and its replacement by a brutal fundamentalist regime was a form of electroshock. Now Islamic women all over the world confronted unapologetic power lust, speciously justified by theology. The most egregious event was the Slaughter of the Innocents: women and girls of the city of Alexandria who had not acceded to new veiling and separation laws were herded into an ancient urban square and publicly gunned down without trial, reenacting a scene that had already taken place in Bosnia, Pakistan, Rwanda, and Thailand, in dozens of refugee camps all over the world. The Slaughter of the Innocents was neither on a larger scale nor particularly more bloody than those others; the difference was that to the Slaughter of the Innocents, the world was eyewitness. The fundamentalist Egyptian government was so confident it could act with impunity that it permitted television cameras to record the entire incident. When these pictures flashed live across screens all over the world, no one could doubt that the issue was misogyny, not theology.

THE JAPANESE ANOMALY

By 2015, Japan seemed to have taken steps toward gender equality. But that was only because it had started out as one of the worst in the industrialized world. In the 1990s, the UN Human Development Index had put Japan at number one, but when figures were adjusted for gender disparity, Japan dropped to number seventeen among nations, in human development.

A decade into the new century, the average earnings of women, which had been about half those of men in the 1990s, now began to rise to the 60 percent mark. The minuscule number of Japanese women in administration and management (7 percent in the 1990s) had tripled to 20 percent. Though Japanese women had been able to vote since the end of World War II, the paltry 2 percent of parliamentary seats they occupied tripled in the first decade and a half of the new century—to 6 percent. There continued to be no women at the ministerial level except for one, Kimiko Yoshihara, who headed health matters for several years at the opening of the new century, though her forthright stand that the AIDS epidemic must be recognized and responded to brought her many enemies and eventually cost her her job.

One consequence of this longstanding gender disparity was that for decades beginning in the second part of the twentieth century, and continuing into the twenty-first, the best and brightest young Japanese women migrated to the West for college and career—the Japanese brain drain nobody ever talked about. Moreover, in a culture that valued form and courtesy enormously, women had always been in the peculiar situation of having to use a special version of Japanese, "women's talk," with built-in self-effacement and deference to men. Women who refused to speak this denigrating language were considered scandalous and uncivil; worse, they were ineffective at accomplishing anything. They had no choice but to emigrate.

However, what seemed like a slow improvement had really stalled. A series of natural and social events in the decade between 1995 and 2005 made Japanese, both men and women, long for and then demand what they called a return to order. These events included the burst economic bubble of the 1980s with its severe follow-on recession, the Kobe Earthquake, the gas attacks in the Tokyo subways, and, perhaps most distressing of all, a devastating attack in 2009 on the extremely well-guarded Tokyo Airport at Narita, where twenty-five large aircraft were blown up simultaneously, more than half of them with passengers and crew aboard. It was not only the monstrousness of the act that appalled the world; it was also that even the efficient Japanese government seemed unable to guard itself and its country against major terrorist attacks.

Outdated pacifism was blamed for the government's ineptitude: right-wing paramilitary groups, already enjoying some popularity, saw a sudden surge in their memberships, rivaled only by recruitments into religious cults. Newspapers admonished citizens to report any suspicious activity, encouraging them to spy on each other. In the elections of 2010, a new militaristic party gained enough votes to become a majority in the Diet, and reforms began. Yet the social fabric seemed to unravel further. Juvenile gang violence against other children was widespread and went unpunished; violence against women by men was even worse, especially because it evoked far less public outrage. Back to Tradition was the slogan, and if that included subordinating women, so be it.

Psychologically, Japanese women blamed themselves for much of this predicament. In the face of past harassment or injustice, they had preferred to overlook it instead of fighting it like their Western sisters. Domestic violence, whether it came from husbands or schoolboy sons, who turned and attacked their mothers as symbols of the unbearable academic pressure they felt, had been quietly ignored for decades. When a singular woman took action, either legally or by complaining, she was ostracized as a troublemaker. It put women in a classic double bind: if they didn't protest, nothing changed, and they had only themselves to blame; if they did, their punishment was ostracism.

Nevertheless, as women continued to enroll in higher education in Japan, their numbers moved up from two thirds close to parity with men. But if they chose to stay in Japan, as soon as these young women graduated from college or university, they faced a life much like the lives their mothers had led: they worked at inconsequential jobs for a decade or so, then reluctantly married and stayed at home, kept house, and reared their child or two children.

The acrimony between the sexes in Japan was palpable. One early indication of this had been the way traditional housewives greeted the first retired "salarymen" from Japan's postwar industrial boom, who began retiring in greater and greater numbers beginning in the 1980s. These men came home to households where they were not only strangers, but contemptible strangers. Their wives referred to them openly as "kitchen garbage" and only gave them pocket money to get them out of the house. Cut off from the fellowship of the office, the status their jobs had once given them, despised at home, this group of men began committing suicide in alarming numbers.

For younger couples, a custom at the end of the century, "in-house divorce," where couples under the same roof led totally separate lives, continued more widespread than ever. Men got their sexual satisfaction elsewhere, and women channeled their sexual energies into volunteer work, sports, and friendships with other women. While this estrangement was based on mutual antipathy, for women it was also self-protection, since AIDS had struck Japan hard, brought in by men who had traveled to Thailand on sex tours.

Women had never been welcomed in Japanese corporations, and this continued into the new century. Japan's relatively late entry into electronic communication (thanks to turf wars fought by the companies and the government ministries) also cut women off from each other, so that networking was more difficult for them than for women in other developed countries. Japan's infrastructure, long neglected in favor of other public investments, was by 2015 in crisis: the antiquated sewer system caused cholera outbreaks; the water system was unreliable; the power grid was given to outages since the lines were almost all above ground and vulnerable to interference—never mind that they were eyesores.

A curious backlash to the Japanese backlash developed. A marginal phenomenon in the 1990s, sex clubs run by lesbians had become an enormous fad in Japan fifteen years later. These were run by "Miss Dandies," lesbians who lived and dressed as men and sometimes took male hormones. They catered to straight women who found men disappointing or unsatisfactory. "Our customers want the kind of attention that men rarely provide," one club owner said, explaining the startling growth of the fad. "We look like men; we act like men; yet we're kind and gentle. We understand what women want." And, the club owner added, "We are disease-free."

THE DEVELOPING COUNTRIES OF ASIA

In the mid-1990s demographers could see that a number of cultural beliefs were converging with government policies to subvert any improvement in women's social and economic status in China, India, Pakistan, and other heavily populated countries where male births were favored over female births. In China, the one-child policy (which effectively translated to one son) produced a surplus of 1 million unmarried men each year beginning in 2010, and this led to a number of drastic remedies.

Foreigners found endless difficulties in doing business in many Asian countries. Business executives had declared that the three most corrupt were China, India, and Indonesia, but the Philippines and Malaysia weren't far behind. Corruption especially hampered businesses, who were prohibited by law from offering bribes and faced penalties if they were discovered doing so. In contrast, businessmen from more worldly nations, like Denmark, wrote off bribes as a tax deduction. Worse, in both China and India, an investor could never be sure that a contract was really binding—the Chinese would change their minds capriciously; the Indians would have an election and the new government would insist on rewriting foreign contracts to suit themselves. As this sort of behavior became typical, foreign investment in both India and China diminished, making what were once rosy projections now a pale gray.

Women were particularly sensitive to their nation's economic climate—if China or India failed to attract foreign capital, there was little at home to provide jobs. But women suffered the most in the countries that had been trapped into the sex industry by the development strategies of the 1980s: Thailand, the Philippines, and Vietnam. And then there was the unusual case of China.

Forgive me. I am sorry to have to meet you here in the Women's Institute, but as my government puts it, I am doing my patriotic duty for these three years. I am happy for an opportunity to practice my English with you. It is such poor schoolbook English—I put so much time into my mathematics studies that I neglected my English. Perhaps you will help me learn to speak more colloquially? I would be very grateful.

How did I get here? As you can see, most of my colleagues are country girls, who couldn't get deferments. I'm one of the few educated women here. I wouldn't be here either but I was orphaned in my teens. Of course, being here, I now understand that the country girls object to this service just as much as well-educated women. Most people don't understand that. Still, it is better than slavery, which has flourished in our country for twenty years.

My life itself raises a major question in the first place. Why am I here, I often wonder, while so many girls and women who should have been here are not? I don't mean here in the Institute, but here on earth, alive. The abortions, the baby girls who were abandoned to die; all this was taking place as my mother carried me. All this had always taken place, in fact, but it was far worse once the one-child policy was put in place.

Consider, please, more recent history. You are aware

that for those people who obeyed the law (not everybody did, especially in the countryside) one child almost always meant one son, by any means whatsoever. No one knew how it would all turn out. Even before I was born, the first products of that one-child policy, the surplus young men, were already reaching adolescence and forming the infamous wolf-packs, as we called them, those predatory bands of unattached males. Unfortunately, this coincided with massive unemployment and made Chinese cities even more dangerous than they already were. Every year since 2010, a million unattached males have come of age. In a population of well over a billion, this may not seem like much of an imbalance. But you must remember that these numbers are compounding annually, and these are some of the most volatile members of society, these wolf-men. As you see, the perfect recipe for gang warfare. For warfare of any kind.

In 1975 when I was born, the ratio of male to female babies was 5 to 1 in the countryside. This is not nature. This is man's interference with nature. It is still thought that nature normally gives a slight edge to little boys, since they are more vulnerable, though we also understand that this slight edge might in fact be the result of bias against females over the history of the human race.

Immigration increased dramatically, though to the countries they tried to immigrate, the wolf-men were as welcome as wolves usually are. They entered the Americas illegally, and sometimes they were given asylum on humanitarian grounds, but their immigration to Australia, for example, was banned. Many of them stopped in the archipelagos, but they were also unwelcome there and hardly improved their lives, much less the quality of life on the islands. They have been executed on the spot in Indonesia. They have begun colonies in various outlying places in Siberia, but an all-male colony is never a pleasant place, nor can it sustain itself indefinitely, even with artificial wombs.

Ironically, you and I may note in passing that these wolf-men, these immigrants, dying on Indonesian beaches, moldering in American jails, are the very sons of parents who had presumably gone to some trouble and effort to ensure that their one allotted child was a son— the son they could count on to keep the family going, both by being a comfort to his elderly parents and by producing further members of the line. History has a sense of humor, no?

I jump ahead of myself. I raised the question of my own existence. Why did my parents choose to let me live when I was born in 1975, why did they rear me, when the bias toward sons was so strong? They were not sophisticated people—both of them worked in factories—and it is absurd to think that they carefully calculated that an excess of males in the population must mean that I would be much more likely to marry and bear children, thus carrying on the family. No. But the value of something scarce? This they understood intuitively.

What they couldn't have grasped, because it is utterly counterintuitive, is that the population in the aggregate began to act in what we would technically call a nonlinear manner. I hope you don't mind some mathematical terms. We still don't understand in detail how genes and culture interact, but we understand it far better now than we used to.

To oversimplify, nature and culture together began favoring male children in the Chinese population to such an extent that the numbers of female babies took a dramatic drop. On the one hand, fewer female babies were deliberately killed now, because more families were producing their desired males. But this collaboration of culture and nature also meant that females were on the verge of disappearing altogether. By 2008, the incidence of female births was nearly subcritical, and instead of population explosion, we worried about population collapse. The rapidity with which this happened is astonishing, but not out of line with what we know about positive feedback in nonlinear systems. In China's case, the effect was accelerated by the great Beijing Earthquake of 2004, and the drought years of 2005–8, which not only affected food production but aggravated the clean water issue, which had been a problem for decades.

Population collapse isn't necessarily a disaster—you can argue that a good weeding out permits the cultivation of long overdue political reform and frees resources for cultural flowering. Perhaps that happened with the Black Death just before the European Renaissance, or even earlier, in some of the late Ice Ages. Population collapse is not necessarily a disaster for the nation or even the planet, but unquestionably it brings millions upon millions of personal tragedies. The social structures for coping with human population collapse are nearly nil.

Like every other Chinese woman who reaches age sixteen, at that time I underwent a mandatory ovarectomy—all my eggs were removed and frozen and are being fertilized in vitro. I am not considered healthy enough or, for that matter, reliable enough to bear my own children. In passing, I might draw your attention to the dreadful morbidity and mortality rates of these compulsory surgeries. They are not conducted under the best of conditions. But you know about this; I'm informed it is an international scandal. Less well known is the problem of organ removal. While the rest of the world can clone healthy, perfectly matching organs for transplant, my country finds it cheaper and less trouble to harvest organs from living persons. Or the newly dead, such as executed prisoners. So—every woman awakens from this surgery feeling first her belly, where the ovarectomy has been performed, and then her back, to see if a kidney, for example, has also been removed. We count ourselves lucky that we wake up at all—obviously our hearts and lungs remain.

Unfortunately for me, my parents and my father's family were taken during the years of the Great Drought. I was effectively alone. I was already studying mathematics at our academic high school here in Shanghai, and if I had been a man I would be at the university now instead of here. Even though I was born a girl, my parents would have been able to argue for a deferment for me. My father, being the man he was, would have bought my deferment.

When girls exhaust their appeals and realize they'll be conscripted into the Women's Service, some 30 percent of them commit suicide. When I knew I must join, suicide occurred to me, I admit it. Perhaps because I would be the very last of my family . . . perhaps because I have an enormous will to live, to survive this . . . perhaps. . . . Anyway, I am permitted books between clients.

My personal future? When my service here is finished, I hope to return to my mathematics studies at the university. If I never see another man again it will be too soon for me. Oh, the service here is less burdensome than girls expect. This isn't Thailand, as we're often reminded. A quota of ten men a day, and if we accept extra men we can reduce our conscription period. Each man above the quota of ten only amounts to a half hour's reduction, but it eventually accumulates. I will say this for the authorities: they are scrupulous about the bookkeeping. But so are we. I keep track for some of the illiterate girls. The whole Women's Institute was set up for men who can never hope to marry yet choose to remain at home to do their filial duty. The men cannot be admitted unless they shower, brush their teeth, and also submit to medical inspection, though we routinely use condoms. There is still risk. Our condoms are barely as good as the condoms the West had thirty years ago. Which is to say, they aren't foolproof.

PROSPERITY COMES TO INDIA

As the new century opened, economic growth seemed stalled everywhere but India, which was quickly shaking off its economic torpor. A sign of new times, a state-of-the-art Indian stock exchange finally opened in 2005, connected to exchanges all over the world. The relative value of the rupee was as common a quote in business news as the value of the yen or the dollar. Satellite dishes received programming from competing TV networks, and a wireless phone system permitted a leap over the difficulties of installing a wired infrastructure. The promise of the 1990s, a large and relatively wealthy Indian middle class, hungry to buy, buy, and buy again, had by 2010 at last arrived, and India's economy seemed to be on the verge of fulfilling the promises that it would be one of the world's largest by 2020.

Unfortunately, what had only been a trend at the end of the century inflated into an epidemic as the new century opened—dowry demands seemed a quick and easy way for young men and their families to join in the buying spree. Families of every religious, social, and economic background saw the dowry a son received from his wife's family not as the foundation upon which his new family would be built, but as a shortcut to material goods. Since the bride would bring these things to the groom's family

home, dowries were suddenly a means to acquire a color TV, a re-
frigerator, a washer, a computer, or an automobile. Even after
marriage, a man's family would continue to press his bride's family for further dowry payments. If the demands weren't met, the
husband and family would begin to abuse the young wife, tor-
ment and torture her, perhaps eventually kill her. Murder was
easy: though laws existed against both murder and dowry extortion, it was commonplace to bribe officials to overlook the death
of just another girl and declare it accidental.

What had been an alarming statistic in the 1990s—seventeen married women killed nationwide each day because of their
family's inability to meet dowry demands—escalated to an appalling hundreds per day by 2015 as the consumer frenzy
mounted. Families were so frightened of these demands, demands
that translated into years, sometimes generations, of debt, that
they usually preferred to abort female fetuses or kill baby daughters rather than face the debt. Inevitably, India began to experience the lopsided ratio of males to females that had already
afflicted China.

When Western images began to flood India from satellite TV
in the mid-1990s, many Indian young people underwent a crisis
of identity. Into this confusion moved two fundamentalist Hindu
political parties, the Bharatiya Janata party and the Shiv Sena
party, offering novel interpretations of the hugely popular Hindu
myths, interpretations that were medieval in their stereotyping of
women. Mythical Hindu heroines were portrayed as having a
nearly infinite capacity for self-sacrifice; they acknowledged that
their only proper role was service to the family, and cautionary
tales showed how women who worked outside could never rear
their children properly. These myths captured the imagination of
millions of Indian young people; their simplicity and obviousness
seemed deeply "Indian," different from and purer than corrupt
Western ideas.

Until the Indian elections of 2006, Hindu fundamentalists

hadn't yielded to the violence Islamic fundamentalists practiced. But in 2006, Hindu fundamentalist policymakers of both parties were confident that a little blood would buy a lot of votes. Though in the election they failed to carry a majority, they did not give up violence against women and women's organizations, but increased it to make the point more dramatically.

> PEARL CHU, 39, SOFTWARE ENGINEER, BORN AND REARED IN SINGAPORE, IMMIGRANT TO COSTA RICA

At first they said it was because the population wasn't growing fast enough. Men wouldn't marry well-educated women (they're not so pliant), and well-educated women resisted taking several giant steps backward into a conventional Asian marriage. That much is plausible, I suppose.

Next they claimed that women were so "over-educated" that they were keeping men from the jobs men ought to have, though nobody explained why men ought to have them if women were doing them just as well or better. Without any opposition, the parliament passed a law—in the interests of the state—to prohibit women from taking certain high-level jobs. That meant a young woman could look ahead and see that whatever her natural cleverness, however hard she worked as a student, she would never get the real rewards she was entitled to once she entered the job market.

I was already at the university when that law passed. I was one of those women who saw that no matter how hard I worked, I'd be frustrated. For a few years I let myself imagine that I'd be the exception. At that time I was considered one of the best software engineers of my generation. How could they do without me?

But, little by little, educational opportunities began

to be foreclosed for girls. In the interests of the state, of course. Everything in Singapore is always in the interests of the state. My daughters were shut out of classes they should have been taking, and while we taught them ourselves, using good educational software, it didn't matter. If they didn't have the credentials, they couldn't go on. But as girls, they were forbidden to get the credentials. They couldn't even be admitted to the academic preparatory school I'd gone to; they were getting messages in the media about how their lives revolved around their wombs. The discrimination was both overt and subtle. Ironically, when we knew I would bear a daughter the second time I was pregnant, we thought we were doing something quite daring and unconventional to have a second girl. If I had it to do over again, I'm not sure I would do the same thing.

Finally, the political pattern—that dissent is absolutely forbidden and rigidly punished—imposed itself on other avenues of life, especially affecting women. We were kept from many courses in school; we were forbidden to pursue certain careers. There was great social pressure to marry early and have a family.

Worst of all, a woman could not be disrespectful to her husband—disrespectful as defined by the state, defined by husbands, defined by anybody male—or she risked jail, even flogging. Even in a loving relationship, which mine was, I could see that my husband had an enormous weapon against me he could use anytime he wanted. What had been a happy relationship between equals gradually shifted into an unhappy relationship between nonequals.

If I'd begun with the assumption that I must be subordinate, maybe I wouldn't have found all this so impossible to swallow. But that isn't how I began. I began by assuming I was as good as anyone; better than most. Suddenly everybody—the state, my mother, my mother-in-law, my employer; even, despite his best efforts, my husband—was saying quite the opposite.

Women are said to be devious, but I consider what I did to be only prudent planning. My daughters and I had no alternative but to get out. To make a very long story short, I planned a vacation trip to Costa Rica, presumably to see the reclamation of the tropical rain forests. In fact, I knew that Costa Rica was becoming an information haven and that they'd probably find my skills interesting. We had two weeks of exploring the forests, and only I knew they might be our last two weeks as a family. At the end, I informed my husband that I'd been granted asylum in Costa Rica and that if he wanted to join us, he could. He chose not to. I don't underestimate the difficulties he had with this decision. He is a good father and loves his daughters. But he is also—basically—Confucian.

After a certain amount of fussing and fuming about my defection, the Singapore government dropped it. It was understood that as an information economy Singapore depends on Costa Rica more than it cares to disclose. The issue died.

By the way, I wasn't the first, nor the last. We're quite a little colony now. Some of us are women dissidents; some are just plain dissidents who need to breathe a little easier. Everyone knows that Singapore executes hackers, anyone who compromises the government-controlled information networks. Not everyone knows that this puts every single person who's capable of programming at risk—and who isn't capable these days? My best friend was accused of encrypting, which in Singapore is plain evidence of criminal activity. In fact it wasn't encrypted material that her transmitter was sending out; it was noise—a bug in a chip. But what a fool she'd be to try to explain. We've all seen what happens when you try to explain. More come to join us all the time here, the cream of that enormous effort to educate a generation in information technology. The best minds need room to stretch, and we have it here.

I've remarried—another boy I went to college with in Singapore. He immigrated here to breathe and stretch too. But I worry about my girls. What if they don't have the stamina it takes to be the very best? Why isn't it enough just to be adequate?

THE TRAGEDY OF THE FILIPINAS

Over the last two decades of the twentieth century, more than 300,000 Filipina women went abroad to work each year, a staggering cumulative number that had some demographers wondering if the Philippine population might collapse. Stroll along the Hong Kong waterfront or through the Piazza Navona in Rome on a Sunday afternoon, and you'd see thousands of household *amahs* gladly visiting with each other on their day off. As in many other Asian cultures, young Filipinas felt obliged to take on responsibility for the debts of their family, and with a per capita GNP of just under US$600, most families were poor.

The majority of these immigrant women traveled as domestic workers (though a significant number signed up for domestic work but found themselves forced into the sex trade); a smaller number went abroad as trained professionals, such as nurses; about 5,000 a year went as mail-order brides, especially to North America and Australia, where mail-order marriages were considered a legal and historically hallowed agreement between consenting adults (though Filipina women were usually coerced into these arrangements by male family members). A large fraction of the 300,000 went abroad as workers in the sex trade to Japan, Thailand, and elsewhere.

Sociologists had often been able to show that high educational levels for women give them opportunities for jobs better than prostitution, so it was an odd and disquieting sign that the Philippines, with a nearly equal ratio of female-to-male educational achievement, dispatched so many of its daughters into the sex trade both at home and abroad. Other sociologists had argued that women with more education could also insist on condom use—though if women were driven to prostitution for survival, it seemed unlikely they could insist on much of anything from their clients. After all, they were only keeping one eighth of the money they earned—the rest remained with pimps, brothel owners, and organized crime.

The local Philippine sex industry owed its genesis to vigorous government promotion, as a means to acquire foreign currency in the 1970s and 1980s. Once the Indochina War ended, and the Americans gave up their Philippine military bases, this official promotion accelerated. Government policies that referred to "hospitality and entertainment" industries really meant prostitution, including child prostitution (in the 1980s, Pagsanjan in Laguna Province had become the Asian pedophile capital).

For several decades, Filipina sex workers at home and abroad accepted the fact that when they returned to their villages, they would be welcomed only for the money they brought to their families. They knew their bounty was received ambivalently: with gratitude, with shame, with guilt. In a passionately Catholic land they would carry forever their reputation as whores; they would seldom if ever marry; and the children they brought back with them would also suffer. But in the 1980s and 1990s it was still possible to return: women did it. They referred to their work, especially abroad, in war terms, a tour of duty; and some made several tours of duty. They became part of a relatively small pool of sexually available women, a circumstance that strongly accelerates the spread of the AIDS virus.

By the late 1990s, the slow-acting AIDS virus had begun to show itself, and the Philippines moved into Stage II of an AIDS epidemic, where large numbers of people sickened and died. Now these returning "soldiers" were seen as something even more malignant: they were sinners, and as a consequence, the bearers of a deadly disease. Since medications to ameliorate the symptoms of AIDS were few and costly, and since clinics had always been unevenly distributed, victims suffered mightily and died. That their disease was the result of sin added to their estrangement from others, including the families they had set out to save.

As the disease became more and more apparent, the government equivocated about preventive measures, especially since condoms were so adamantly opposed by the church, whose support the government relied upon for whatever moral authority it had with voters. Exhibiting a hypocrisy monumental even by the standards of the sex trade, government spokesmen blamed "the foolish and wicked women who had succumbed" to working in the very sex industry it had itself vigorously promoted. By making scapegoats of women who had "succumbed," the Philippine government succeeded in hiding its own corruption, as well as its policy failures in economics and in health care.

Sadly, even among the plethora of Filipina women's groups that existed, few felt self-confident enough to stand up for the "soldiers" who had sacrificed their lives for their families and their country. The AIDS Magdalenas, as they were called, became more and more isolated, left to suffer and die like biblical lepers. Convent schools, which had traditionally condemned the sins of the flesh, especially female flesh, grew more and more strident, and a new generation of young women grew up with the frightened but unshakable belief that their sexuality was by definition sinful.

Yet this delayed-action disease manifested itself in widening circles and in larger numbers of people. High government officials began to show symptoms, as did chaste wives who had been infected by their straying husbands. Returning Filipina immigrants who had worked hard and honorably, leading blameless lives in foreign countries, were accused of harboring the virus: they were shunned by neighbors, discriminated against by employers, even attacked physically. Immigrants abroad who had intended to return home made what arrangements they could to stay where they were, no matter how obnoxious the conditions.

By 2005, a compost heap of fear and superstition had nourished a new political demagoguery, sweeping out of the city slums and the country villages, led by men and women alike. It condemned women as the source of all social evil and demanded that they stay at home and be good wives and mothers (though nobody had any idea how families would survive without the earnings of all adults). The demagogues spoke about working to rescind women's civil rights, beginning with the vote.

Though this demagoguery failed to find enough support to survive more than a few years, its misogyny infected every level of Philippine discourse. By 2015, every Filipina had become a potential AIDS Magdalena.

SEXUALITY DENIED AND EXPLOITED

When the UN Cairo Third International Conference on Population and Development closed in 1994, many women were jubilant that the United Nations had finally affirmed women's rights to comprehensive health care, education, and autonomy as necessary first steps toward population control. Though they well understood that the document produced by the Cairo Conference had no legal force, it stood as a model for nations to measure themselves against, and it was sure to be influential in national legislatures in the future.

Women rejoiced too soon.

The counter-chorus began and grew louder: what really ailed the present world was women's libertine behavior. By 2000, a celebrated slogan had found its way around the world, in many languages: "When women go for it, they always go too far." Put a stop to that, went the arguments on talk shows, in electronic discussions, and letters to the editor—arguments taken up at once by politicians—and you would soon eliminate illegitimate births, wayward children, insubordinate women, crime, unemployment, disease, and poverty. The family would be restored; men would be able to be real men again, if only women were forced to be proper women.

Abortion had long been the premier symbol of promiscuity and social failure. Though dressed up in language about protection of life, in fact anti-abortion sentiment stood as much as anything for a revulsion against the female libido, something that growing numbers of men and women were determined to control, deny, and even eliminate—a possibility that was even being tried chemically in certain religiously controlled regions by 2008.

The right to legal abortion had been rescinded in eastern Germany when it reunited with western Germany at the beginning of the 1990s and in Poland when it gained independence. Here the language was protection of the unborn and sacredness of life, but what really drove this policy was the Catholic Church, flexing its political muscle by promulgating its traditional misogyny.

In the United States, an ever-more bitter battle had been fought around this issue since abortion was legalized in 1972. A quarter-century after that Supreme Court decision, abortion had become a focus of protests that turned from words to terrorism, often lethal. Terrorism succeeded where reason failed: as the century drew to a close, fewer physicians knew how to perform an abortion, and those who did were too frightened to. Though the morning-after pill was potentially available for contraception, it was so carefully regulated in most states that "morning after" was a ridiculous misnomer. Other forms of pharmaceutical abortifacients were also banned.

Thus by 2003, misogyny, pro-natalism, and genuine frustration with social failure converged in recriminalizing abortion where it had once been legal, including the United States and most of Western Europe except Scandinavia. Since the United States had also never been able to admit that adolescents were sexually active, and thus could not bring itself to provide them with contraceptives or educate them in disease and birth prevention, a pattern continued that was first established in the 1970s, nearly half a century earlier: 50 percent of all pregnancies were unintended, and one in three were terminated. After 2003, they were terminated illegally.

Now, with abortion illegal, it was far more dangerous, and many victims ended in hospital emergency rooms. In the 1990s, half of U.S. women's emergency room cases were the result of domestic violence; in the next decade, after the recriminalization of abortion, the proportion shifted. A quarter of women's emergency cases were now caused by complications from illegal abortions and a quarter by domestic violence—though what this meant in fact was that the real numbers in both had risen: domestic violence cases were gradually matched by abortion complications.

When U.S. emergency rooms began to turn away cases related to "suspected abortions," mainly because no medical plan would pay for any procedure even suspected of being related to abortion, the statistics could be read to say that the incidences of illegal abortions were finally going down. Social commentators congratulated themselves on the success of a policy that kept women chaste and saved the unborn by making abortions once more illegal.

The reality was more complicated. Abortions were sought and practiced as desperately (and wretchedly) as ever, but continuous reports of women being refused medical assistance and bleeding to death in emergency rooms told women in need that they couldn't look to hospitals for help. They simply survived or died at home, where their deaths were conflated with the growing numbers of female suicides. Worse, when scores of women who died from natural miscarriages came under suspicion of having induced them, women understood that *any* pregnancy, wanted or not, put them at risk. The artificial womb, a relatively underused invention and plaything of the rich since its introduction in 2007, became by 2012 much more popular with Western women.

With their massive success in recriminalizing abortion, anti-abortionists turned to what had always been their real goal: to reverse and then eliminate a century's progress in birth control, which they argued fervently was not only contrary to natural law, but gave women a sexual freedom that they could not use wisely, a sexual license that undermined the entire social structure. The momentum from the abortion ban was the driving force behind an equally successful state-by-state campaign to eliminate contraceptives, chemical or mechanical, except for in "grave medical emergencies." This campaign was eagerly supported by pro-natalist legislators, obsessed by the need for young workers who would enrich depleted pension funds.

At the same time, what had been absent for decades—the great shame attached to unwed motherhood—now reemerged in the United States. Though religious and pro-natalist impulses played a role in this new attitude, there were practical reasons for its emergence too. Partly it grew from public frustration with millions of young American unmarried couples who had heedlessly borne children that they were in no position psychologically or economically to care for. These children, problems from birth, represented a high cost to society in every dimension.

None of this might have mattered had new fertility regulators from the laboratory been developed. Human fertility had been under intense study, and a number of experimental contraceptives, including both male and female hormone blockers, mono-clonal antibodies, and directed molecular evolution, seemed promising. But the same arguments made against abortion—it permitted a sexual freedom to women that would undermine the whole social structure—carried the day against newer, safer, more reliable contraceptives. What was legally available even to mar-ried persons didn't look very different from what had been legally available a half century earlier.

By 2010, an underground network to supply both newer and older forms of birth control began to spread throughout the United States, with contraband drugs and devices imported from European and Asian laboratories. But these were costly and often dangerous, since quality control was nonexistent. Users also risked fines, even jail. The law, however, was spottily, almost whimsically applied, with arrests rising to a crescendo at election time, and, as usual, well-off white men and women fared best.

SOLACE AND REFUGE IN WORSHIP

In a desperately hostile world, some women turned, as they had in the past, to religious faith. Because they promised reward in the hereafter, traditional religions and new sects alike became refuges for women who could no longer hope for help or justice in this world. Some women found it easiest to accept their subordination as part of a religious discipline. But if some women found comfort in the same faiths that subordinated them, even more withdrew into a world without spiritual sustenance of any kind.

A small number of women actively rejected the same old misogyny and the same old promises for the hereafter and sought solace in reborn women's religions, particularly worship of the Goddess. Uncovering the old, lost, and suppressed practices of women's religions had begun in happier days, but as times grew harder for women, these investigations took on a new urgency. When archaeologists uncovered new sites where the Great

Mother had been worshipped, some women made pilgrimages there, savoring not only the long connection with woman-worship, but also the thrill of defying the patriarchy. Others actually found vestigial practices and symbols inside established churches, and they defiantly walked the labyrinths and worshipped at the Mother shrines in their own way.

Though the numbers of women involved were negligible, the clergy of established religions felt distinctly threatened; they tried to stop these pilgrimages, these appropriations of established religious practices, and called in local police to break up the marches, if necessary, by force. But as the Goddess-bombers, who had turned their malice from gynecological clinics to women's worship groups, had already discovered, such actions only transformed the victims into martyrs. Word spread widely and quickly, through the networks, even through underground comic books where the illiterate could read them. The death sites became hallowed, and the authorities came to understand that their actions only strengthened the very practices they aimed to curb.

A Golden Age of Equality

First they gave us a day, International Women's Day, then they gave us a year, 1975, then they gave us a UN Decade for Women, 1975–1985, and maybe if we behave, they may let us into the whole thing. Well, we haven't behaved, and that's why we're making progress.

—Bella Abzug, 1994, at a break from negotiating the terms of the UN Cairo Third International Conference on Population and Development

In this scenario of a Golden Age of Equality, the Western notions of individual rights, rule of law, and personal privacy take hold and prevail in a globally integrated growth economy, a result of the passage of trade agreements in the 1990s, the development of regional trade areas—Caribbean, Middle Eastern, South African, Mediterranean— and the prosperity associated with widespread use of information technology. Simultaneously, some degree of differing traditions are accommodated even if they don't prevail, owing to a spreading belief

95

that, like biological diversity, cultural diversity is very valuable in its own right. The nation-states remain relatively stable, and it has come to be widely held in the international community that war is not a sign of patriotism, but instead an irrational waste of resources, although short-term regional conflicts are not unknown. Funds long used for defense and aggression are at last freed for peaceful uses. Environmental protection is universally acknowledged as a long-term economy even when it seems like a short-term expense. Communications thrive without impediment among the world's governments and peoples, encouraging nonconfrontational conflict resolution, a set of techniques that is beginning to be taught to schoolchildren as commonly as personal hygiene. Great technological advances, a deepened understanding of the natural world, together with the strong economy, sustain moderate population growth and prevent massive, forced cross-cultural migrations, which would be socially and politically destabilizing. A profound shift in consciousness has permitted both women and men to begin to think of women as different from, but not less than, men. The search for equality in the workplace not only has brought about a new balance between family and work, but has generated new energies and adaptations that increase creativity and productivity, and eased pressure on men as the primary providers.

MAJOR TRENDS

In retrospect, you might argue that the great shift of consciousness that overtook the planet by 2015 could be described by what scientists call self-organized criticality, better known as "the sand-pile effect." A sand pile is usually stable, even as sand is slowly drizzled onto its peak. Then without warning, a single additional grain of sand suddenly produces instability: the change begins with shifts and cascades; on rare occasions it moves on to major instability: landslides and collapse. The cone is reconfigured swiftly and irrevocably.

This is what had happened for the women in the world.

It was a popular game among intellectuals to try to name the single revolutionary grain that had demolished the sand pile, the idea or event that had led to this wholesale, swift, and apparently irrevocable change of international consciousness. Some argued that it must have been the near universality of swift communication, which now made of the planet a single, pulsing entity. Others argued that information technology had been only indirectly responsible for the change, that the significant "last grain" was the arrival of general prosperity, which had long been promised by information technology. Prosperity gave people leisure, with time to reflect.

Certainly related to those two was the voracious universal appetite for playing the sophisticated games that had evolved from on-line games in the 1990s, MUDs (multi-user domains). Like their ancestor versions, the games of 2015 permitted, even encouraged, participants to take on new identities, especially new sexual identities, as they collaborated with other players on-line in creating free-form, ongoing electronic settings and dramas. The 1990s versions had all been text-based, and though they were international, the text was almost always English. By 2005, however, not only were elaborate graphic effects commonplace (which meant that the representations players created of themselves were astonishingly varied), but automatic translation programs permitted anyone speaking any of the major European or Asian languages to play.

Perhaps it was this wildly popular international game playing, a form of participatory electronic theater, that by 2015 had demolished not only the divisions between nationalities, but also the rigid divisions once constructed between the sexes, first in the games themselves, and then in real life. Enough critics arose to worry aloud (for fun and profit) that electronic life (EL) was influencing, even replacing, real life (RL), and this could only end badly. But then such critics of new technology had a genealogy that stretched much further back than the computers they attacked.

Another possible "last grain" was the popularization of neo-Darwinism, whose ideas were already affecting scientific research in many fields in the late 1990s. By 2015, nearly everyone recognized that what was "natural" to human beings, namely their genetic endowment and the behavior it produced, was far richer and more varied than had once been thought.

Another proposed "last grain" was fractal geometry, invented in the late twentieth century, but only coming to influence, even saturating, popular culture in a general way by 2015. Fractal geometry made the old dualisms seem like an obsolete way of apprehending the world, defying as the fractal view did categories of organic versus geometric, abstract versus real, holistic versus reductionistic, regular versus irregular.

Yet another "last grain" was the emergence of complexity studies in science, which revealed that most of the natural world—and much of human design, including the behavior of economic and political systems, the behavior of business organizations, and the evolution of languages—could be understood most fruitfully in terms that might puzzle traditional scientists, but terms that expressed very well what had always come naturally to women in the way they related to each other and to nature. Complexity was devoted to dynamic systems, and dynamic systems behaved the way women did—their hierarchies were fluid; they swapped information freely; they embraced multiple interactions and multidirectional paths; and control, or domination, in their old meanings were irrelevant.

The "last grain" could even have been the "Dagger in the Heart of the Dragons," which had begun in the late fall of 2007 as a protest against the death of a young Bangladeshi woman sold by her father into the Thai sex trade and then found murdered and mutilated six months later. Women all over Bangladesh protested the indifference of both their own and the Thai government to the exploitation of women in the sex trade. When these women failed to get satisfaction, Bangladeshi seamstresses then took the protest a step further and boycotted Thai goods. Thanks to international electronic organizing, that local boycott not only grew to include other issues affecting women, but swelled to embrace the Philippines, Indonesia, Malaysia, and most of India, ending in late 2008, a year after the initial protests, in a nearly total shutdown of East Asian manufacturing. The Dagger Episode gave Asian women an astonishing, heady taste of their own international power, and when work resumed, they enjoyed higher and more equitable wages, as well as the kinds of health and pension benefits taken for granted in the West for almost a century, along with new opportunities for education.

Some events that changed things had nothing to do with women specifically. For example, just before 2005, partly in response to successful lawsuits arguing that the complete prohibition against narcotics was unduly arbitrary and that their use was no different from the use of alcohol and tobacco, and partly because the costs of policing and punishing had far outstripped the benefits, several nations in Western Europe declared that they would decriminalize narcotics and regard their use as a private, individual decision, no concern of the state's. Addiction or abuse were now considered medical problems alone. Crimes committed under the influence, however, were crimes, and drugs were no excuse. Whether from pragmatism or desperation, when the U.S. Supreme Court ruled along approximately the same lines in 2010, the United States slowly followed the European lead.

Each country now found itself free to address a host of other problems. Tax revenues from narcotics sales could be devoted to medical treatment of addiction, and countries saved the money they had formerly used to interdict drugs and punish drug traffickers. Addiction and abuse were complicated and not always curable, but with the help of new pharmaceuticals and other therapies, such problems could now be vastly ameliorated. Their incidence was falling anyway, as individuals took more personal responsibility for their own health, a responsibility made easier by the flood of new personal diagnostic tools that became available after the turn of the century, for everything from nutritional deficiencies to cancer.

The decriminalization of drugs wiped out the profits that had driven the main part of international organized crime, a plague that had infected nearly every aspect of government and business. It was only as the profits disappeared that citizens learned the full depth of the corruption; they saw that the corrupted included some of the loudest and most sanctimonious public voices against decriminalizing narcotics.

• • •

It hardly mattered which particular incident had toppled the sand pile. Many things, after all, had converged: the failure of the old ways, the pressing need for new ways; the arrival of genuine fertility control; the novelty of a critical mass of educated women worldwide; the recasting in 2000 of the UN System of Common Accounts to take cognizance of women's economic contributions that were either unpaid or part of the informal economy; and especially the social leadership of Western women and those non-Western women who had been exposed to Western ideas of equality. Women in both the East and the West were acutely aware of their own histories, the battles that had persisted for more than a century.

There had, of course, been many gradual changes, changes in quantity that began to make a change in quality, pushed shades of gray into black and white. Women in the United States, for example, had been joining the workforce steadily since at least 1890, but by 1990 they constituted more than half of the workforce. Moreover, in the years between 1970 and 1990, their job profiles had changed dramatically. In 1970, only 14 percent of American economists had been women, but by 1990, 44 percent of economists were women. In 1970, only 6 percent of lawyers and judges had been women; by 1990, 27 percent were. In 1970, 3 percent of industrial engineers had been women; in 1990, 27 percent of them were women. And among younger workers, the proportion of women in formerly male-dominated fields was far higher than in the workforce generally, a proportion that kept increasing toward parity in most fields, especially those requiring higher education.

Elsewhere in the world, what lent impetus to the inevitable was the sudden ease, thanks to cheap, widespread, broadband communications, with which women in one place saw with their own eyes how freely women in other places lived. In the mid-1990s, international observers had already noted what they called "an impatient urge of peoples everywhere to participate in the events and processes that shape their lives." If this urge could be properly nurtured in a responsive national and global framework, it might become a source of tremendous vitality and innovation for the creation of new and more just societies. But, those observers warned, when the irresistible desire for participation clashes with inflexible systems, ethnic violence and social disintegration result. At the end of the twentieth century, the world had known more than a taste of that violence and social disintegration and had in the main chosen justice, flexibility, and community instead.

What was known for certain was that the flattened economic growth patterns from the early 1970s to the mid-1990s proved to be the sign of an economic restructuring that has historically taken place worldwide (and particularly in the developed countries) every fifty years or so and from which economies have always rebounded much stronger than they were originally.

By the late 1990s the world economy had begun to grow robustly, led by the developed countries whose information infrastructure was most advanced. For, as nearly everyone predicted, the new economy was an information economy, the application of knowledge to work in many unexpected ways. Productivity grew apace, yielding surpluses that could be directed toward pressing human problems: education, social welfare, medicine, the arts, the revitalization of cities.

Women played a central role in the economic transformations. Enjoying their prime earning years was the first generation of women to assume from the beginning that they would have a serious wage-earning career alongside any family responsibilities. The buzzword was "work cycle." It was nothing more than the recognition that as human beings move through their lives, different issues impel them at different stages. Young single professionals have different appetites for work than young parents; people in their sixties hold values different from people in their forties. Couples planned their families with the work cycle in mind.

Yet everyone in the American workforce of 2015, men and women alike, would have been puzzled and repelled by the grinding hours their parents once took for granted. Men and women in the 1980s and 1990s had desperately longed for more time outside work—time for their families, time for their communities, time for themselves. By 2015, working smart had replaced working long. Telecommuting, "hot desking," temporary task teams rather than full-time employment, all ideas that had been experimental at the end of the twentieth century, were now the usual mode of work, and this meant that all workers, men and women alike, controlled their time, set their own priorities, and sought balance. Higher productivity from information technology led to higher wages, allowing families to manage on two half-time salaries and to prosper on two full-time paychecks. The one-dimensional man, whose life collapsed upon retirement, was as anachronistic as the manual typewriter.

By the turn of the twenty-first century, most women were

acutely aware of their sex's vital contributions to national economic development: little girls from Seoul to São Paulo memorized the numbers—"women make up 52 percent of our country's population, but account for more than 55 percent of our country's prosperity"—the way they had once memorized their multiplication tables. This was also the first generation to take full advantage of the decentralized workplaces made possible by information technology. Work itself was accomplished not only by brain, but by the acknowledgment that there were many styles of thinking, and all styles, including the style that relied on wisdom, intuition, holism, and flexibility, once known as "feminine" (though it could be found in any human head) was as important as every other.

With the Scandinavian countries leading the way, women almost everywhere were lobbying for or had succeeded in passing legislation that mandated fifty-fifty representation in their national parliaments and congresses. One reason this proportionate rule began to be widely accepted was that nearly everywhere women comprised more than 50 percent of the population. To guarantee them only a 50 percent proportion in fact underrepresented them and acted as a cap, thus guaranteeing men that they need give up no more than half the parliamentary seats. Mechanisms to ensure gender balance in appointed government bodies were also falling into place. This had enormous implications for education: where women had a say in how money was spent, girls were educated. Balance and fairness alleviated many tensions, and the rocky fights over affirmative action that had bedeviled both the United States and Europe from the late 1990s into the beginning of the new century faded away.

The problems with producing cheap fusion had been solved, and using fusion instead of petroleum meant that the deference with which the Western democracies had once treated the petroleum-producing states, turning a blind eye to their human rights abuses, was no longer necessary. Pressure from outside, coupled with Arabic, African, and Asian women's exposure to Western media (which acutely raised women's expectations) and Islamic women's reinterpretation of Islamic *shari'ia*, the legal commentary on the Koran, meant that the worst excesses of cultural misogyny were driven out.

Scholars and psychologists had provided ample evidence that the root causes of violence against women—across cultures, ethnic groups, religion, or age—were nothing more than patriarchal values carried to excess, provoked by the threats men felt from changes outside. Inside families, what had often sparked battering was competition among family members about who would be taken care of, father or children; or traditional demands for domestic services from a man coming in conflict with a woman's resistance and assertiveness. Outside families, the same notions of male entitlement and female subordination had been institutionalized, and women's resistance again provoked violence. Though it had slightly different manifestations in different cultures, the pandemic violence against women had at long last become a public issue worldwide, no longer something that was hushed, private, and acceptable.

Women's legal rights became synonymous with human rights: what had once been ignored or unenforced was now noted—and enforced. In the developed world, this translated into a new recognition that the nuclear family was indeed as valuable as its most ardent supporters had long declared, but its vitality depended on a sophisticated and intricate web of support from the state, the community, and employers, only beginning with care for children and the old. So-called women's issues were recognized at last to be important to all members of society, especially children. Healthy, well-educated children were essential to sustaining a robust economy.

The monetarization of work, although a fact of life for nearly two centuries in the developed world (with the developing world coming up fast behind) had presented a problem for traditional women's work. A modest effort was begun in some countries toward compensating women for the work they had always done for nothing: cooking, cleaning, taking care of children, the sick, and the old. The reality of even token pay brought men into the business of caregiving, especially as they grew older. Because no certain measurement of competence or productivity existed here, the best were paid the same as the inept.

・ ・ ・

Thanks to educational systems that went everywhere (cheap, broadband, intelligent—and independent of paper) girls and women all over the world had access to education for the first time in unprecedented ways. It had often been said snidely: no wonder girls did so well in school when they were so docile, so obedient, so compliant, so eager to please, such good rule-obeyers. Little goody-two-shoes went the subtext; prim and virtuous, but without adventure, energy, or an independent spirit. Anyway, girls' success was only in school, wasn't it? Beyond school in the real world—well, history told the real story.

Yet as the artificial barriers to women's achievement in the real world came down, opening up places in a knowledge economy that depended on citizens who would take on the responsibility to educate themselves all their lives, those snide descriptions were shelved. Little girls and grown women showed themselves to be enviably adapted to the new knowledge society: they sat still and concentrated when they had to, and they learned. They bridged new fields and made new connections. They roamed cyberspace with imagination and daring. And, since much of knowledge work was a combination of formal schooling and manual dexterity, the age-old women's skills were at a premium: little girls could read; little hands could sew; they offered models for robotics technology as they themselves grew up to be superb knowledge workers, combining their aptitude for abstract learning with their manual dexterity.

It was not that boys couldn't learn or lacked manual dexterity. But the gender shift had taken place because work not only seemed to favor what women did very well, but it permitted them to work unimpeded, stretching their strengths and developing their weaknesses. So-called smart drugs, pharmaceuticals meant to improve cognition, which were a joke in the 1990s, had returned and were generally effective in increasing cognitive speed and originality. For an age that put a high premium on human imagination, this was important.

. . .

Of course in a world where every human was considered different—but equally valuable—boys and men had the same happy experience. *Tired of holding that pose?* The stressful stereotypes men had been forced to live up to through the ages dissolved and released them. For the first time in Western history (and in much of the rest of the world) both men and women were free to express a wide range of traits. Nobody pushed little boys to play sports if they preferred to cook instead; nobody mocked little girls who collected spiders.

Not only did the old rigid divisions between male and female break down everywhere, especially in the "living theater" of online games, sophisticated international descendants of the old 1990s MUDs where men took on the personas of women, and women passed as men. The borders between living and not-living proved just as permeable, as "bots" and intelligent agents—pieces of code, after all—took important roles in these theatrical games.

Despite the growing prominence of conflict resolution, and the satellite surveillance systems that tracked troop buildups the better to prevent wars before they began, regional conflict still flared up from time to time. Neither terrorism nor crime had disappeared. But defenses, especially weapons, now offered a wider array of choices. Aggressors could be immobilized—

either electronically or physically—without necessarily being killed.

Fitfully but earnestly, human beings were teaching themselves to cherish their many communities, embracing diversity by learning from it. Indeed, as the stereotypes dropped away, humans astonished themselves with the ranges of behavior they could thrive within. The tapestry of human life grew ever richer and more surprising.

BONOBOS MAKE LOVE, NOT WAR

At the end of the twentieth century, new scientific studies about one of our nearest genetic neighbors, a kind of primate called a bonobo (sometimes misnamed the pygmy chimpanzee), had amused and then startled social theoreticians. Humans and bonobos had diverged only 8 million years ago, and the subsequent divergence of the chimpanzee and the bonobo had come much later. The bonobo shared more than 98 percent of the human genetic profile, and for a variety of reasons scientists argued that bonobos had undergone less transformation than either humans or chimpanzees. They probably come closest to resembling the common ancestor of all three modern species.

In fact, some of the studies about bonobos were less new than newly unearthed. Bonobo behavior had so shocked and embarrassed early researchers that they had hidden their observations in a dense Black Forest of scientific German. Only toward the end of the twentieth century did behaviorists begin to observe bonobos in the African wild (the forests of Tanzania and Zaire) and overcome their sexual squeamishness to publish in plain English (though in scientific journals) how bonobos behaved.

"The species is best characterized as female-centered and egalitarian and as one that substitutes sex for aggression," wrote a researcher in a 1995 issue of *Scientific American*. "Whereas in most other species sexual behavior is a fairly distinct category, in the bonobo it is just part and parcel of social relations—and not just between males and females. Bonobos engage in sex with virtually every partner combination (although such contact among close family members may be suppressed). And sexual interactions occur more often among bonobos than among other primates. Despite the frequency of sex, the bonobo's rate of reproduction in the wild is about the same as that of the chimpanzee. . . . So bonobos share at least one very important characteristic with our own species, namely a partial separation between sex and reproduction."

Bonobos were praised for their intelligence, their emotional sensitivity, and their imaginative sense of play, but their most striking characteristic, from the human point of view, was their female-centeredness—females were the central sex, around whom bonobo society built itself—and their deep commitment to making love, not war.

Sex—on every possible occasion, in every possible erotic variety, and with nearly every possible partner—serves a profoundly important social function for the bonobos: it is used to avoid conflict. Anything (not just food) that arouses the interest of more than one bonobo at a time tends to result in sexual contact. In most other species, such situations lead to squabbles, but bonobos seem to use sex to divert attention and diffuse tension. Sexual behavior is indistinguishable from social behavior and creates the unusual social structure of the bonobo, in which young female bonobos migrate from their birth group and use sex to smooth their way into a new group of adult females, who among bonobos are the dominant and closely bonded sex.

These observations about one of our closest genetic cousins dramatically altered arguments about social behavior based on "the natural," arguments that had always supported male dominance, war making, and sexual chastity (at least on women's part) as biological imperatives. Animal behaviorists who had argued complacently from chimpanzee models were now forced, if they were intellectually honest, to admit that humans had sprung from a quite different set of behaviors than what had prevailed among us for thousands of years. So-called aberrant behavior, in particular lesbian and homosexual behavior, was shown to have a natural precedent and a genetic basis. The bonobos also engaged in adult-to-young sexual activity, which gave researchers insights into the power of drives that can lead to sexual abuse of children.

The best behavioral science moved forward to reconstruct human evolution based not on chimpanzees or even bonobos, but on a three-way comparison of chimpanzees, bonobos, and humans.

THE TRANSFORMATION OF SEX

News of the bonobos served to illuminate, even legitimate, transformations in sexual relations that were already under way. Instead of a means to power—his over her, hers over him—sex had become a personal and pleasurable transaction, privately agreed upon between two (or more) persons. Women still sold and men still bought sex, but nearly every government had decriminalized prostitution; many actually adopted the Dutch model; and the profits that once attracted organized crime no longer existed as sex work became a regulated, taxed, but independent cottage industry.

The industrial devolution of sex came as an enormous relief to women in Asia, where the sex industry had reached some kind of miserable pinnacle. In Japan, for example, during World War II, government-licensed brothels had been taken over by the military to become "comfort stations." First Japanese women and then women of conquered nations had been forced into sexual slavery. This model had been adapted by the postwar sex industry in Thailand, the Philippines, and other Asian countries and continued until, at the turn of the century, the entire system came apart.

The Asian sex industry shattered for a number of reasons, but among the most important was the growing economic independence of women everywhere. A woman with her own bank account answers to nobody and makes her own sexual choices. At the same time, vastly improved barrier methods of preventing sexual disease, and improved male and female contraceptives, meant that those who did choose to participate in commercial sex stayed healthy, thus obviating the constant need for new recruits.

An idea long argued by persistent Asian women scholars became common currency, that the entire Asian sex industry had been built upon some of the worst excesses of patriarchy, particularly the phallic myth, which defines male lust as uncontrollable, and its negative twin, the maternal myth, which defines women as mere reproductive machines in the service of that uncontrollable male lust for sex and power. (These myths, or their variants, were familiar to women who were forced to veil themselves in the desert heat so that no more than their eyes showed; they were familiar to women who were forced to pray in seclusion so that they wouldn't distract men from their conversations with God; familiar to women upon whose chastity alone masculine, even family, honor rested: a life-and-death matter for her.) The Japanese government's official apology to its comfort women of World War II—choked, reluctant, and grudging as it was—was the first breach in the myth, at least in Japan, and more was to come. By 2005, Asian women felt sufficient self-confidence to define themselves well beyond their reproductive functions, and five years later, uncontrollable male lust had become an enormous joke.

The old sexual taboos, and with them, the old myths that underlay those taboos, had disappeared. But people now recognized that with those taboos had also gone the rites and rituals through which the wisdom of many cultures helped youngsters to learn how to live with the power of their sexuality. The rites and rituals for a new world could not be the same as they had been for the old world, but slowly they began to emerge: with men as well as women taking pleasure, and taking responsibility.

POPULATION: FIVE BILLION TAKE RESPONSIBILITY

"Men have more babies than women do." Stop to think about it, and you could see it was true—women could only have a baby a year for a limited number of years, but men could father many babies from the time they were fertile until the ends of their lives. But until the famous UN Cairo Third International Conference on Population and Development of 1994, no population planners had been willing to say that, let alone face its implications. Cairo began that turnabout.

Many nations began pursuing measures that took this discrepancy into consideration. The Netherlands, with one of the lowest adolescent birth rates in the world, offered a model of sexual education, confidential information, and easy access to counseling and services. But countries moved ahead in other ways too.

For example, among the unmarried in Western Europe and many parts of Africa and Asia, contraceptive responsibility was customarily assigned by age bracket. Though it was often argued (as it had been when the fifty-fifty representation laws had been proposed) that to mandate such a thing interfered with individual rights, the response was that such mandates served a greater good—indeed, like old-fashioned traffic lights, certain laws such as these acted to preserve everybody's individual rights. Thus, up to age twenty-one, men were charged with the responsibility to prevent conception. Government and religious leaders all over the world concurred that this responsibility was an important rite of passage for young men, who had long been permitted an irresponsibility in these matters that would have shocked their forefathers.

In practice, then, most young men opted for reversible vasectomies at puberty (the so-called silicon slug), though they could also choose antifertility implants, or even use the new supercondoms that had been developed to protect against sexually transmitted diseases. They were moreover encouraged to form open, legal relationships with postmenopausal women (a cultural custom once widespread among European tribes and the Polynesians), the so-called Silver Foxes—relationships that contributed not only to their sexual maturity, but their social maturity as well.

If a young man failed in his contraceptive responsibility, remedy was sure, swift, and protracted. He was well aware that highly accurate biological tests would disclose his responsibility. Whether he lived in a nation that assumed his contraceptive responsibility as a matter of custom, or whether he lived in a nation where it was mandated, he found himself with the choice of contributing financially to his child's support throughout its minority, or running up a bill with the state, which he would eventually have to pay in installments at the same time he paid his annual taxes. He could reduce his bill by looking after the child himself, either full- or part-time.

From age twenty-one to thirty-five, contraceptive responsibility became young women's. Again, most young women opted for temporary surgical sterilization or contraceptive implants. The penalty for unscheduled children was the same as young men's: financial contribution to her child's upbringing, with full- or part-time care reducing the out-of-pocket costs. In practice, intelligent young lovers took responsibility for backup contraceptives even if it wasn't their turn for primary responsibility. After age thirty-five, contraceptive responsibility was considered a matter of mutual responsibility.

These periods of contraceptive responsibility were chosen to approximate the libidinal peaks of each sex, and in fact they worked to remind humans that their hormones were only one part of them. Indeed, cyclical responsibility for contraception was only part of the cycle of responsibilities human beings now acknowledged and ritualized, responsibilities of caretaking over a lifetime, whether of family members, the community, or the earth. Law only followed after sentiment, or new consciousness: the concatenation of phenomena that had caused the "sand pile" to collapse had already stimulated change.

Many traditional religions initially had difficulty adapting to these changes, especially since so much dogma had been devoted to scriptural justification of hierarchies, in particular patriarchy. But just as the studies of the Gnostic gospels had permitted a legitimate and acceptable revision of Christianity, other faiths began to discover new, or somehow overlooked, or somehow misinterpreted scriptures in their past. Building anew on the old sacred texts, these innovations brought a spiritual renewal to every major faith.

GERDA HOFFMANN, 33, DATA BASE MANAGER, LINZ, AUSTRIA

My first on-line persona was "Terry," short for Teiresias, the Greek mythological figure who had been both man and woman in turn, meant to imply that my persona was sexually ambiguous. I graphed the figure ambiguously too, so you couldn't tell by looking. Terry wandered through a number of domains, lurking more than participating, until finally she-he-it got involved with another player's rep called Bébé, romantically and then sexually involved. Bébé understood Terry to be male, and Bébé presented herself as female, so this was an interesting chance for me—then a twenty-one-year-old female—to play a male lover to a female beloved. At the time, I was working as a low-level data processor, and it was no trouble to switch screens between the work I was getting paid for and the Game—though when I think about it now, my boss certainly could've monitored all that. Maybe he did. Maybe he enjoyed it.

The affair with Bébé was without doubt the most intense erotic experience I'd had until that time, and I was hardly inexperienced in RL, real life. It went on for several months, this unprecedented intensity mediated—no, amplified—by the distance between human and screen personas. It was not only voluptuousness; it was the kind of beat-the-world feeling you have when you're deeply in love: you can do anything. I was involved with Bébé, in love with her in a sense, but I began to love my Terry persona too—his assertiveness, his self-confidence, seeped into my own RL, Gerda's RL. I got a better job. Then I was promoted there. Inside months, all this happened, and I believed it was my Terry aspect guiding me in some sense, or acting for me, or I was becoming Terry. Who knows?

After putting it off for a long time, Bébé and I finally decided to meet. In RL she lived in France and I lived in Austria, but we decided to meet someplace neutral. We chose Prague. I was apprehensive—I rehearsed little speeches about why I'd deceived Bébé into thinking I was a man. Do I have to tell you that my beautiful, my lush, my kittenish Bébé turned out to be hetero male? And very attractive? Marc and Gerda began a whole new love affair, which was almost—not quite—as good as the on-line love affair between Bébé and Terry.

Now this happened to me again, believe it or not, a year or two later. This time I'd presented myself as het female, no ambiguities, and got involved with Roger, who presented himself as het male. The erotic aspects of our relationship happened very quickly and they were again extremely intense for me. This part was common—you can have affairs in the Game all the time, and I do, using three quite different personas, actually. Yes, I become that persona for the half hour or hour I'm making love. Sex kitten. Dominatrix. Shy virgin. It's great sport, these fantasies shared with dozens of people.

Anyway, with Roger it was more than lust. We had a whole set of interests in common, including mountaineering and mountain-biking. We finally agreed we'd take a mountain-biking trip together in America, where Roger lived, and he suggested the Rocky Mountains.

In RL Roger turned out to be Emmy, gay female. I was slightly taken aback. After all, I'd grown up in the most conventional bourgeois home, with the most conventional bourgeois attitudes. I was supposed to like boys, not girls. But Emmy was a revelation to me—even better in RL than as Roger in the Game. Not just as a lover, though she was—I can't begin to describe that.

No, it's Emmy herself. If I could be anybody else, I'd be Emmy. She has such integrity, such an ethical, high-minded view of what the human spirit can attain. She follows a path, as she says—a kind of American version of Tibetan Buddhism. At the same time, she hasn't a gram of pomposity: she may be the funniest human being I've ever known. Emmy has been lover, guide, teacher, companion, model. I have no embarrassment in saying that I love Emmy without reservation. I feel honored to know this woman.

The physical distance between us has made it unrealistic to do much more than remain friends and sometimes lovers. She's come here to Linz a time or two.

We meet in the Game, and we both know that we have other romantic interests there. It's fine. The real point is how our various personas infuse our RL personalities. You think personality, gender, is something fixed, a given, but it's not. It's quite protean. I am not the same person I was when I first signed on to the Game, and I keep changing. I love it. Everybody else is changing too, *growing*, I think it's not too far-fetched to say. We help each other grow. We're all co-evolving. I haven't let go of what it means to be a woman. The woman I am is a wiser, better human being than the girl I was.

WHY EQUALITY HAPPENED "OVERNIGHT"

A massive change of public sentiment is always overdetermined. People decide to recycle, stop smoking, drink less alcohol, and eat more fiber for not just one but a half-dozen reasons. Along with the "last grains of sand" that collapsed the sand pile of strict sexual dimorphism was another: the obvious failure of the same old policies.

For instance, population control, which neither involved women nor took their point of view into consideration, had failed utterly. But the 1994 UN Cairo Third International Conference on Population and Development took another approach. It produced initiatives meant to educate women worldwide, to ensure their good health (including reproductive health), to give them choices about if and when they would bear children, and alternatives if they chose not to. A year later, the UN's Fourth World Conference on Women in Beijing reaffirmed the statements of the Cairo platform and added women's right to choose or refuse to have sexual relations.

At the time each of these initiatives seemed at best like well-meant statements of the ideal. Nobody realized how determined the women who'd met in Cairo and in Beijing were to turn those well-meant statements into action. Ten years later, you could look back and see how those promises had been translated into reality, by patient but persistent and effective efforts at every political and social level all over the world, from the tents of Arabian Bedouins to the villages of Aborigines in Australia's northern Queensland.

By 2005, as the UN Fifth World Women's Conference took place, dramatic results could be read in birth rates, as promised. Partly they could be read in the health statistics, which showed that women everywhere were living longer, healthier lives, thanks to good nutrition, preventive medicine, and cheap diagnostic tests that gave early warnings about many diseases when they were most amenable to remedy. Women in the developed world still had better access to medical care than women in the less developed countries—but the gap was closing, as women bore fewer but healthier children, as cheap devices replaced expensive physicians, and as telesurgery meant that even the most complicated kinds of procedures could be done remotely.

But less tangibly, those dramatic results could be read in women's new self-confidence and ambition. In the midst of all the profound changes and reordering under way all over the planet, women's new roles were only one of many great changes and therefore no longer evoked quite the hostility they had in the past. The idea that women's gain might be men's gain too was gradually taking hold.

Yet another possible "last grain," a reason for the great change, was the coming of age of more educated women than ever before in history—by 2015, in the developed countries, more women than men pursued higher education, and in the less developed countries, women were almost equal in numbers to men in higher education. This critical mass of women had learned how to ask questions and think for themselves, how to puncture overweening authority, and how to say no to traditions that bound them just because they were women.

An unglamorous but undeniable reason for the change in sentiment was the patient, fundamental, and skillful work of organization that women had done for over three decades, slowly transforming the face of government and nongovernmental organizations. By the turn of the century, a unique international generation of women had arrived at senior status. This generation had come of age working on practical issues of feminism, pacifism, civil rights, and environmentalism. They had no illusions that anybody would do it for them: they would have to do it for themselves; and now they represented an old-girl network of women who had been on the barricades and in the mail rooms and on the telephone trees together, who knew and trusted each other. They had money, they had organizational skills, and they had long ago lost the girlish need to please. They not only had the power of age; they sensed that this was their last chance to achieve the equality they had long sought for their daughters and sons as well as themselves.

That all women for the first time could control their fertility safely, easily, and reliably was another reason for change. That women could see outside their own cultures, and even communicate with other women outside, was yet another reason. It was a revolution from within as much as from without.

And finally, that men got something out of this—something they found deeply valuable—accelerated the change. Equality not only released them from anachronistic assumptions about their proper roles as men and lifted the unfair burdens those roles had forced on them, but it offered them interesting, richer new roles as well, founded in balance. It offered deeply satisfying relationships with women, who were now their colleagues and partners instead of their subordinates, their companions as well as their lovers.

THE GODDESS RECLAIMS SCIENCE
(AND THE ECONOMY AND COMMERCE AND
GOVERNANCE AND RELIGION)

Much of the work observing the bonobos, the close-to-human primate whose behavior called into question what had once been unquestionably assumed about human nature, had been carried out by women. Following the example of their mentor, Jane Goodall, a number of young women scientists in the 1970s and 1980s cast away the certainties of academic employment and went off to live alone in the African forests to observe their subjects over sustained periods of time—years—instead of on summer field trips or one-year sabbaticals. It was a new method of observing animals in the wild, but it disclosed continuities and insights that the old methods could not.

This was only one small way women changed the way science was practiced. Throughout the last quarter of the twentieth century, women had been slowly penetrating science's monastery, especially in the biological sciences, and as the new millennium opened, those small numbers became significantly larger numbers. When, in the United States, the postwar baby boom generation began retiring during the first five years of the new century, women were recruited in yet larger numbers by universities, laboratories, and scientific enterprises of all kinds: a technological society needed every scientifically trained person it could get. With this enfilade, women helped to transform the aridity, the one-dimensionality, that characterized much of science.

A persistent complaint had been heard earlier in the twentieth century about the poverty of the scientific method. Some felt that the old analytical approach to science had been played out, that a new approach was called for. Others blamed "the expulsion of the Goddess," by which they meant the exclusion from science of the female principle: the silent partnership with war making, the elevation of reason (and often force) above all other things—though in fact an authentic appeal to reason would suggest that reason should play a central (but not a solo) role in the scientific enterprise.

The story of science at the turn of the century both symbolizes and illustrates the loss to the world when women are expelled from their rightful place, when the feminine is forcibly excluded, whether from science, the economy, the arts, or governance. Moreover, this particular story tells how the new century acquired one of its most illuminating models for understanding some of its own most interesting aspects, the model of complexity. Complexity became for the twenty-first century what Heisenberg's Uncertainty Principle had been to the twentieth—celebrated, misunderstood, seized upon by poets and politicians alike. Therefore the story is worth telling in some detail.

WHEN THE GODDESS AND SCIENCE PARTED

Once upon a time, the Goddess was inextricably identified with knowledge and knowing how. The Goddess, called Athena in ancient Greece; Shakti, the feminine and creative principle in Indian cosmology; Isis, Oldest of the Old from Whom All Becoming Arose; Erda, as she appears in Germanic mythology; and Cerridwen, goddess of intelligence and knowledge in Celtic mythology. Her name was Ishtar; Metis; Sophia, goddess of wisdom; Gaia; or simply the Mother; sometimes Queen of Heaven, sometimes Mother Earth, as she appears in Native American cultures. Whatever she was called, the Goddess was understood to be the creator and repository of knowledge about nature. She shared that knowledge with her human children, but in return asked reverence and care in preserving her bounty.

But comes the division, the opposition, between science and (Mother) nature—most explicitly and dramatically in Europe in the sixteenth and seventeenth centuries, a millennium and a half after the beginning of the destruction of Goddess worship in the Mediterranean and Northern Europe—and Nature is to be subordinated and conquered, her secrets revealed and taken away from her. Though misogyny goes back to Aristotle, it became especially sharp when the methods of Western science were first laid down and began to embody a central metaphor that defined science as male, in opposition to the subject of science, which is Nature, or the feminine. This important change, when Nature becomes an other, even an adversary, to be conquered, marks the end of the feminine principle in science, indeed, the end of humility and reverence in the face of knowledge. Knowledge is no longer sacred but secular. Knowledge is pursued, nevertheless, upon the model of the Christian monastery: men alone in search of truth, determined to know, to fill their minds and mortify their flesh, without the distraction, indeed the pollution, that women represent in that misogynistic tradition.

So matters remained for more than three hundred years. The handful of women who found—or fought—their way into the practice of Western science were only permitted to stay on masculine terms. In the United States, as late as 1991, women represented less than a quarter of Ph.D. scientists in math-based fields, and about a third of the Ph.D. scientists in the life and social sciences. Few were in the top echelons, and they regularly fell behind their male colleagues in promotions and salary increases.

But so what? Women were systematically excluded from many aspects of public life. It's no surprise that science only reflects the culture it grows in, so why should it change, any more than corporations, or religious establishments, or governments?

THE ABSENCE OF WOMEN IN SCIENCE

Until the early 1970s, science seemed invincible. New discoveries and their applications, new inventions, arrived regularly, each bearing the promise of the infinite, controllable future. Men had gone to the moon; computers got dramatically smaller and cheaper; biology promised an end to all disease, and we would feed millions with the Green Revolution. Biology even promised to control world fertility with the Pill.

Indeed, science seemed a glorious and very well-funded adventure, and when serious questions were first raised, they came from people who loved and honored the scientific tradition. The questions were relatively simple. Why weren't there more women scientists? Why weren't women permitted to take part in all this intellectual glory?

Once the easy, the traditional answers were disposed of, the real answer was simple: science was embedded in the larger culture, and the absence of women wasn't very mysterious after all.

A larger, more complicated set of questions then came to replace the first simple questions. The new questions had to do with the very nature of science and the scientific method. Yes, women were excluded, but worse, schisms had arisen between masculine and feminine, subjective and objective, understanding and control. In traditional macho science, scientific explanations stressed hierarchies and unidirectional causal paths. In more balanced science, with different views of nature, explanations would encompass multiple interactions and multiple directional paths, hierarchies of a provisional kind, and differing kinds of explanations for different phenomena.

Had science suffered from its monosex culture and outlook? More important, had its monoculture impoverished the world outside science? Was science as it was practiced nothing more than a white male, Eurocentric construct which must be dismantled before it collapsed and crushed everyone? Such questions, preludes to significant changes in the composition and practice, the very ways of knowing and doing science, would never even have been raised if everything had been satisfactory.

GROWING DISSENT

In retrospect, we can see that the first dissents actually came at the apex of science's glory days. In her book *Silent Spring*, published in 1962 and warning of the dangers of unregulated pesticide use, Rachel Carson was only the first to raise the alarm about the unexamined side-effects of science as it was practiced in the twentieth century. At the time, many of these distant early warnings sounded overheated.

Yet the dissents accumulated weight and evidence until they threatened to destroy the credibility of science altogether. One critic argued that the spread of the European enlightenment was in fact the beginning of darkness for many cultures outside Europe. You didn't need to agree altogether with that to see how the imposition of Western models of economic development, based on the idea of nature as something to be subdued and exploited, had led to horrifying, poisonous ecological destruction, and the same assumptions had pushed women and children, who farmed the land and tended the forests in the developing countries, into the economic, the social, and in some cases, the biological margins, all over the world.

Even scientific innovations with benign intentions had unintended consequences. The Green Revolution, one of the proudest creations of biological science, was introduced in the 1960s, intended to feed a growing number of hungry mouths with high-yield seeds. Unfortunately, those high-yield seeds required large amounts of water, fertilizers, and pesticides; in the Philippines, for example, their use poisoned large tracts of land and seriously undermined the health of farmers, mostly women. The Philippine economy was distorted, and whereas all fertilizer was once local, 70 percent of it had to be imported at the end of the century. In some parts of India, the Green Revolution lethally amplified social injustices that already existed.

Women stood up to all this. In India, in Brazil, in Malaysia, in dozens of other places, they led in the struggles to conserve forests, land, and water, because they were engaged in a life-and-death battle to preserve their livelihoods, their actual lives and the lives of their children. In the developed world, women led the grass-roots organizations to clean up, protect, and preserve the environment (though it was true that once those organizations formalized, men led them).

So there was a compelling *push for* change in science. There was also a strong *pull toward* change.

COMPLEXITY REVEALS THE HIDDEN GODDESS

In the last two decades of the twentieth century, a new approach to science had begun attracting the intellectually curious. In a way that was completely unintended, the sciences of complexity began to answer some of the complaints about the Goddess's absence from science. Feminist critiques of science as it was traditionally practiced emerged as an illuminating parallel to the working hypotheses of complexity researchers.

Old science's chasms between masculine and feminine, subject and object, understanding and control, were falling out of date. So were scientific explanations that stressed traditional hierarchies and linear causality rather than myriad interactions and multidirectional paths; this produced a tension that grew out of very different views of nature, domination, and control.

The science of complexity, on the contrary, embraced multiple interactions and multidirectional paths; it was highly skeptical of control, or domination, in their old meanings. This dynamic, provisional understanding of natural and artificial systems was useful because the old ways simply didn't work for most things that scientists wanted to study and understand as the new century opened. In the computer, they had a new laboratory instrument to study dynamic systems. (Even more interesting, the idea of both growing something and designing it—so-called directed evolution—was applied to some of the most difficult problems: computers and their software were being evolved, rather than designed, and so were pharmaceuticals. By 2015, so was art, so was clothing, so was entertainment.)

Now a new vocabulary revealed new phenomena: structures and patterns in many places—biology, physics, the evolution of language and cultures, the dynamics of economies—emerged from self-organization, in a rich mixture of negative and positive feedback, often under the influence of small but significant historical accidents. These structures and patterns could (usually) be understood, even explained, but not always predicted; they were path-dependent, they evolved, they co-evolved with other systems outside themselves, in an elaborate dance of cooperation and competition.

The ensemble behavior of these systems was very different from what might be expected by looking at the components of the system individually and in the abstract. Contrary to systems that could be understood by old-fashioned reductionism, these dynamic systems exhibited emergent behavior. That is, their full behavior was something beyond the sum of their parts. They were hierarchical, yes, but they expressed a fluid kind of hierarchy that hardly resembled the rigid power structures that the old science (and economics and commerce and religion) had held in reverence. The new systems were dynamic: some systems moved from state to state, from order to complexity to chaos, ice to water to steam. Most telling, the boundaries between these phases constituted the point where the system made its choices; it was at the boundary between the phases of complexity and chaos that learning—change and adaptation—took place. The wrong choice might throw the system back into frozen order, which meant that it couldn't respond to changing outside conditions; the wrong choice might throw the system into chaos, where it might never recover. But the *right* choice would lead to learning and adaptation to changing outside conditions. The component systems of a complex system were loosely coupled, the component parts relatively autonomous. Nobody was in charge; nobody was boss.

How could this be? What was the general law of pattern formation in nonequilibrium systems (as such fluid systems are technically known)? This was the puzzle that preoccupied scientists concerned with complexity. As the new century opened, many more questions than answers existed. Even the provisional answers advanced by workers in complexity relied on an intricate give-and-take between real world knowledge and observation and the use of the computer as a laboratory instrument for simulation, theory building, and confirmation. Out of these general queries some valuable concepts began to emerge. They didn't look much like the old science, and many traditional scientists found it all very interesting—but not quite convincing.

For women, however, these novel models evoked by complexity studies—fluid, nonhierarchical, suffused with give-and-take—were welcome and not the least strange. On the contrary, these new models simply expressed in mathematical terms the ways that had always come naturally to women, ways of working with and relating to each other and to nature.

Thus, pushed by the obvious toxicity of old science and the impossibility of sustaining former ways, and pulled by new, more attractive, more inclusive ways that promised to address the rich complexity of nature more comprehensively, science was forced to welcome back what it once drove out: the Goddess, the feminine principle.

. . .

Thus we return to *mythos*, to female divinity and wisdom. At the beginning of the new millennium, the major themes once associated with Goddess worship, and systematically destroyed over the centuries by an anxious and threatened patriarchy, were being unearthed. The Goddess tradition, it seems, emphasizes process rather than dogma. It embraces diversity; it celebrates connection and integration. Here is a deep reverence for the earth, the literal mother of us all—whose food we eat, whose air we breathe, whose water we drink, to give us life. (Other themes of human pleasure and human comfort emerge too: the Goddess *wanted* her children to be happy.)

In contrast, the whole point of view of old Western science, reflected in its language, was one of object versus subject. Abstraction and disinterest were prized over concern, or even fitness with the real world. Precision was more important than inclusion. Knowledge for its own sake was valued over knowledge within a context. Yet if, for example, Western scientists had considered the Green Revolution in a real world context, they might have been able to predict the potential damage it would do to the world's soils. Perhaps they might have been able to predict the further damage to social structures it was going to cause. But perhaps not.

Imperfect as it was, this objective versus subjective point of view had often served science and society very well, which accounts for its durability. It continued to have much to teach us. After all, the most bracing and revealing criticisms of science had originally come from people who had taken science and its methods at their word, demanding genuine—or at least stronger—disinterest and objectivity; people who had called for genuine meritocracy, genuine rules of reason, had begun the transformation.

As the new century opened, then, science was under stress and would be pushed and pulled to change for its own salvation. It was obliged to admit the feminine principle, permit the Goddess to reclaim her share.

What did that mean?

To begin with, the Goddess means *balance*, not hegemony. (After all, it does us no good to trade one imbalance for another.) A balanced science does not discard objectivity or focus or disinterest or meritocracy. Instead it puts its inquiries into a larger, richer context. It examines objectivity with a skeptical eye and demands more of it; demands more of focus, of disinterest, of meritocracy. Whose knowledge? a balanced science asks. Whose science? To what ends? Though scientists were forced to admit with unaccustomed humility that they could not foresee all outcomes of their research, they could at least ask the questions and try to answer them.

Balance meant many other things too. It meant a representative number of women practicing science as well as men; a representative number of nonwhite, non-Euro-Americans. The ways of accomplishing this were simple to state—revised education methods, authentic equal opportunity, for example—but very difficult to achieve. However, they were not impossible, and the changes began to yield a great payoff for all as new ways of thinking by both women and men brought new breakthroughs. *Above all, this new science was not a zero-sum game.*

GENERAL AMY BROWN, 52, U.S. ARMY

All those organizational changes you see around you? Everything from the corporations to the government? We led the way. In the armed forces, it laid itself out loud and clear: what had once been the ultimate hierarchy (we invented chain-of-command, okay?) was going to have to do it differently, but do it right. The Gulf War of 1991 was transitional—there you saw privates on the ground with cell phones, night vision, and the first primitive intelligent agents; one moment they were talking to their commanding officer; the next moment they were calling home: "My mom says we've taken Kuwait City. CNN says we're near the border." Enlisted personnel were not only getting information they never had before, but they were expected to make many more independent decisions than any foot soldiers had ever made, and by and large, they were prepared for it.

But many of us saw what the Gulf War was a preview of, that we were going to have to rethink command-and-control to make it congruent with a new kind of organization that was emerging, thanks to technology. We had been a pyramid. Big base, tiny top. Women almost all somewhere in the lower echelons.

What was the new army going to look like? We didn't have big defeats that would make us rethink and re-design, like after Vietnam. But a few of us were running simulations, checking the possibilities. On one side was the old command-and-control organized army. On the other was the new army. We didn't even have a name for it, but it was something like a nexus, a multidirectional net, where power was decentralized, information flowed in every direction. There were hierarchies, yes, but they were temporary: who was up might be down next time, depending on circumstances.

Now what? This is completely contrary to chain-of-command, need-to-know. Plenty of the old boys just couldn't handle it. Change the whole philosophy of warfare after 2,500 years? Forget it.

But our simulations told us that no matter how we sliced it, dollar for dollar, resource for resource (weapons or foot soldiers) an intelligent organization outdoes centralized hierarchies. When everything's centralized, the new technologies just won't be effective, and an overwhelming force becomes an overwhelming vulnerability up against an intelligent organization. If the old boys can't handle it, okay; we bring in the new girls.

We groped for a metaphor. Organism? Network? I don't think we have the right metaphor yet. But we can't afford to fail.

At first the changes weren't real. One grunt in the Far East read one of my papers. She e-mailed me to the effect that for all the electronic goodies, the system of rank—pay grades, officer versus enlisted responsibilities—was still the same old-boy network. Her rank confined her to making only certain kinds of decisions officially, though in reality she still had to make other, more urgent decisions; and when she did, she got no credit for them. Distributed power sucks, she said, because you do the work of a higher rank, have that kind of responsibility, but don't get the rank, pay, or respect. Plus, the more electronics we get, the more paper we generate.

I'm human. I was *really* offended. Soldier, I thought—And then I rethought. This gal is telling me the truth. Don't shoot the messenger. What happened—today's "flat military"—sure shook up the services, but anyone who'd been in for more than a day could buy into that. Frankly, it was a pleasure to watch those funds switch toward rebuilding the civilian infrastructure instead. Somewhere in the defense buildup of the 1980s, people lost track of the idea that they'd better have something worth defending.

We were also in transition, and we needed to learn that. We needed to learn that from now on, we would *always* be in transition. First, no technology is foolproof, especially electronic technology; we still need very old-fashioned backup systems. Second, we must start from scratch every time to decide what kind of war we are fighting, something Karl von Clausewitz understood in his bones and laid out in the very first chapter of his first book of *On War*. We must neither mistake a new war for an old one nor try to turn it into something that is alien to its nature. At the same time, every war is deceptively similar. And every time, we are using technology no fighting force has used before.

Why do military disasters happen? They happen because of a failure to learn, a failure to anticipate, a failure to adapt, and a combination of those. How can we learn? First, by being open to it. Lifelong learning, my old undergraduate college used to say. More than a slogan—it means the military becomes a learning organization. It shares intelligence. It communicates among its constituent parts real fast.

How can we anticipate? We think holistically; we think inside our enemy's head. We not only study what happened and learn from it, but we study what might have happened, and we learn from that too. How can we adapt? Since we've encouraged sound initiatives at every level, when chance presents an opportunity, we can recognize it and seize it. This is not always successful; that is the risk we take. But the old way wasn't always successful, either.

EDUCATION YIELDS HIGH RETURNS

In the large-scale reformations taking place at the turn of the century, girls' and women's education and training were particularly prominent. Females should be educated, the practical argument went, because it benefits the nation. At the end of the twentieth century, the World Bank had produced figures that showed the returns on a female's education both to households and to society at large were actually higher than the returns on a male's education. In Kenya, for example, simulation studies showed that if men and women shared the same educational characteristics, farm-specific yields would increase between 7 and

22 percent. Increasing women's primary schooling alone would increase yields by 24 percent.

Cross-country research for seventy-two developing countries showed that total benefits to society from investments in women's education were significantly higher than similar investments in men's education. Educated women had lower fertility rates, and the children they did have were significantly healthier. If you halved the ratio of population per physician, you reduced the number of infant deaths by 2.5 percent. If, however, you doubled secondary female education, you reduced infant death by an enormous 64 percent. Teachers, it emerged, made a much more significant difference to a population's general health than doctors.

But how to convince ordinary people that this was so? You began by educating parents. In Morocco, school participation rates of rural girls increased by 55 percent when the male head of household's education increased from none to primary, but rose by 135 percent when his wife's education changed from none to primary. If you had to choose who would be educated, choose females: in Bangladesh, the death of a father increased the mortality of children under age five by 6 deaths per 1,000, but the death of a mother increased mortality for those same children by 50 deaths per 1,000 for boys, and 144 deaths per 1,000 for girls.

Though the high correlation between women's education and their fertility rate was well established by the 1980s, the linkage between management of resources, productivity, and conservation, and women's education and rights was not clearly understood until the turn of the century. Here, a vicious circle emerged: women without education or property rights had insecure land tenure, which kept them from adopting new technology and discouraged them from efficient land management.

The World Bank also publicized economic winners and losers and offered reasons. For example, a comparison of Gross Domestic Products of Kenya and Korea showed that in 1970, although their GDPs were approximately the same, public expenditure per child in Korea was three times higher than Kenya's. By 1985, as a result of Korea's lower birth rate and directing a larger percentage of its GDP to basic education, Korea was spending twenty-seven times what Kenya spent on basic education. In 1995, ten years later, Korea was projected to become one of the world's seven largest economies by 2020; while Kenya was barely surviving. World Bank analysts showed that a supply of well-educated labor, complemented by a pattern of export-led growth, explained the successful transformation of the East Asian economies.

The World Bank went on to show that although public expenditures on social services and infrastructure seemed to be allocated on a gender-neutral basis, they were actually used differently by women and men, a difference that perpetuated inequalities. For example, subsidies to higher education in most developing countries benefited more men than women, since at that level, female enrollment was lowest. But reallocating such spending toward primary education and the early years of secondary schooling had the greatest impact on girls' education and yielded higher social returns for the society as a whole.

• • •

The new education wasn't just the three R's. Beginning with early childhood education, gender stereotypes and biases were identified, the first step toward their eradication. Community-based organizations that worked with women and girls were better recognized; policies that directed money away from girls' education and training were changed. The aim was not necessarily to train girls to be professionals, but to train them to take charge of their own lives and destinies, to become active agents in their own welfare.

Thanks to its successes in the Balkans, where ordinary

women, trained in conflict resolution by a small group of foreign mediators, had picked up the pieces and begun rebuilding a society after the devastating civil wars of the 1990s, conflict resolution as a technique began to be taught routinely all over the world. It was a healthy and sensible alternative to dispute, or, on a larger scale, war. As nations slowly disarmed, the $600 billion that had been spent worldwide on arms each year began to be transferred to social needs.

The collapse of public education in many developing countries (or its absence in the first place) had threatened all children there. But enterprising local women had moved into the vacuum, and, operating on shoestrings without any bureaucracy to support, they had opened a number of model schools in the 1990s, which by 2015 were serving populations that had never seen a teacher or classroom. Global corporate needs for integrated communication had inspired cooperative licensing of bandwidths everywhere, and now the ubiquity of cheap, broadband electronic communications meant that children in the poorest countries were often receiving the same kind of education that children in the developed countries did.

BIRGITTA UHL, 23, TEACHER-TRAINEE, SWEDEN

I wouldn't be who I am today without the education I was lucky enough to have when I was a kid, the education I expect to go on having the rest of my life. The descriptions I give you here aren't a kid's-eye view, but what I know now.

Scandinavia was always known for its excellent schools, and it still is. Even though the United States has dominated the information industry, we've taken their products and reshaped them in ways we think are, frankly, far superior to the original.

For example, central to every Swedish—every Scandinavian—child's education is the collaboratory, the electronic learning environment. It isn't just that you learn in collaboration with other children, though that part is true and, it goes without saying, deeply valuable. During a given project, the collaboratory notices and re-members which of us are good, even facile, at which tasks. While it rewards those natural skills—very gratify-ing—it also pushes each of us to develop where we aren't so good.

For me a weak spot was "look-ahead," or what you might call envisioning. I was always very good at figuring out the meaning of the concrete details in front of me, an excellent pattern-recognizer, so to speak. But to look ahead, to picture what *might* be—I'd have been perfectly happy to let somebody else do that. The collaboratory gave me plenty of positive feedback for being good at the here-and-now, but it didn't stop there. It insisted that I develop where I wasn't so good. To keep me from being too frustrated, I was offered relatively easy envisioning tasks—what will happen if you do this next?—while the members of my collaboratory who were good at look-ahead got more interesting challenges. In other words, this customized learning environment brought us along where we were weak and pushed us even further where we were strong.

The collaboratories I grew up with were designed to develop not only our cognitive skills, but also our social skills. Behind all the pretty visuals, the music, the fun and games, an expert system soon detected which chil-dren were shy and provided opportunities for them to shine (which of course increased their self-confidence and helped get them over their reticence). It picked up who was too aggressive, and it presented those children with tasks that challenged them sufficiently to preoccupy them and teach them alternatives to aggression.

The collaboratory has sensors to detect physical skills, and these were developed in the same way as the cognitive and social skills: encourage the skilled to be better, help the less practiced to be better too.

Children were, and still are, assigned to each collaboratory on the basis of a complicated algorithm, which makes sure all have the experience of working with different children of different ages, temperaments, skills, and backgrounds. Already by 2005 Sweden was no longer quite the homogeneous place it had been for centuries, so those differences weren't inconsequential. One set of schools in Lund experimented with keeping the same children together in the collaboratory for prolonged periods—a couple of years—but the experiment was judged a failure because while the children certainly bonded into family-like groups, they missed the range of human interactions that new collaboratory partners provided.

You see, we taught each other at the same time the collaboratory and the teacher guided us. It was a wonderful way to learn the patterns of how we'd be working for the rest of our lives—in teams, helping each other, prompting each other, improvising, probing beyond the givens.

Some people complain that this method of learning might equalize things among children, but it also makes everything bland. What nonsense. I'll never be a whiz at envisioning, but I'm very much better at it than I would have been without this special tutoring. Nobody would ever sign me up for the soccer team, but the collaboratory pushed me to be as strong and graceful as I, at least, could ever be. The whole purpose of education, it seems to me, is to fix your weaknesses. Your strengths take care of themselves.

I now work on a team to design the next generation of collaboratories. Our expert systems are much better, much more adaptive than the first generation, and since they make better use of randomness, they're—well, we hope they're even more imaginative than the first generation, though as kids, we were pretty happy with what we had. We're incorporating better graphics, but not that much better. We believe that tokens work to exercise and strengthen a child's imagination better than presenting her or him with a full-blown picture.

Gender differences? I'm not about to declare they don't exist, but for pedagogical purposes, they're negligible. We find the differences between individual children are far more interesting than the differences between classes of children, whether girls and boys, or ethnic backgrounds, or whatever.

The Swedish educational collaboratory is being adopted in many places in the world because it works. It also happens to be cheaper than the human-intensive education previous generations grew up with, but that's only a bonus. The best thing about it is that it works. There's even some talk about using it in the huge American prisons.

WHOSE MONEY?

With its mandate to reduce poverty, the World Bank, once the target of both disgruntled contributors and clients, had responded to criticism by changing its focus in the late 1990s. Instead of financing dams, highways, and airports (megaprojects that all too often degraded the natural environment and padded the pockets of a powerful few), the bank turned its attention to human capital development and was soon its largest international financier, with 60 percent of its projects for human capital development addressed specifically to gender issues. The bank worked at expanding options for women in agriculture and natural resource management, and it set up training programs that would increase women's participation in the labor force at full fair wages. In imitation of the highly successful rural banks, like the Grameen Bank begun in Bangladesh in the 1970s, the World Bank even began to supply direct financial services to women. All this meant that the bank had to bring its considerable influence to the task of persuading client governments to modify laws and social customs toward equal opportunities between women and men.

Thus, as the new century opened, countries that sought World Bank help had to show that their land and property rights, their labor market and employment laws, their family laws, and their financial regulations treated men and women evenhandedly. The bank increasingly addressed gender issues in urban development, and in water and sanitation projects, and it involved beneficiaries, especially women, in the direction and execution of the projects it underwrote.

Above all, the World Bank identified two policies that underlay any nation's sound economic and employment growth. One emphasized macroeconomic stability and the removal of price distortions. High inflation acted as a regressive tax on the poor, on low-paid wage workers, and those with fixed incomes—in other words, women. Overvalued currencies kept the price of imported goods low, crowding out locally produced goods. Women's businesses, often concentrated in the informal sector, were particularly vulnerable to competition by cheap imports.

The second policy emphasized the promotion of labor-demanding growth in industry and agriculture, and broad-based investments in human capital. Trade reforms tended to benefit women directly, since women formed a significant part of the labor force in manufacturing, and female earnings there were higher than earnings in the rural sector. Moreover, the remittances women sent back from the cities were an important supplement to household income.

The dynamic model of development, with national economies moving from a cheap-labor production base (a stage where corruption was tolerated, and the environment might be severely impaired) to a healthy infrastructure and prosperous GDP, was far from ideal as models went, but it had the great virtue of working, and nobody had any plausible alternatives. All the bank could hope to do was move a nation through the early, cheap-labor stage as quickly as possible toward the promised land of healthy prosperity.

Though not every client nation was as assiduous as it might be in complying with World Bank policies, by 2015, the bank's new focus was already paying off handsomely. For example, one pernicious custom that had persisted in the developing world was now disappearing: the disproportionate amount of money that women contributed to their families, compared to men, who had typically kept money back for personal consumption. Study after study in the 1980s and 1990s had shown that though women earned far less cash than men, their money went entirely to their families; whereas men, who earned much more, had kept their money for transistor radios, bicycles, cigarettes, and other personal indulgences. By making loans directly to women, and organizing support groups so that women kept their profits themselves, the World Bank helped equalize incomes between men and women.

In 2009, the unwaged work of women was formally recognized, along with their double-day burden. Men, who had remained disengaged from work in the home, were enlightened as to the value of homemaking work when accounting procedures changed and unwaged work became part of the Gross Domestic Product.

DEVELOPING THE WAGE EARNERS

When it was first revealed by international measurements, the magnitude of the contribution made by Thai women to their national economy had come as a big surprise. Among young rural migrants to Bangkok, women outnumbered men 2 to 1. Women constituted 80 percent of Thailand's manufacturing workforce, and they outnumbered men 4 to 1 in the workforce that produced five of the top ten export items, the source of precious foreign exchange. In tourism—all too often the sex trade—they predominated. Women's earnings were generally returned to their parents or families, circulating millions of baht and invisibly narrowing the income disparity between rural and urban areas.

It took no great insight to see that if these workers were better trained and their skills developed, then the contributions they already made would increase. As northern Thailand became the biochip nursery of the Pacific Rim, it demanded a better-educated workforce, and women's education became a compelling national priority. By 2015, the relatively well-educated and hard-working female labor force of Thailand had became the economic engine of the Thai economy.

RETHINKING THE ECONOMY

• • •

I learned that in the UNSNA (UN System of National Accounts), the things that I valued about life in my country—its pollution-free environment; its mountain streams with safe drinking water; the accessibility of national parks, walkways, beaches,

lakes, kauri and beech forests; the absence of nuclear power and nuclear energy—all counted for
nothing. They were not accounted for in private
consumption expenditure, general government expenditure, or domestic capital formation. Yet these
accounting systems were used to determine all
public policy. Since the environment effectively
counted for nothing, there could be no "value" on
policy measures that would ensure its preserva-
tion.

Hand in hand with the dismissal of the environment, came evidence of the severe invisibility
of women and women's work.

—Marilyn Waring, former chair,
New Zealand Public Expenditure
(Public Accounts and Budget)
Select Committee, New Zealand
Parliament

• • •

As early as 1980, mainstream economics seemed to be floating
further and further away from whatever ties it had once had to reality. It was neither predictive nor descriptive, but scholars and
government analysts argued passionately that the assumptions
upon which it was based must not be changed, or it would be impossible to compare where we were to where we had been. A
number of young economists, impatient with such fusty arguments, began searching for economic models that would permit
them to look at the whole instead of the parts, the dynamic
whole of the economy instead of its static aspects.

By 2015, several of these models had emerged as more predictive, more descriptive, and more germane to real life national
economies, but since no single model dominated, the field of economics continued to operate on two levels, giving lip service to
classical models but often acting on the basis of new models. It

reminded observers of the difference between written and spoken languages.

So although the formal underpinnings were muddled, the facts were not. In the new economic models, women and their work were counted as part of the GDP. Raising (not just giving birth to) children was assigned a value. Noncash-producing work, such as farming to feed a family, or hauling water to slake its thirst, was assigned a value. Cleaning the house and preparing meals were assigned a value. Leisure was assigned a value. A negative value was assigned to pollution, and stripping the forests and poisoning farmlands. National budgets answered such questions as who does what work where—paid and unpaid? What is the position of the nation's children and the aged? Who has adequate housing? Who enjoys good health? What are the changes in water and air quality, and why? Who relieves the state of the burden of caring for others?

EQUALITY IN THE WORKPLACE

In the developed countries, and increasingly in the less developed countries, the nature of work had been subtly but decisively transformed. In retrospect, it could be seen that brains had been replacing brawn for more than a century, but at the beginning of the new millennium, this changeover was stark. The United States led this change, with its high (and often painful in terms of unemployment) investment in information technology during the 1980s and 1990s. The investment had seemed slow to pay off, but when it did, it paid off enormously. Service-sector productivity rose, along with service-sector wages. The investment's hidden payoff was a generation of workers who took information technology for granted; they knew how to leverage it to add value in places that simply didn't occur to latecomers to the knowledge revolution.

Whether for cultural or biological reasons, women excelled

at the work of the information economy: gathering, trading, re-combining, and reimagining information; multitasking and improvisation. Women worked themselves into key jobs that paid best, giving them an economic advantage for the first time in history.

Conventional wisdom had held that work was more central to men psychologically than to women, and therefore job-related stress was more likely to affect men. Moreover, went conventional wisdom, men were better able to compartmentalize work and home—if there were crises in one or the other, men's productivity was less likely to be affected.

But conventional wisdom proved wrong. Research in the 1990s began to show that men and women were equally stressed by work, and, more important, they experienced equal pressure from events at home that might have an impact on their work. A high level of concern about children was the main factor in psychological stress among men as well as women.

Toward the end of the century, a number of innovative firms began to study issues of work and family for all workers. It became clear immediately that work and family were inextricably linked for men and women alike. But, ironically, so-called family-friendly policies only reinforced the status quo because most people were afraid to ask to use them, believing (correctly) that their managers would question their commitment to the job. Thus unspoken assumptions about work actually interfered with business goals. Employees "jiggled the system," using sick leave or vacation time, which cost the firm in terms not only of unplanned absences, but in employee cynicism about a firm that claimed it had such benefits—but made using them so difficult.

When work-family benefits were opened to all employees, however, regardless of family status or manager discretion, work teams came up with collective approaches to ways of getting the job done, with dramatic results. A 30 percent decrease in absenteeism was coupled with greater customer responsiveness; measures of employee satisfaction improved; while friction between employees decreased, since apparent favoritism was reduced. These new responsibilities advanced self-managed teams into yet new responsibilities for further gains to the firm.

Not only had workplaces that operated in continual crisis mode been stressful to family life, but they tended to value long hours at work and high-visibility problem solving. When new management models were introduced, when problem prevention was identified as desirable and was rewarded, when periods of quiet time were formally designated so that individuals could devote attention to their own tasks, then crisis management finally gave way to planning and crisis prevention, dramatically more effective work, and shorter hours.

By looking at work through a work-family lens, by collectively designing solutions, by challenging deeply held assumptions about gender roles and the place of work and family, people began to share more and more new ideas, new ideas that benefited everyone. The workplace began to change profoundly. It was a process of collaboration, listening, reflection, and mutual learning; solutions were tailored for each site. Everybody gained in the end.

· · ·

As the first decade of the new century progressed, there was massive resistance to the long hours corporate workers had endured in the 1980s and 1990s. Better technology made working smarter a sensible alternative to working harder. This was played out most starkly in the American legal profession, where controversy raged over billable hours. Why should women lawyers, who, studies showed, worked more effectively (and therefore accomplished more in fewer hours) be penalized by a system that rewarded time-clocking? Shouldn't they be rewarded for productivity? For avoiding trouble instead of expanding it to force-feed the bottom line? This dilemma went to the very heart of legal practice and restructured it, as women-dominated firms made bids for work based on a job-cost estimate instead of hours billed. The valuable professional became the professional who practiced preventive law, preventive medicine, preventive engineering, not the one who ran up billable hours.

People with full lives, who had time to enjoy their children, and even sing in a choral society, while they held a responsible job, were shown by scores of studies to be more valuable to their employers. They were healthier, more productive, more innovative than workers who were consumed by jobs. People looked back and wondered why this commonsense observation had needed science to validate it, but it had. By 2015, workaholics were considered as socially handicapped as the chronically unemployed.

At the same time, it was widely acknowledged that both the "mommy track" and the "daddy track" had unfairly penalized the very people who were investing in and developing the world's precious human capital, its children, especially in the developed countries. A new generation of men and women executives refused to do business the way their corporate fathers and grandfathers had done. They took more time—and pleasure—in their families, and as fathers moved closer to their children, they were sensitized to their children's well-being. No egalitarians were more militant than the fathers of daughters.

Simply hiring women had not been enough to assure genuine equality. By the 1990s it was clear that women in large organizations were being confined in service-oriented staff positions that prevented them from achieving top positions. Line, not staff, positions traditionally produced senior executives in corporations. At women's instigation, corporations began to see the value (to both themselves and their staff development) of placing women in line positions at mid-career, and job rotation became routine.

To their surprise, corporations also found that what mattered to women—good benefits, like long-term health insurance, flex-time, day care for sick youngsters and the elderly, investment advice for families with college-bound children; stress-management workshops, nutrition courses; on-site exercise classes—also mattered to men. These workforce-centered benefits helped businesses retain their most valuable employees.

Sick leave policies changed. Employees who didn't use allotted sick days were permitted to extend their vacations, or even contribute those days to a pool for other employees undergoing long-term illness. Where there were corporate sites (not everywhere, because the virtual corporation predominated) on-site conveniences became commonplace, such as child-care centers, dry cleaners, clinics, pharmacies, and ATMs.

Business hours stretched to include evenings and weekends, just as retail hours had, but the average workweek per worker actually dropped, thanks to team-organized work time, flextime, the leverage that information technology supplied, and distributed work places, which all but eliminated the long wasteful daily commutes of the twentieth century.

THE ROLE OF DIVERSITY

Workforce diversity played a significant role in bringing about equality. As one consultant put it, diversity wasn't a problem to be solved, it was a powerful force to unleash in changing markets. Spanish-speaking employees opened new markets and adapted products in Latin America for their North American companies; while Asians opened new markets in Southeast Asia and China. Unspoken assumptions were teased out in corporations and examined. Did the phrase "we are a corporate family" really translate into "father knows best," thus subtly keeping women from decision-making responsibility? Did working long hours signal diligence and dedication? Or did it signal that face time was being given credit over productivity? Good management was being rethought.

These questions only mattered in terms of corporate bottom lines: arguments from ethics and morality had not worked, but arguments for profit did. Just as in nature, heterogeneous groups produced better solutions to business problems—they came up with more varied ideas—than homogeneous groups did.

Though the United States had the most carefully documented diverse workforce, immigration from the South to the North all over the world had diversified workforces everywhere, especially in Europe. Though it was less prepared, Europe took the lessons the United States had learned earlier the hard way and adapted them to its own situation. Franco-Arabs and German-Turks became invaluable to their firms. Chinese women flowed into Italy where they set up small businesses—and began to add their distinctive contribution to the genetic stew that Italy had always been.

Most envied of all was the United Kingdom, which had uncovered astonishing new markets everywhere by abandoning the Victorian old-boy hiring policies that had obtained throughout the twentieth century; instead Britain cultivated its radiant rainbow of minorities. There was jocular talk about the new British Empire, a gigantic trading place where everybody spoke the same language, English, and once again, at last, the sun never set.

THE PAPERLESS SOCIETIES

Toward the end of the twentieth century, the cost of paper began to rise precipitously. While this was an inconvenience for the developed countries, it might have been disastrous for the less developed countries, struggling as they were to modernize themselves and educate their people. What averted catastrophe was the introduction of widespread electronic communications, especially for education and entertainment.

India, for example, had wired itself up almost spontaneously to receive satellite television in the mid-1990s. Well-educated Indian engineers soon sensed a voracious demand, which inspired them to develop and in 2002 bring to market small, simple, solar-powered wireless computer/receivers that could be used to access the other communications satellites orbiting above the earth. This eliminated the need for costly lines that transmitted power or data.

Introduced experimentally to villages in the Indian state of Karnataka, home of India's Silicon Valley in Bangalore, the idea of cheap "handies," as they were soon known, was seized and refined by the Brazilians, who found an enormous market in Latin America. The Indians found themselves in competition not only with Brazilian suppliers, but with several of the East Asian Tigers, a competition that drove hardware quality up and prices even lower, and (to the consternation of many traditionalists) invited jazzy Anglo-Saxon content beamed by satellite into every village of Asia and South America.

FROSTED DOESN'T HAVE TO MEAN COLD WAR

Not surprisingly, the general graying (dejuvenation, to use the technical term) of the industrial world also helped usher in equality: as men and women grow older, they grow more like each other, it seems. The Netherlands was typical. Though population remained almost constant in numbers between 2000 and 2015, the country's changing proportion of young to old transformed many other aspects of Dutch life ranging from housing preferences to the most important daily activity (it had once been shopping for groceries; now it became socializing), from traffic to leisure activities, from social justice to educational opportunities.

For example, though the population remained constant, the

number of households nevertheless grew, especially one-person households, and that growth would accelerate between 2010 and 2030, although the population had actually begun to decrease slightly. The reason: older persons tend to form one-person households both by preference and owing to widowhood.

On the other hand, a drop in the labor force, to be expected in an aging population, did not take place, since not only did women join the workforce in ever larger numbers, but they worked longer throughout their life. These older workers were healthier and more active than their predecessors had been; they had more interests and more skills; since they had fewer claims on their time (their families were mostly grown and independent) they were more valuable to their employers. Moreover, they had been born into and come of age in a changing milieu; for them, change was a natural state of affairs; they cheerfully retrained and retreaded whenever necessary. A late twentieth-century California scheme that devoted 1 percent of the unemployment tax paid by employers to outside training and retraining was adopted all over the world and helped to keep workers at the frontiers of usefulness. But workers also understood that part of this retraining would be their own responsibility: they put money aside for it just as routinely as they put money aside for the mortgage.

Phased retirement, pioneered by the Scandinavian countries, also became widespread. Older workers did not retire abruptly: sometimes they returned at peak times, or for special projects, then went back to leisure. The Western developed countries greeted this set of independent personal decisions with relief, since the 1990s drop in the birth rate had created a temporary but severe shortage of workers to support the social security system. These older phased retirement workers also helped ease the integration of young skilled workers from abroad, whose temporary stays had become commonplace.

Women had long been accustomed to taking time off from a

career for family responsibilities, then retooling to come back. Now the rapidly changing workplace meant men had to retool routinely too. They usually took sabbaticals for this and returned to something quite different—a different job, a different location. These sabbaticals were often life-changing: they gave men a new perspective on their work, so they enjoyed new energy and brought refreshed insights to tasks.

AGING CHANGES THE WESTERN WAY OF LIFE

In the decades between 1995 and 2015, more women went through menopause than in all of previous recorded history. Menopause became a rite to celebrate (dozens of homegrown rituals sprang up all over the world), a passage for women who strode out of the Moon Hut and into new freedom, self-realization, with fresh, unimpeded energy and high self-confidence.

National policies on population had adopted an ancient practice of several cultures: they strongly encouraged liaisons between these Silver Foxes and inexperienced young men, partly as a population control measure, but also to give young men experience, social polish, and a mature sense of sexual and social responsibility. The Silver Foxes became symbols of what all women aimed to be—independent, knowing, witty, candid, clear-eyed, generous-hearted, and self-composed—and what all men, young and old, yearned for. It was universally believed (and expressed in popular songs and dramas) that the man who met the demanding standards of a Silver Fox was extremely accomplished.

· · ·

The numbers of students in full-time education in the West had been dropping since the 1970s, and this trend continued. But higher education found other students and reached them by other ways: all men and women, no matter what their age, needed to retrain continuously as the nature of work changed. Crime dropped (older persons commit less crime), but people afraid to open the door at night increased (older persons are more fearful). People took more interest in their community by joining voluntary associations, boards, and committees (older persons have more time for volunteer work). The picture was similar in other developed countries, such as New Zealand, where families began later and were smaller-sized, born to older parents who could give them more advantages than younger parents could.

In Sweden, however, though the indigenous population aged, thanks especially to lower mortality rates among women aged sixty to ninety, a flow of immigrants in the last part of the twentieth century rejuvenated Sweden's demography.

DOMESTIC VIOLENCE

When the frightening crime statistics of the 1990s were unpacked, they revealed that a significant amount of the rise in violent crime that had exercised American and European voters and politicians alike could be accounted for by domestic violence. As late as the 1990s, the World Bank reported that in the developed countries, women of reproductive age lost one healthy day in five because of domestic violence and rape. These were crimes that had never before been reported, because women were afraid of reprisal, of not being taken seriously.

But as women were encouraged to think of these batterings as a criminal act against them and to report them officially, instead of enduring abuse as something inevitable, even as something they somehow deserved, the reported "crime rate" rose—but women's safety increased. One brave woman after another stood up and bore witness across the Northern Hemisphere. As the perception took hold that violence against a wife or girlfriend or child *was* a crime and *would* be punished, violence between intimates didn't disappear, but it diminished considerably.

In other parts of the world, where domestic violence was still commonplace, men were put on notice by women's protective groups. Governments followed their lead: men could no longer batter at will, but would be held accountable for it, would even serve time in jail. A quasi-religious movement among men in the developed countries sought to find ways to make other men deal with and take responsibility for their own violence against women and against each other. That it was a kind of religious movement was fortunate, because traditional religious authority had time and again undermined itself with its support of social and religious policies that sanctioned violence against women—policies that women perceived, questioned, and eventually rejected.

BRAZIL AS SUPPLE AS A DANCER

By the end of the 1990s, the business leaders of multicultural Brazil, South America's largest country, had revised long-held attitudes at record speed. From a virtually closed economy to a world economy, from wildly fluctuating inflation to steady economic growth, Brazil's private sector had adapted so smoothly to extremely divergent circumstances that its amazing adaptations went almost unnoticed. Politicians, bosses, and union leaders regularly sat down together to identify their common goals. What became more and more clear in these discussions was that one of Brazil's biggest problems was the widening gap between the rich and the poor that had yawned so dramatically in the last decade of the twentieth century. At the root was education—Brazilian workers were badly educated in poor schools and remained desperately poor and unproductive because of it. Health care was second to blame, with a two-tier system that treated the wealthy generously, but starved the poor of preventive treatment and needed care.

In the 1990s, conditions in the rich southern part of Brazil approached first world standards, but conditions in the poor north were desperate. Tax revenues allocated for education disappeared into a swamp of corruption. Only in a few places, where schools were perceived as actually pertinent to life, did students flock to them: at the federal technical schools, for example, there were regularly three thousand applications for two hundred openings.

Recognizing that bureaucracy and competition were inimical, governors of the *estados* both rich and poor began to push the responsibilities for the schools onto the municipalities. Schools now had to compete for funds, offering their achievements as incentive. Under these circumstances, the new computer-based learning programs were widely and eagerly adopted. Brazil's own computer industry rivaled India's in producing small, strong, handheld, solar-powered receivers and computers; generations learned together.

The difference was apparent in every part of society, most especially in the equality between men and women. With the same adaptability Brazilians had shown toward fiscal matters, they moved toward changed attitudes about each other. Led by a well-organized network of women's groups that had been inspired by UN initiatives to fight for political and economic fairness, Brazilian women had begun making their voices heard as early as the drafting of the 1986 constitution. They had continued to experience discrimination, especially because of the machismo cult, which put women on the bottom of a ticket as tokens to win women's votes and silence their demands, but with no real power. Despite their political troubles, Brazilian women flocked to three organizations that made a difference: the feminist movement, the Base Ecclesiastical Communities movement, and the Neighborhood Associations movement.

Brazil's indifference to domestic violence had been internationally criticized. Its courts had customarily accepted any violence toward women by their partners, even murder, as legitimate defense of honor if the man claimed that he suspected infidelity. Feminists began by organizing protests outside these trials, demanding that the killers be jailed. In response to the protests, Brazilian states established nearly 100 police stations, modeled on Japanese neighborhood police posts. These stations were staffed entirely by women; women victims could file charges here with confidence that they would get a fair hearing. The number of charges and convictions for domestic violence rose dramatically.

Another wildfire movement was liberation theology, expressed in Base Ecclesiastical Communities. Many of these groups were formed by feminist theologians, who operated consciousness-raising sessions that identified the patriarchal structure of society and the traditional church itself as two baleful influences on women's lives. Finally, Neighborhood Associations gave women valuable grass-roots practice in getting things done and began to train women for political office.

With a newly resurgent Chile anchoring the western coast of South America, ecotourism generated new prosperity in the impoverished north, and Indian cultures became new centers of world spiritual renewal.

NINA KRASNIC, 36, PROFESSIONAL MEDIATOR, NEW YUGOSLAVIA

When people ask what it was like here, I have to ask when. Under Tito? I may not be young, but I'm too young to remember that. Before the war? Sometimes I confuse the happiness of childhood with what I remember of peace, but—it was lovely here. We thought we had everything. We didn't, but we thought we had. We made plans for the future. The university. The seaside. We hung out at the coffee houses and the discos. We loved Western music.

Then came the war. Living hell. In my high school class, only 4 of us survived. Four out of 160. Of those four, one of us is completely deranged. No medicine, no therapy, can bring her back. She was a beautiful young woman, and now she's a crazy old woman, so her life is as good as gone.

The rapes and the torture. The killings. Rape as an act of war—a conscious, deliberate act of war. All that's part of the historical record. We cried for help. We waited for Godot. That's history too.

In the worst of it, a group of well-meaning foreign women came here very quietly with an extraordinary, an absurd message. You must plan for the future, they said. We had no future. But they persisted. They said, this land will go on; it will need you; women always pick up the pieces after men have destroyed. We listened because what else could we do? Some of these foreign women were professional mediators; some of them were only ordinary women whose hearts were breaking at what they saw.

We came together in a room, Serbs, Croats, even Romas, Gypsy women. We hadn't spoken to each other in years. Their men had done unspeakable things to us. We faced each other and spoke about the war. We opened our hearts and wept. Women's tears are the salt of the earth. And eventually each of us said: yes, my side is responsible for atrocities too. For a woman who has suffered as some of us suffered, you can't imagine how difficult that is to say.

We were sick of being victims. We didn't need a road map to see that the old diplomacy hadn't worked, wouldn't ever work. We must have something new, we said, or our granddaughters will be picking up the pieces like our grandmothers once had. We began to understand that we must take power ourselves to prevent war. This was frightening. Women had been fearful of power because in our experience power could only be abusive.

We started simply. We started with talk. We found women of like mind. Some of us witnessed silently in black. This was terribly dangerous—a statement that we protested our government's aggression with all these trigger-happy idiots swaggering around with their assault weapons. Would they shoot an unarmed woman? Of course. What could be more tempting? Our safe places were attacked by hooligans, and the authorities looked the other way. But we persevered.

The foreign women said they were here to learn from us. We thought we had nothing to teach but sorrow and rage. We were wrong. We had much to teach each other. The foreign women had techniques—conflict resolution, it's called—and these were vital. We took it from there; we began to develop political strategies right for us so that when it was over, we women—Serbs, Croats, Romas, Macedonians, Montenegrins—could offer a vision that was so compelling that people would choose it gladly.

We discovered new ways of working together. Old stuff now, but nobody had done it that way before. We learned how to build conflict resolution right into the political process, part of public policy. We managed to insert it into the schools: conflict resolution becomes as ordinary as brushing your teeth. We learned the hard way, but we learned—how to be democratic without falling into the trap of hyperdemocracy, where everybody has a say, but talk substitutes for action and nobody takes responsibility. How to move ahead. We discovered for ourselves that hierarchies are neutral; it's when they're infected with authoritarianism that they're bad. Our hierarchies are evanescent; they revolve, they evolve, and then they disappear. We take power, use it, then give it away. Nature is the example here: nature is full of hierarchies, but they're temporary, fluid, your brain rules your feet—until you stub your toe. This is nature's way, and it's our way too.

We had help. Help from women's groups all over the world. Money from German women. Money from Dutch women. Scandinavian women. Money from the Americans. But more important were these ideas, seeds that have grown into a harvest of peace.

Our first test came when the peace was declared. There was still bickering about winners and losers. No winners, we said. Only losers. Let's get on with it.

Proud? No, that's the wrong word. But a sense of accomplishment, yes. Teams of New Yugoslav women go everywhere as mediators these days. We're what you might call famous for it. It's no longer shocking to see women on government negotiating teams. We know how to listen deeply, hear the pain and emotion. There's so much pain in the world. We know how to find common ground, how to resist judging, how to tease out the traditional means any culture has of ending discord—any culture that's survived more than a week has some traditional means of making peace. We know how to find it. We know how to teach other women to do it too, to leverage their natural expertise as peacemakers. I say "natural" without blushing. We do think differently from men; if mothers weren't natural peacemakers the human race wouldn't have survived this long. We know how to unlock creative thinking, because we had to do it ourselves. We're especially good because we have Christians and

Muslims on our teams; we come from the place where Islam and Christianity have traditionally met in blood-baths. We understand hatred in our bones, and we've transcended it. We come with moral authority, because, as the world knows, we women picked up the pieces of our own country and glued it back together again.

THE NEW LIGHT IN THE CENTER OF THE WORLD

• • •

Women have already taken flight.

Pale and grave, they are performing the pilgrimage that their grandmothers dreamed of for so long: to dance without a mask, with eyes riveted on a limitless horizon. . . .

What is certain is that women have decided to listen no longer to *khutaba* (sermons) they have not had a hand in writing. They are ready for take-off. They have always known that the future rests on the abolition of boundaries, that the individual is born to be respected, that difference is enriching.

The imams are irate because if domestic *ta'a* is challenged by weak women, how can men be expected to lower their eyes in deference to the leader? The modesty of the Arab woman is the linchpin of the whole political system.

—Fatima Mernissi, Moroccan
author and distinguished scholar
of the Koran, 1994

• • •

Looking back, no one would have anticipated the radical changes that swept across the Islamic world. The West, long believed to be the place of darkness, *gharb*, had fought and easily won a well-publicized war in Kuwait against Iraq in 1991. In doing so, it seems, Westerners had introduced two ideas. The first was that no border could finally protect Arabs from the West. The second idea was that the East and the West must understand each other. Understanding the West, however, meant understanding democracy, an idea that frightened the traditionally powerful, but ignited the Arab masses: unnoticed by Western media, Arabs had poured onto the streets of their cities during the Gulf War, calling out for democracy.

If the Western media failed to notice, Arab intellectuals and artists did not. They saw it was their task to round out Arab history, to place beside the traditions of strict obedience to authority, of rich autocrats and masses of poor ordinary people, the equally true, equally enduring traditions of individual dignity. They wanted to show how such individual dignity had once thrived in Islam's history, and what great leaders in the arts and sciences the Arab peoples had once been and might be again.

By the opening of the new century, the failure, the decay, the corruption of autocrats had yielded to a fresh breeze that, after a decade, became a windstorm, sandblasting away the old. The scholars—many of them women, some of them fundamentalists—who had insisted on a reinterpretation of Islam, who had insisted on a renegotiation of the contract between themselves and the state, had changed the face of the Arab world once more.

Intellectuals had spoken out, at first hesitantly, and then more boldly. They risked their lives and signed petitions even in the most repressive states. They took a new message abroad. Sometimes it was very simple: that in the history of Islam, the ideal imam is just, because he is attentive to the needs of the community, involved in people's well-being. He is just because he is vulnerable and challengeable. Sometimes the message was considerably more subtle, rediscovering the rationalist tradition of Islam, purposely hidden for years by those who had everything to lose if it came to light.

Some went further. Petrodollars, they said, had financed the propaganda that "encouraged submission and repudiated reflection." Arabs must reclaim the humanistic tradition that they alone had kept alive when the West had deserted it in the Middle Ages, a humanistic tradition they had not merely preserved, but enriched, before they passed it along. In the 1980s and 1990s, the writings of these philosophers and historians were read hungrily by young Arabs and taken to heart. It was Arab feminists who insisted on speaking aloud the oldest truths, bringing upon themselves the most ferocious repressions.

Women, it was traditionally said, were the gravediggers of dynasties. Over hundreds of years, in many places, when women came out on the streets, dynasties fell. It was an argument about to be proved again, as Arab women, by now literate, earning money (in some places, like Saudi Arabia, controlling nearly half of the assets), began to claim their rights as individuals not only in words, but by unveiling and going out into the world. The 1990s hypocrisy of the two-skirt suits (a stylish skirt for Western travel, a dowdy long one for home wear) and all that the two-skirt suits stood for, was cast off with the veil. Khadija, the first wife of the Prophet Mohammed, whose business and earnings had supported her husband in his meditations and when he went out to preach, became a symbol of the Arab woman in the business world, economically and politically engaged.

Thanks largely to the tradition of the harem and their own recent suppression, Arab women had a strong sense of sisterhood. When Iraq's rebuilding began, it was women who led the way, shaping a state that was neither unduly influenced by the West, nor in the grip of repressive theology. In the new state of Palestine, the factional women's political organizations that had existed earlier coalesced. Drawing on the lesson of Algeria where women had fought alongside men for freedom from the French colonialists and then were dismissed, Palestinian women refused to return quietly to the private sphere. They stubbornly demanded and eventually took their part of political and economic power in the nation they had helped win. Believing that "taking care of women will take care of the nation," wealthy businesswomen all over the Arab world formed an association called the Sisters of Khadija, which established small, highly successful one-to-one development projects for other Islamic women in former Yugoslavia, Bulgaria, the Islamic states of the former Soviet Union, and Arab Africa. They were no-nonsense, results-oriented, and markedly successful: in 2009, the Sisters of Khadija, the private consortium of Arab businesswomen dedicated to economic development, won the Nobel Peace Prize.

NEW AGRICULTURES

In areas that had once been deserts, modern water-smart, pesticide- and fertilizer-spare agriculture began to take hold. Genetically engineered plants, disease-resistant and water-stingy, were introduced. This was especially true in parts of Syria, Iraq, and Iran, the old Fertile Crescent. Real peace with Israel, thanks to the Jerusalem treaty of 2007, had meant that resources could be rerouted from war. Even better, the loans that had long been granted to Middle Eastern governments only on the condition that such money be used for buying weapons were at long last available for development instead of arms.

The Israelis, who had spent years developing high-yield crops that used minimal water and chemicals, were invited to send expertise, which they transmitted over the Internet to any farmer in need, help that came along with up-to-date weather and market forecasts. Along the Euphrates and the Tigris, fruit and citrus trees bloomed once more, wheat, barley, and cotton fields yielded bumper crops, and just-in-time distribution systems brought local fresh fruits and vegetables from Middle Eastern markets to world markets for the first time in centuries.

In the Sahel, nature's buffer between the Sahara Desert and the fertile plains and forests of Africa, new agricultural methods also took hold. The new agricultural exchanges between the Sahel and the Arab world brought a renaissance of the traditional cross-fertilization that formerly existed between North Africa and the Arab world. What had begun as an agricultural flowering became a cultural flowering as well, a source of pride all over the Arab world.

The bounty of new agricultures, combined with the fresh points of view that flowed in on the crest of new information technologies, released increasing numbers of Middle Eastern and North African tribal women from customs that had once been rationalized as the result of an economy of great scarcity. Women who had endured time-consuming, backbreaking labor as subsistence farmers were now blessed with time to educate themselves, care for themselves; they were blessed with time even to do nothing, which was the greatest luxury of all.

IRAN'S VELVET TRANSFORMATION

It's an old law of physics that for every action there is a reaction, and nowhere was this clearer than in Iran. By 2010, a cohort of thirty-pluses who, along with younger people, made up more than 60 percent of Iran's population, represented what might be an extreme in cynicism. They had been routinely taught to lie since childhood, they had been forced in adolescence to give lip service to the fundamentalists to secure a place in the university or a good job, and they had come of age only to discover an appalling hypocrisy and corruption among their mullahs. In short, they had been in reaction to religious fundamentalism for so long that by now, fundamentalism itself was negligible, the domain of the very old, the very poor, or the very pious.

Beginning in the early 1990s, satellite TV had brought them Western music and entertainment, which in turn had nourished a hunger for Western clothes—and then Western ideas, especially ideas of free thought and expression. These pressures led to a peaceful secularization of Iranian society between 2010 and 2015, which in turn opened a prosperous new era in Iranian history.

The Iranian diaspora provided rich cross-fertilization for those who had remained at home. For example, women reclaimed the old skills—the famous Persian carpets had always been women's work—but they adapted new methods. The "evolving garden" Persian rugs, based on genetic algorithms, became as famous and desirable as the original tribal rugs had once been; weaving nourished an efflorescence of other crafts that were the envy of the world.

Grateful for the disappearance of truly oppressive religious laws, Iranian women spoke sympathetically of the deep psychological resistance, the intense fear, that men felt toward change, and how women must help them through this time. They argued openly for women to keep up the old roles at home, to help men through the adjustments they had to make at work. Did such a strategy sound patronizing to Western ears? Did it mean women had to negotiate between their own very different roles at home and work, and add the "second shift" of unpaid household labor to their professional day? Iranian women laughed. This was nothing compared to what they'd been through.

Diaspora scientists, many of them women, returned with new ideas for the petroleum that was left in Iran's oil fields. Rather than burn precious fossil resources for fuel, polluting the environment and contributing to destabilized global weather patterns, they said, we can leverage the value of Iran's best natural resource. Through their work, a great array of new petro-products, far more valuable than mere fuel, began to emerge from Iranian laboratories.

THE CALIFORNIA MICROCOSM: EQUALITY STILL HAS WINNERS AND LOSERS

As the millennium opened in California, two populations of roughly equal size shared the state of California, whites and nonwhites. But that picture concealed a finer-grained set of divisions among haves and have-nots, a set of divisions that corresponded more to education, and hence household income level, than to ethnic identity. All Americans were getting older as a group, but by 2010, California's median age, thirty-six, was nearly three years younger than the U.S. median. Single-parent households continued to grow, to 2 million by 2000, 3.5 million by 2010, 5 million by 2015, three-quarters of them headed by women.

Between 2000 and 2015, well-educated, well-off Californians had more to bring them together than to divide them. Certainly a majority of them were in the white half of the population, but the group also included many Asians (especially second-generation Asians, who continued to be overrepresented in the professions and managerial classes), a much smaller but nevertheless identifiable proportion of Hispanics, and an overrepresentation of black women.

Though members of this cultural alloy maintained an ethnic identity at home and for holidays, those identities were blurred by larger commonalities. The Alloids acquired their information and entertainment from the same kinds of high-tech home media centers, made the same kinds of decisions about leisure, traveled to the same resorts at home and abroad, and had the global awareness to be concerned with the same mega-issues: the environment, the economy, and public education.

They treated their ethnicity as a strong flavor in their lives but not the whole banquet, and they tended to see separatism, or even ethnic solidarity, as a strategy whose time had come—and gone. When asked, they'd say that one of the reasons they were in California was to reinvent themselves: the old ways (whether the old country's or the old generation's) no longer worked—if they ever had.

The Alloids were just as likely to order tacos for lunch as lemon-grass soup, and they shared a colloquial English rich in borrowings from Spanish, Chinese, Japanese, and technojargon, with sprinklings of Tagalog, Vietnamese, Farsi, and Hindi. Their tastes in music were wildly eclectic, ranging from European classics to Senegal rock to Taiwan blues. If they stopped to think about it, they were living examples of the synergy of multiculturalism.

Because so many of the Alloids were children or grandchildren of new immigrants, few were inclined to be nostalgic about what their forebears had abandoned. Anyway, worldwide travel made it easy for them to go and see for themselves. They would return home from these sentimental journeys reconfirmed in their Americanism. They were goal-oriented rather than ideological, and their politics reflected their pragmatism: *whatever works, okay?* Black, Hispanic, and Asian Alloids defied the traditional voting behavior of their ethnic groups by voting at the same high rate as the rest of their well-educated cohorts.

This voting behavior translated into political decisions—whether on foreign policy or on local issues—that reflected a kind of triage: leave alone what will get better by itself, help what can be helped, and abandon the rest. The ideological flaming that had characterized the 1990s was a puzzling piece of history to them.

Though they represented just under a third of California's population, the Alloids were by far the state's most influential population segment, the pace-setters that everybody else, younger and older, imitated. They had the highest household incomes and the fewest children (though they did have children, in contrast to the nonfamily households that predominated among this age group in the past) and their households often included an older relative, integral to the family, a result not only of demographics but also of cultural heritage.

As attractive as their lifestyle was, it rested firmly on years of family and individual sacrifice, formal education, opportunities seized, and individual wealth accumulated. This experience shaped their social conscience in unsubtle ways: Alloids were willing to hold a hand out to the less fortunate, but not much more than a hand; they supported projects and policies that offered second chances, but not third, or indefinite chances. As a group they were unmoved by chronic social problems that wouldn't yield to decentralized, often privatized, solutions.

The Alloids were generally convinced that if the broken institutions could not be fixed and made to work, it was sheer sentimentality to try and preserve them. They were to be dismantled and replaced with institutions that worked: the public schools, social welfare, health care, and large parts of the state government all came under scrutiny. (The school systems were a particular target of their impatience. When growth in the numbers of entry-level workers resumed in the late 1990s, their lack of preparation for work was blamed on the schools—somewhat unfairly, since most of the growth came from recent Hispanic and Asian immigrants.)

Because they saw a pressing need and a big payoff, the Alloids were willing to invest in educational experimentation, from high-tech computerized learning to the "samba school" model, where learners teach other learners; and they simply bypassed entrenched bureaucracies (teachers' unions, for example, who found themselves in the same position as air traffic controllers once had under President Ronald Reagan: dismissed and unmourned). The triage strategy was applied to other social problems, and it was seen as a means of community consensus building and collaboration rather than being divisive.

The Golden State was not golden for everybody. Those who failed to share the values of the Alloids were worse off than ever. In 1990, for example, American-born blacks were already complaining that the new immigrants reaped a disproportionate share of society's benefits and then leaped ahead economically. That complaint was well founded, and the trend only intensified. The success of black women in middle and upper-level occupations, however, suggested that racism wasn't the whole answer. Other losers in the multicultural game were those Asians and Hispanics who could not or would not participate in the socially upward mobility that might propel them out of low-skill occupations.

Alloid pragmatism considered each of these groups as unsalvageable, and the barrios and shantytowns that characterized Latin American and some Asian megacities became small, permanent, and brutal fixtures of the California landscape, sources of social stress that, unfortunately for the stressed, were generally ignored by the contented majority.

PAMELA McCORDUCK, 75, WRITER, UNITED STATES

Though I'm born in the middle of the British blitz of World War II, the bombs screaming down around my mother in childbirth, nothing between her and the night but a flapping tarpaulin, I'm the new baby in a family that hasn't had babies to pamper for many years. I'm the first child of my father, who himself had been the favorite youngest child. Love and attention are everywhere I turn. (Among my toys, my first computer: a child's counting frame, a small abacus with nursery-colored

beads mounted over a blackboard: I only remember playing with it when I see one in Munich's Deutsches Mu-
seum nearly a half-century later, and the memory comes
over me in a wave of warmth, how I loved that abacus,
that blackboard, how I precounted and prescribbled like
a drunken Neanderthal.)

Everything is rationed, so I go to bed—or the bomb
shelter—cold and by candlelight. Petrol is nearly nonexistent too: deliveries are made in dray carts. On my first
day of school, I wake to the clop of a dray horse's shoes
on the cobblestones. I don't know life can be different,
that once it was. Unlike the grownups, I don't feel suddenly and unfairly shoved backward in history. (Just how
far back have we been shoved anyway? At the German
invasion, the Polish cavalry had valiantly rushed out on
horseback to attack the tanks. Only twelve days after I'm
born, the U.S. War Department announces that the use
of sabers by officers on duty with troops will be discon-
tinued.)

No, I'm born into a transitional moment, past and
future pulling away from each other like mismatched
lovers, yearning for what has been and what might be,
but confounded by what is. My first but not my last experience with this.

Sometimes my mother takes me to the village outside
Liverpool where she grew up. Aughton is placid, nearly
untouched by the war, its church and village green as
peaceful as when she'd been a girl. We gather at Auntie
Lucy's cottage, the stuff of calendars and biscuit-tin tops:
whitewashed, thatched roof, hollyhocks and fuchsias in
the garden. In the long English summer twilights, I
make up stories about the ballerina fuchsias and pick
raspberries (as elemental to me as fish and chips) while
the women talk low and laugh softly. My mother in-

cludes me in her life as if I were an honorary grownup. Though she stopped working when she married, she'll still do the hair of friends as a favor, carrying her hairdresser's case like a doctor's bag. And I go with her, sit quietly, watch the women talk and primp, speaking their hearts the way women do as their hair is being fussed with. It's an act among primates so basic, so relaxing, so begetting of trust, so finally loving, that the anthropologists even have a phrase for it, mutual grooming.

I'm not yet five when my mother tells me the war is over. She's jubilant; now we can go to America. On my usual twilight ramble (a different world, where a little girl can wander safely alone) I'm drawn through a Tudor-style portecochère into a large grassy field, where a great bonfire burns. Orange light against half-timbers, shadows of countless people milling, gathered on the grass, singing that peculiarly British mix of patriotic and sentimental songs, dancing the Hokey-Pokey ("You put your right foot in / You put your right foot out / You put your right foot in / And you shake it all about." Is it possible the phrase comes from the streetcry of the Italian immigrants who sold ice cream in Victorian times? *Ecco un poco. Here's a bit.* That's why they were called the hokey-pokey men.) It's V-E Day, victory at last over the hated Jerries and Hitler. (Strange but true that nearly all the significant men in my life will be Germanic; I will spend some of the happiest times of my life in Germany.)

I join in, dancing and clowning too, still a four-year-old outsider. I don't know anybody, but I strain conscientiously to feel something in common with this jolly crowd. Around our piano, I've learned all the words to all the songs, mouth them perfectly. At the same time, I scrutinize those faces: are people *really* that happy? Or—dark thought—are they just faking it like I am?

In America, I make a great effort to become the All-American Girl. I change my language (treacherous mother tongue); I learn to play by girls' rules (only two bounces; only half the court). Girls' rules follow me relentlessly: by the time I'm grown up, it takes me a few years to see that Freudianism, the unquestioned dogma of my sophisticated college crowd, is just the same old two bounces, half the court.

At twenty-eight, my life is a sum of ex's: ex-wife, ex-secretary, ex-fat girl. I've lost other skills too. I can no longer speak the language of don't-tell-your-father, All-American sweet and deferential girl-talk. On the other hand, I'm in love with a man who will be partner, pal, and lover for a lifetime.

Very slowly, I realize I can break the rules I hate. I can make up my own. I go back to science, which the English major in me has always secretly loved; I discover the optimism of scientists, which suits my temperament; I discover the computer and begin to write about it as seriously as if it were literature (and lose a tenure battle for my impertinence). I refocus on artificial intelligence, not a little because (though I don't know it then) it seems to say that intelligence can exist outside the male cranium. What I *do* know is that the whole enterprise strikes me as a wonderful intellectual adventure, and I'm going to be up for those the rest of my life, win or lose.

I write, I publish, I travel. Of course: partner or not, I have a room of my own, know how to close the door, and have enough guineas to keep going. I awaken each morning and thank Providence for my good fortune in doing work I love. I'm always ready for the new, though I live in old places that honor the old ways.

My mother danced—in public—into her eighties. I'll dance there too until my knees give out.

Two Steps Forward, Two Steps Back

Every single one of you in this room knows what it's like to work like a dog to move things forward and then have some whiner come in there and say, "This isn't right, that isn't right." How many of you have stood over a stack of white shirts—you know the kind I mean—and you've sprinkled 'em down real good the night before and you iron them and when he gets home he has plenty of nice white shirts folded in his drawer, and he comes in and he says, "There's a wrinkle right here." And he says, "Why did you fold 'em and put 'em in the drawer? I like 'em on the hanger."

> —*Governor Ann Richards of Texas, during her unsuccessful 1994 race against George W. Bush Jr.*

In this scenario, Western notions of individual rights prevail, but the world economy is largely depressed and sluggish. Environmental protective measures are suspended in the name of the economy, disrupting what had begun as a movement toward global sustainability. The age is characterized by huge international migrations, people in search of jobs, housing, even food. New technologies are unevenly distributed, permitting wealth to accumulate in the hands of relatively few. The long-established international network of experienced, activist women is so hard-pressed to address the most basic needs of the world's women, such as nutrition, child spacing, protection from domestic violence, and workplace safety, that little other progress is possible. We call this stagnant state of affairs Two Steps Forward, Two Steps Back.

MAJOR TRENDS

Nearly everyone in the last part of the twentieth century who had peered into the future predicted that the knowledge society would soon be global. By 2015, this was a fact. The Internet—already known as the Net by 1995—spanned the globe, a hybrid of fiber (though not fiber as it might have been known ten years earlier), satellite, and wireless systems, but always carrying bits: storable, transferable, malleable.

In nations that permitted uncontrolled exchange of information, democracy flourished. It was typical of the tensions between the rights of individuals and the needs of society that conflicts still arose—did citizens have an absolute right to freedom of expression, or encrypting their private messages, or did the state have legitimate right to censor some documents and have access to others? If one brought on one's own poor health or injury (by smoking, or drug or alcohol abuse, or even by failing to exercise, or by choosing dangerous exercise, like mountaineering or hang-gliding) did the society still have to pay the medical costs of that risky behavior? (This tension played out elsewhere, as we will see, in questions about entitlement to various kinds of medical care, for example.)

An international pact, promoted and signed in 2002 in the spirit of preserving national sovereignty, permitted each nation to scrutinize telecommunications at its borders and prohibit material a government considered unsuitable for its citizens. Invisible but highly effective electronic barriers kept people in many parts of China, Indonesia, and some of Southeast Asia from accessing anything but the most sanitized, government-approved bit stream. Those national governments that went to the trouble to apply electronic sealant around their borders (and often within them) were serious: lawbreakers—hackers, encryptors, pornographers—were dealt with severely. In Singapore, for example, encryption was prima facie evidence of criminal activity, and encryptors faced heavy fines and jail.

As predicted, then, power and wealth accrued to knowledge workers, although across the globe they were a minority (perhaps some 40 percent) of all workers. New knowledge-based services and industries emerged that had been unimaginable even a decade earlier; old industries were transformed almost beyond recognition as they reorganized themselves around their information flow bits, instead of their product flow atoms.

Education was fundamental to any knowledge worker's career. Women's experience here was mixed. When they had access to education, they prospered, because they were excellent knowledge workers. But although the numbers of the world's women who were literate had dramatically increased, from 40 percent in the late twentieth century to 60 percent by 2015, many women were still outside the information age, farming and running small enterprises that barely allowed them to stay in place economically.

Pressed by the growing disparity between themselves and the developed countries, whose businesses had led the way into and now dominated the information age, and pressed too by a total workforce of some 2.5 billion, the less developed countries desperately tried to catch up by adopting the new, cheap, broadband intelligent technology for education in ways the developed countries, on the whole, did not.

In most countries of the developed world, in contrast, the tradition (in some cases only the memory) of a good education was the enemy of the best. Information technology had been adopted by the schools early, but it was a cosmetic adaptation: educational bureaucracies resisted the kind of wholesale restructuring in schools that businesses, for example, undertook at the end of the century.

The situation in the developed countries was further complicated by two salient problems: the Age Bulge and what came to be called "prison-mania." The Age Bulge refers to the rapidly aging population of the developed world, where people over sixty-five, now comprising 20 percent of the population, required more from social services (pensions, medical, and home-help assistance) than any population cohort except the very young.

Prison-mania was not unrelated to the Age Bulge. In the United States, expenditures on prisons had, for the first time, matched spending on education. California, as usual, had led the way: in 1995–96, the sums the state spent on prisons exceeded the amount spent on higher education, and within a few years, on education generally. Though critics pointed out the grave consequences of this emphasis on prisons at the expense of schools, especially in an information economy, by 2005, the pattern prevailed all over the United States, spurred by fearful citizens who were growing older and feeling more vulnerable to that only slightly larger cohort of the 21–24 age group, the source of most violent crime—and not coincidentally, competitors for social resources. (Ironically, a scheme begun in California in 1991 was copied all over the United

States and eventually in Europe, where higher education had traditionally been fully state-supported but now demanded student co-payment. Tax-exempt college savings bonds were promoted to middle-class families to save for their children's college education, but the money raised by these bonds actually helped finance prison construction.)

Starving the schools (and the highway and transportation systems and public services) to pay for the prisons would seem, on the face of it, to force the adoption of new educational methods and technologies, especially if they would be cheaper; but that didn't happen. An entrenched workforce of teachers and administrators accepted innovation only grudgingly and gradually, successfully arguing that though productivity might have gone up everywhere else, from manufacturing to services, productivity gains must not be expected of educators, since no electronic form of teaching could ever substitute for the hands-on human element. Educators pointed to their past success—weren't their schools essentially responsible for the knowledge society?—and they persuaded skeptics that this was the solid foundation for future success. The result, in the developed world, was educational stasis.

Of course different cultures and nations approached the problem differently. In Sweden and the Netherlands, the willingness to experiment and adapt continued. In India, where state governments had, by law, become one-third women, it was no coincidence that with the new century, girls had begun to be educated in almost the same number as boys, and the great illiteracy gap between females and males was being closed. But in certain parts of Africa, especially Muslim North Africa, and in rural China and Latin America, as cheap as the new means of education had become, many girls were still denied access because "they had other work to do," which meant they continued to be raised as household, agricultural, and sexual drudges.

· · ·

For as long as we have had written records, equality between the sexes has seldom been a social goal anywhere on the planet. Theorists have attributed this to various aspects of their own cultures—the Judeo-Christian patriarchy, or the Confucian worldview—without acknowledging that in fact those traditions only codify what is nearly universal among humans, whatever their culture. Sexual inequality might not always have been a human cultural fixture (as archaeological and even evolutionary, but not written, evidence suggests), and there's no reason why sexual inequality must always have been. But for thousands of years, inequality, sometimes acute, has prevailed, and its very persistence makes it that much more difficult to change.

Approaches toward equality have always come as the result of enormous effort, often pain: a battle by individual women, women working together, and the unusual, occasional man. What history does tell us is that each time or place women came closer to achieving equality—for example in early medieval Europe—powerful forces decisively pushed them back.

So though hopes were high for equality as the new millennium opened, and though many individual women had changed their lives and the minds and lives of everyone around them, the fact is that as the second decade opened, progress stalled. All over the world, women were saying: "I cannot go backward and be my mother." Every woman in her heart of hearts understood that a bell had been rung that could not be unrung; a horn had blown that could not be unblown.

Yet as women worked harder, longer, sometimes even better; as laws were passed that seemed to insist on the right actions; as women achieved what they'd never achieved before, real equality eluded them. Men still controlled the public sphere and often the private. For example, awakened by their defeats at the 1994 UN Cairo Conference on Population and Development, religious and political conservatives had marshaled themselves into alliances that would enfeeble the UN meetings that followed. Though the conservatives weren't very successful there, their intransigence absorbed energies that women might have spent on reenvisioning their futures, instead of fighting rearguard actions.

Worldwide, the situation was muddled by pious rhetoric and confusion about the nature of economics. International experts at the United Nations and the World Bank, for example, declared that in the less developed countries, for maximum economic development to take place sexual equality was indispensable, but once that was said, so what? Left unsaid was that the powerful were willing to settle for far less than the maximum if they could then evade difficult and painful social change. Global economists fiddling with their formulas and simulations didn't know how to factor in the reality that, in a patriarchal culture, every man, no matter how feckless, flatfooted, silly, or unlucky, could take comfort as he laid his head down each night, as he prayed each morning, that come what may, he was better than any woman.

Oversimplified and idealized Western classical economic models didn't work in the developed world either, for that matter. Some men might concede that everyone might eventually be richer in dollars, Deutschmarks, and yen if women had genuine equal opportunity, but why strive for the maximum when the present system satisfied, at least for those who already had power? Moreover, if you looked at the wealthiest countries—Switzerland, Japan, Germany—just where was the real world evidence for this equality-makes-wealth theory, anyway?

With money taking a more and more central role in village as well as urban economies, rural villages did not become small textbook examples of equilibrium economics. Identical agents did not arrive with perfect rationality at shared, logical conclusions or expectations. Instead, the reality principle prevailed: families understood quite well that males would acquire prestige and power, *plus* make more money, so males continued to be favored—they were better fed, got better health care, were better educated. Women followed the Matthew Principle: what little they had, that too might be taken from them. Women's work, essential but unpaid and thus unvalued, was often women's worst enemy.

Among themselves, women joked about men pointedly ("the invasion of the Cassocks"), and their personal conversation could be vicious, but this only reflected their frustration: they were working more and more as men did, yet they were still second-class citizens.

Partly, women sensed they didn't really understand the unwritten rules of power. Partly, the rules had changed. Partly, tokenism gave the appearance of equality without its reality. Partly, women were burdened with hours of essential but unpaid labor that had been theirs for centuries: child care, household work, family sustenance. Those who worked for wages added that unpaid labor as their "second shift." Partly, women held themselves back, either refusing to play by those rules (but therefore forfeiting much) or acting as their own worst enemies, yielding to age-old tactics of divide and conquer that men consciously or unconsciously exercised. Partly, women saw no choice. Whatever the reasons, it was not too far-fetched to say that for most women in the world, sometimes even where women had achieved the most, they might be compared to men in a prison: their hope was to get through the day, to avoid being a sexual victim, to survive.

AN AMERICAN CASE STUDY

The structural and demographic changes brought about by the maturing of capitalism, changes that have permitted women to join the paid workforce all over the world, were already evident in the United States by the 1920s. Demand for female labor grew rapidly after 1900, as the clerical and sales industries flourished. Married white women joined the paid workforce relatively late (black women, married or unmarried, had long been in the paid workforce); but by 1930, 20 percent of all clerical workers were women. During the 1930s, the heart of the Great Depression, the proportions of women in the workforce continued to increase, despite scarce jobs, despite federal laws and business practices that confined women to female work ghettos and applied last-hired, first-fired policies to them with impunity. Moreover, what small advances women had begun to make in the professions earlier in the century were now lost to them in the depression. With wage and other kinds of discrimination against women, the 20 percent difference in earnings between men and women in 1900 soared to a 55 percent difference in 1940.

During World War II, the female labor force increased by more than 50 percent; a large proportion of these women were married, and a majority were mothers with school-age children. Federal and state child care was suddenly deemed feasible and eventually served 1.5 million children by 1945. The war also temporarily eliminated the barriers to the employment of wives, mothers, and older women, who moved into well-paying and challenging jobs.

But for women a reversal took place after World War II. They were laid off or downgraded into dreary prewar women's work, clerical and service jobs. Wage discrimination was reinstituted. Despite these barriers, after a brief drop, the proportion of women in the workforce continued to climb throughout the 1950s and 1960s. "The increasing integration of women's workforce participation with marriage, then, preceded the growth of feminism, as did the shortening of the period of life in which women made a full-time commitment to motherhood," Stephanie Coontz points out in her book, *The Way We Never Were*. Thus the high visibility of women in the workforce in the

1970s was hardly a sudden eruption but instead the result of several long-range trends.

American feminism reinvented itself once more in the 1970s and seemed refreshingly effective, at least with the help of enforced affirmative action in business and government. Women continued to move steadily into the workforce, equaled and then passed men in college enrollments, and at least in a few cases, began earning big salaries.

By 1995, 400,000 American women could boast they earned $75,000 per year or more. But some 3 million American men earned that much. A male CEO of a major corporation might be paid $200 million a year, but the poverty level of a mother with two children was $11,000.

Though women's participation on boards of large corporations increased from the near nil it had been a decade earlier, by 1993 the 60 percent of corporations with women board members stopped with one token woman. She could not effect much change, and she was often regarded as exactly that, a token, not a role model or even someone to be taken very seriously. "The woman's seat" became common on corporate boards for the next decades until 97 percent of large corporate boards had one. But there was only one.

Also by 1995, a stunning 59 percent of top-level women executives told a Korn-Ferry survey they had experienced sexual harassment. But only 14 percent of them bothered to report the harasser to a supervisor; while 37 percent confronted the harasser privately. Half of all those harassed just tried to ignore it. These women were still expressing hope that at the end of the century, when the World War II generation of men had all retired at last, issues around what businessmen called their "comfort level" would have gone away. But comfort level issues didn't go away—if anything, they got worse, for a variety of social and psychological reasons.

The Korn-Ferry survey had cheerfully concluded: "There is

now a concentration of accomplished, proven senior women executives and it is our view that our next study a decade hence will show them breaking through the 'glass ceiling.' The '90s truly will be the Decade of the Executive Woman."

But the glass ceiling in businesses and most professions proved to be shatterproof: women watched in despair and rage as less qualified men were still paid better for the same (if differently named) work and were still promoted above them. The pattern could be found in business, in the law, in the sciences. It didn't happen as inevitably as it once had, but it happened often enough to exhibit what women called a clear pattern of discrimination—and what men called the breaks. Experts had declared that affirmative action was no longer necessary; in a move with some precedent, the Supreme Court followed the election returns and in three major decisions in 1995, 1997, and 2000 declared affirmative action to be unfair to individuals. Thus as affirmative action laws were dismantled, neither the courts nor the legislatures could offer women redress.

By the year 2015, 85 percent of all American women in the 18–49 age group were in the workforce. They could see that women held better jobs than before, but each woman knew a story of some woman, perhaps herself, who had been suddenly and arbitrarily barred from a job she'd earned and deserved. They could see slightly more women in state and federal legislatures, but a number of these were unsympathetic to the difficulties any woman faced in rearing children and working for wages, a lack of sympathy they ascribed to honoring family values. Ominously, women could see that in fields where they had finally achieved equal representation, such as medicine and law, those fields had restructured, and women were no longer offered the well-paying, high-prestige jobs they once had. Women—especially the Hispanic women who now comprised the dominant minority of U.S. women—were still crowded into lower-paying women's work.

Yes, on the whole, things for women had improved. But not by much.

MARIA SELKIRK, 71, RETIRED BUSINESS EXECUTIVE, CHICAGO

It never occurred to me at the time that I was anybody's token. I'd stopped keeping track of my "first woman to's." Well, seventeen significant firsts, including some big awards. Honorary degrees from business schools. Part of achievement is making it look easy. Maybe I made it look too easy, but the truth is, I'd worked my ass off for everything I'd achieved—why shouldn't I be invited on boards? Who better? Yes, I was well connected, but I made those connections: it was me with my Rolodex at four in the morning to Eastern Europe, eleven at night to Tokyo. My power, my money, was payoff for a lot of lonely nights in cookie-cutter hotel rooms. Not always alone, but almost always lonely.

At first I was naive in some ways. Later, people accused me of being fundamentally cold, of using them. In retrospect, I guess I thought I was just playing the game the way the boys played it. You've got something useful to tell me, great; if not, let's not waste each other's time just because we happen to meet at this sales conference or board meeting or whatever. A good mentor might have taught me that even in business, some people resent that kind of utility-function relationship. My thought was—no, honestly, it still is—if you want friendship, get it from your friends; if you want love, get it from your lover. I'm here for business. But it turns out that attitude can actually be bad for business.

At my peak around the turn of the century, I sat on, oh, I don't know, twenty or more boards. Yeah, I remember thinking: twenty for 2000. Not including my own company's board, where I took the chairmanship after we hired somebody else to be CEO. I was the only woman on all but two of those twenty boards. It didn't strike me as odd. Being the solo woman was situation-normal for me. At the same time, I sometimes felt, and deeply resented, my status as "only" a woman, at least in the eyes of some of my colleagues. The usual stuff: the we-don't-hear-Maria, the interruptions without apology, the dismissiveness, the patronizing, the plagiarism. But I never felt moved to ask that more women join me. Why should I? I didn't need allies; if it could be done, I'd do it myself. Let them earn it, the way I did. Other women would dilute my uniqueness, but this was buried way deep, let me tell you.

When did it change for me? At first, I began to notice I was getting a bit stale—the fresh ideas were fewer and further between, and that was partly because when you become a professional board member, you don't have much time to renew your intellectual capital. In place of real thought, you recycle what you've heard over there to fit the situation here. In other words, I was racking up the frequent-flier miles and making easy money, but I was facing the same old questions posed by more or less the same old guys: I used to joke that only the four walls and the four seasons changed. Then, another sign: as my term ended on some boards, I was inevitably replaced by another woman. That's when I got it: I'm perched in the Designated Woman's Seat; they don't want me for my smarts, my wisdom, my insight; they want me for my XX chromosome, my Yin, my yoni.

You'll laugh, but at first my feelings were hurt. Really! Then I thought, what the hell. Better mine than somebody else's. But I went nonlinear when I was actually named in a nasty little article in one of the business weeklies back in 2003 that called this token-woman-on-the-board a kind of high-class whoredom. Now I think, you bet: street corner or boardroom, it's just business.

No regrets. I made a lot of money, and guess what, money is a great magnet. The messages still flood in. I have my own foundation. I may as well give it away, since I can't take it with me. Yes, people are using me, but we all use each other all our lives, don't we?

WOMEN'S WORK AND EARNINGS IN THE DEVELOPED WORLD

Bouncing around the Internet in an infinite journey:

• • •

ANDY: Hey, John, I hear you got that sex change operation!
JOAN: Yes, and the name's now Joan, thank you very much.
ANDY: Did it hurt?
JOAN: I took a demotion, a 40 percent cut in pay, lost my benefits package, and was placed on temporary contract status. You BET it hurt!

• • •

In biblical times, according to the book of Leviticus, women at work were valued at thirty silver shekels. Men, however, were valued at fifty. Six thousand years later, little had changed.

In the first decade and a half of the new millennium, women in the developed world had nearly reached parity with men in terms of their percentage in the workforce. Their salaries, their benefits, and their opportunities had not. In the 1950s, American working women as a whole, for example, had earned between 60 and 64 percent of men's earnings. But that percentage slipped in the 1960s and never achieved 1950 highs again, resting at be-tween 57 and 58 percent of men's earnings for the rest of the cen-tury and even into the new millennium. Though white American women did better compared to other American women, earning in the 1990s about seventy-two cents for every dollar men earned, their gains came mainly because men's earnings had dropped. Moreover, all over the developed world, a discouraging pattern emerged of women moving into jobs which, when men held them, had been relatively well paid, but as women's work were less valued.

Though an elite group of American executive women had seen their salaries double between 1980 and 1990, they still earned only two thirds of what men earned in comparable jobs. That ratio held steady until 2010, when such women inched up to 75 percent of what men earned in comparable jobs, a ratio that did not alter in the next five years.

Worse, executive or professional women who took time off to have children and spend a few years rearing them found unwel-come news when they returned to the workplace: they were soundly penalized for their time off. It wasn't merely a matter of refurbishing old skills or learning new ones. These women de-tected first a skepticism among their colleagues ("if she's stopped to have a baby, how can she be serious?"), followed by what women described as a meanness, a vindictiveness that hobbled their careers. Moreover, mothers found that returning to work in an uneven, sometimes depressed economy meant fewer choices, often a significant cut in pay, and that postchild, they were no longer willing to bleed for the company in the form of vast num-bers of personal hours spent on work. They came to understand that their earnings and responsibilities would always lag, that their sacrifice was permanent. The belief would not die that wor-thy workers never, ever stopped working for any reason whatso-ever.

Within the United States—and this was reflected in Great

Britain, Germany, France, and to a lesser extent, Scandinavia and the Benelux countries—was its own "third world" of poor women. At the turn of the century the richest 1 percent of Americans, 2.5 million of them, averaged annual incomes of $400,000 after taxes. That 1 percent had almost as much as the bottom 40 percent of Americans, 9.3 million of them, a vast majority of whom were women and children. These proportions remained unchanged by 2015.

THE PARENT TRACK

Always—always—women were forced to make concessions that men never had to face. In the 1990s, 91 percent of U.S. executive men were married, but only 60 percent of executive women. That percentage had, if anything, dropped by 2015. Of those executive and professional women who did marry, most chose not to have children or deferred them until very late. In 2015, a typical professional complained that she didn't have enough time to spend with her spouse or her children—the same complaint she would have made twenty years earlier. She worked the same nearly sixty hours per week as her male counterparts did, and if she took leaves of absence (her male counterparts took nearly none) they were brief.

Not surprisingly, executive and professional women were the main users of the artificial womb, perfected in 2007, which meant they needn't take time to carry their own babies. They could also take advantage of *custextrap* (for custom extrapolation), a new technology that permitted certain regions of the mother's DNA to be sequenced and examined, so that properties of a candidate egg could be transferred to a computer which then presented a visual "mock up" of the potential child, from childhood into early adulthood. This extrapolation could be customized—features could be changed and added or subtracted—hence the term.

Rearing a child was so labor-intensive, many parents said, that it was only sensible to be sure this was exactly the child you wanted.

Whether a mother was a professional, an executive, or a worker of another kind, she continued to have prime responsibility for her children. In addition, she was typically responsible for household management, even if she earned more than her husband. Other innovations in medical care, like long-term prevention instead of crisis intervention, community clinics in the schools, and internal biochips that permitted distant readout of vital signs, all helped lift some of the burden. But it was widely held that if adults might cure their colds and minor influenzas with rain forest infusions, children must contract these minor diseases and let them run their course to train their immune systems. A mother—or her hired help—had to be there. The extra responsibility of a family led to burnout, and women workers tended to retire earlier, not only a loss to all concerned, but an extra burden for her society, since she was likely to live longer than her male colleagues.

Women in the developed world (for by now nearly all women worked outside the home) ached for help with balancing their work and family responsibilities. For one brief moment, women thought they saw hope. Studies in the mid-1990s showed that the workplace was no friend of fathers, either, unless their wives were at home shoring up the support structure. Those executives— men *and* women—whose spouses worked found themselves earning less, advancing more slowly, penalized for being unable to dedicate themselves entirely to their jobs.

"We often used to say if men had to face the discrimination women faced, that would be the end of it," one working feminist remarked. "But we were wrong. Traditional businesses weren't just antiwoman; they were antifamily too. I wonder where they thought their future clients and customers were coming from."

Hope died when nobody seemed to have the will to act on what amounted to indifference to family responsibilities, even an implicit antifamily bias. It grew even grimmer when those European countries that had traditionally supported families through government policies began to withdraw that support as unaffordable.

ITALY: A DISTANT EARLY WARNING

By 2015, the Pope was once more Italian-born, but it seemed as if the last people to listen to him were the Italians. As early as the mid-1990s, demographers all over the world had been watching Italy as an example of what might happen if population control went awry. Once the capital of *La Mamma* and *Il Bambini,* in the mid-1990s, Italy had the lowest birth rate in the world—1.3 babies per woman of child-bearing age. Demographers predicted that if those trends continued, Italy's native population could never recover.

Not only was there a scarcity of babies, but the graying of Italy was dramatic and pervasive—already by the mid-1990s more people were on pension than worked, and the numbers of people working dropped steadily as the new century opened. The national pension and health system was in crisis, and revenues that would have gone to the schools went to help support the old instead. Worse, the population varied from region to region. Most of the elderly lived in the already prosperous north; while most of the young lived in the high-unemployment, impoverished south. Italy's retirement age was the youngest of the industrialized nations: fifty-five for women and sixty for men, giving women especially nearly thirty more years of pensioned life.

Women were blamed for all this. They were accused of materialism, wanting designer clothes instead of babies. But women retorted that, first, the decision to have children or not was a joint decision with a man. Italian men were just as reluctant to father more than one child, a concept that seemed to elude critics. Next, the workplace—where women not only earned money, but found an independent identity—made no accommodation for mothers. Flextime was unknown. Child care was problematic: most women, entirely responsible for child care, relied on their own mothers since professional child care was spotty, but the older generation of women resisted taking on the care of more than one child, arguing that they had already done their duty rearing their own children.

Italian women were nearly absent from government, and as a consequence, whether in the relatively prosperous north or the hardscrabble south, women had no say in how government funds were allocated. Flinty—or notoriously corrupt—local governments had refused to put money into parks, playgrounds, and nursery schools, providing children and their mothers with no social nor physical space. The schools were being looted to pay for the old. Very sensibly, parents asked themselves whether this was the right world in which to bring up children.

Into this youth vacuum rushed a flood of immigrants. Some of them were ethnic Italians from the Americas, whose own great-grandparents had journeyed away from Italy a hundred years earlier. These immigrants were legal and welcome, lured by special scholarships and stipends the Italian government offered in the hope of reclaiming its own. But others, fleeing the Balkans, Eastern Europe, Africa, India, and even China, arrived illegally. The government turned a blind eye to these, with the unspoken hope that they would eventually assimilate and help pay the cost of the elderly, but by 2015, the situation was highly unstable, with a core group of immigrants rebelling against their own exploitation.

UTE MARC, 37, ARTIST, MUNICH, GERMANY

I thought with my name it was inevitable I would be an artist, make my marks. I've worked in all the media—passive (if you can say such a thing about art), interactive;

I've done solo work and I've done work with collaborators. I continue to think of myself as an outsider, though of course these days I need a human accountant and a human manager—not precisely the sign of an outsider. My work is represented in the major contemporary museums here and abroad, and there are collectors who will buy anything I put together. It's despicable, really. But what can you do?

About five years ago, I backed off my antiestablishment stuff. It seemed to me that much of it was posturing, not authentic; I mean, we were selling to the highest bidder, right? My colleagues can tell themselves that's fleecing the bourgeoisie, but it bothered me at some fundamental level. I went through a period of embracing the establishment, then mocking it. I did work for play-malls and theme-environments. That sounds very up to date, but we have a long tradition of that here in Germany. Mad King Ludwig is my hero in that regard.

It's strange but wonderful that Germany's most notable kings have all been queens—I mean Frederick the Great, Hitler, probably Charlemagne. The greatest was Mad King Ludwig, at least from a theatrical point of view.

That's why I appear in public as Queen Ludwige. I've appropriated one old queen's fantasies and transformed them into fantasies for today. I make socio-political-sexual statements with my art. For the last year or so I've been preoccupied with the endless embrace of Eros and Thanatos. Did you see my installation at Dachau?

JAPAN: ANOTHER DISTANT EARLY WARNING

By the early 1980s, the Japanese government was already fretting about the numbers. Wealthy as the country seemed, it was not producing enough babies to replace its population. The government was right to fret: by the mid-1990s, Japan's fertility rate had dropped to one of the lowest in the world. The problem, government officials complained, was Japanese women, who kept putting off marriage until later and later. In the 1990s, 40 percent of Japanese women between twenty and twenty-nine were still single. In the first decade of the new century, that number rose to 75 percent. Moreover, in the 1990s, 95 percent of Japanese women had eventually married by age forty. By 2010, that number had dropped to about 60 percent.

Women made no secret about why staying single was better than getting married. Life as a married woman in Japan was tough, frustrating, and lonely. Japanese men still worked the twelve-hour day their fathers and grandfathers had worked, and if their commuting time had dropped thanks to new high-speed trains, this only meant one hour's commute instead of two. Stubborn turf wars in the 1990s among government bureaucracies, and also the inherent difficulties of entering Kanji text by keyboard, had caused Japan's information infrastructure to fall behind both American and European networks. Not only did Japanese workers still have to present themselves to offices every day, since telecommuting was nearly unknown, but the more subtle problems of information lag were beginning to have an impact on the Japanese economy.

Virtually no Japanese man would share the housework or child care just so that his wife might continue her career. Men declared that after such a long workday—which still included evenings out with the boss—they had no time for housework, especially not so that women could continue working at what for most of them were still low-level clerical jobs. But women, out in the workforce more and more, had long pointed out that the typical Japanese firm valued face time over productivity, and no man really needed to work such long hours if he worked effectively instead. However, the whole issue of long work hours was so embedded in the culture that few firms dared break the pattern.

Moreover, continuing the pattern begun in the 1970s, in the opening decade of the new century more than half a million Japanese men were posted abroad to tend Japan's vital global business. For a number of reasons—the most important being the difficulties children had adjusting to Japan when they returned from abroad—more men went abroad without their families than ever before, leaving wives at home for three and sometimes four years, women whose only task was to shuttle one or two children from school to after-school classes and sports events. It became fashionable for Japanese women to refuse to marry men who hadn't yet done their overseas service. More important, these women demanded evidence that their prospective husbands had tested negative for HIV, given the popularity of prostitutes both in Japan and abroad.

To be sure, Japan's wholesale cultural denial of HIV and AIDS had altered since the 1990s when the country was still in Stage I of the HIV/AIDS epidemic, where the disease is invisible. By 2015, the country had already passed through Stage II, where people had begun to sicken and die, and had arrived at Stage III, where AIDS had been acknowledged as a public health problem and was slowly being dealt with. The sheer numbers of AIDS patients, nearly a quarter of all men between twenty-five and forty, had forced a new realism.

But behavior change, Stage IV, was slow to come to Japan. Men who couldn't marry, men who were apart from their wives, and men who were estranged from the women they had married, took a samurai's fatalistic view of life and continued to find sexual solace with prostitutes both in Japan and abroad (on sex tours). Such conditions were ideal for spreading the disease; men contracted it in growing numbers and brought it home. Among Japanese women, there was widespread conviction that once a woman married, she could no longer demand that her husband use condoms or be tested for HIV, and she had no control over whether he was unfaithful to her. Understandably, then, Japanese women did not approach marriage lightly.

Thus though Japan led the world in roboticizing, it felt the people deficit more and more, especially since it still refused to permit immigrants in any significant numbers. But males and females stared implacably at each other across an unbridgeable chasm, women more and more aware of their unequal status and determined not to succumb to the marriage prison.

PATRICIA BATES, 68, RETIRED BUSINESS EXECUTIVE, LONDON

We've never solved the problem of accountability. British history can proudly lay claim to some of the most splendid feminists ever to put pen to paper or self to sacrifice. Yet for women, our country is still among the most backward in Europe. I don't see much chance for real change, at least anytime soon.

Whether politics, business, the judiciary, the civil service, or the arts, here in Britain we've always begun with a kind of obstacle race, a species of apprentice system as obsolete as any eighteenth-century indenture. It's meant to produce winners—*suitable candidates*, as they're officially called.

At the end of the obstacle race—one's late thirties, early forties—the suitable candidates indeed emerge. By curious coincidence, the suitable candidates are somehow always chaps. Really? Well now, a regular chap just *feels* better with other chaps, doesn't he? A chap's proper job is to look after other chaps, isn't it? Promotion panels, search committees, nominating bodies, nobody calls them to account. It's all secret, don't you see? Britain has a long history of official secrecy, and that's how the Other Ranks are kept down and out. Occasionally we women have entered the race, even more occasionally we've emerged as suitable candidates; but always one by one, excruciatingly slowly. Far too many of us have taken the Thatcher model to heart: I made it here on my own and bugger you.

It was no help that women's natural allies, the Labour and the Liberal parties, persisted for years in pretending that real work was done by real men and required a broad back. Not only did the trades unions continue to nominate only white men to run for office, but they rabidly resisted any equal-pay legislation as interfering with collective bargaining. The whole shift from industry to information went right past them, and by the time they understood, it was too late.

Women have brought some of this on ourselves, I must say. In the last part of the century we squandered our energy on endless quarreling over reproductive rights, women bitterly against women. Comes the morning-after pill with its sweet discretion, and that's that. Think of us as medieval theologians who'd thrashed each other to the death over how many angels can dance on the head of a pin. It was all over, and we'd all lost.

Male violence. It's been a continuing theme of women activists here for half a century or more. For reasons that looked eminently sensible then and look just mad now, we framed the issue in terms of pornography. Dirty pictures, naughty words are easy to understand, and who'll stand up for the principled right to depict naked women in chains with needles in their breasts? Kiddies being graphically buggered? But when we'd been able to gain laws suppressing pornography, pornography didn't go away, it simply went underground. That's something, I suppose, but the desire for pornography didn't go away. Violence—the casual, everyday, blacken-her-eye, knock-her-to-the-kitchen-floor kind of violence—certainly didn't disappear.

By the 1990s many feminists had allied themselves with the New Right, who had an entirely different set of concerns, retro for women in my opinion. Feminism and prudery became confused with each other, not only in the public's mind, but in the minds of feminists themselves. We were seen as against sex, against fun; all for high-necked dresses, cold baths, and colder porridge. By the turn of the century, feminism was all but discredited in Britain.

I ask you: Why did women think they could suppress a literary tradition of hundreds of years? *Why did they think it would change matters if they did?* The fight against pornography was one more example of routing out the symptom in the forlorn hope it would cure the disease. Our country has a long cultural tradition of male violence against women, if not its acceptability, certainly its inevitability—particularly domestic violence. People shrug. That's the way it's always been. Me, me mum, and her mum before her. Not that you should think this is entirely a working-class matter. "The husband is prohibited from using any violence to his wife other than that which appertains legally and reasonably to the husband for the governance and correction of his wife." Mr. Justice Blackstone, if you please.

In 1994, Norwegian women kept Norway out of the European Market because they were afraid it would be a big step backward for women. British women, on the contrary, must be grateful to the Treaty of Rome for giving them something their own nation wouldn't. No, say what you will, I'm afraid that here in Britain we won't come anywhere near the equality women elsewhere in the developed world enjoy for a long time to come.

ANNETTE BROWER, 36, INFORMATION VALIDATION SPECIALIST, UNITED STATES

I'm on an Edge City school board. It seems hard to believe that, in principle, I'm fighting for the same things my mother was fighting for twenty-five years ago. She was fighting for books and pencils. We're fighting for workstations, networks, and downlinks. She was fighting for salaries. I fight for salaries. She was fighting for quality. I fight for quality.

One difference: the building where I went to school was, oh, fifteen years old, I guess. My kids, on the other hand, are going to a school that's over fifty years old. Even if education hadn't gone through these wrenching changes, which of course it has, you get inevitable—and big—problems with a fifty-year-old building. The heat is balky in the winter. The windows are warped and won't open anymore, so the kids don't get fresh air when the weather's good. The plaster is peeling. The wiring? Please.

In my day, education was pretty much the same as it had been for centuries: a bunch of kids trooped into a classroom under the supervision of a teacher and they read books, recited, wrote on paper, and learned together. Sure, the PC was over there in the corner, but nobody used it except for playing games and maybe a little word-processing. It was part toy, part symbol, part

alien from outer space. Now, with all the wired possibilities, education has changed enormously. The private
schools have ubicomp, ubiquitous computing—computing everywhere. The private schools have computing
walls, where when we were kids we had blackboards—
and my kids still do. My kids are still stuck with the old-
fashioned model because the old buildings can't be
brought on-line in any easy, cheap, safe way. If we could
find the money to do that, the teachers resist because it's
a threat to them and the way they've always done
things. I would gladly buy my kids their own computers,
but it's forbidden to use them in school. The teachers
wave these fake studies that claim computers impede
children's motor and cognitive development, their social
skills. Anyway, not every parent can afford to supply a
personal computer; therefore nobody can have a PC.
Democracy!

Even without the possibilities of wiring up, my kids'
schools are dreary little minimum-security prisons, that's
what they are. What were these people thinking of when
they designed and built them? I guess they meant well,
and maybe when the buildings were new they looked
okay. We don't exactly live like royalty, but my little girl
cries when she has to go back to school after the weekend.

The public schools get the least and the last—the
least money, the least equipment, the least of everything. Some people would say the least of the teachers
and students too, though I don't believe that—necessarily. Anyway, my kids have no choice: it's the public
schools or nothing. But as if we didn't have enough
problems with our technology deficit, we're stuck with
the BPs, the behavioral problems. The private schools
don't have to take those. We get the so-called special ed

kids, too, what *my* kids call the wet-the-bed kids. Children may not be subtle, but they're honest. Special ed kids don't exactly help the learning process, frankly. With no special ed teachers, they suck up the regular teacher's time unfairly and lose any chance for the education they deserve. But this is how it is: the public schools are the warehouse of last resort. When I'm feeling optimistic, I tell myself the kids are getting an education in spite of the schools, not because of them. When I'm really depressed, I feel as if I'm consigning my kids to the basement forever. They'll never catch up, and it has nothing to do with their intelligence. They're normal kids. Not geniuses, just normal. In these bad old schools, that's barely enough to let you hang on to your place in the basement.

You can't blame the good teachers for wanting to go where the good technology is, where the good pay is, where the everyday rules don't seem like that thick, overgrown forest where the prince found Sleeping Beauty. I mean they go to the private schools, of course. Better pay, better benefits, better everything. There isn't a chance in the world I could even think of sending my kids to a private school. My education was basically empty, but if I could afford it I'd school my kids at home. I can't; that's a luxury for two-parent families.

The picture isn't entirely bleak. We have a few dedicated people in our schools. We're grateful to them. But when you think what people who can afford it do; when you think of how public education is supported in other countries, it breaks your heart.

Sometimes I feel very alone. Most moms really care, but they don't have the time to fight this fight for their kids. They've got their hands full with work and putting a meal on the table, doing the laundry, paying the bills, fixing the roof. They expect the schools will educate their kids. Every mom I know works; at the end of the day she's not exactly brimming with energy to participate in meetings. I hear that word "community," and I just want to puke. Community is a luxury for people who have time for it. My job is more flexible than most, so I've taken on the responsibility of the school board. But it's wearing, really tiring. If it isn't the county auditors, I'm up against these religious nuts, my board colleagues.

The utter low point for me was when Spark Computer Company offered to donate twelve computing walls to our elementary school, along with teacher training. Only twelve; it wouldn't have changed the world; but it was twelve more than we had. Two of the people on the board said they wouldn't take them because the Spark Company is gay-neutral, and this means that sinners could have designed those motherboards! Hey, I'm not making this up. They lined up two others who said that Spark was dominated by Asian interests, so it would be un-American to accept the machines. We three sane ones didn't have a chance. I went home and cried that night. I just cried. I came *this* close to resigning, but who'll stick up for my kids if I don't?

I don't have any kind of life of my own. My life is my kids and their schools. Sometimes I think I'm going to wake up and I'll be forty-five and what will I have to show for it? Survival, I guess.

Then I think about the long line of teachers I'm descended from. In the black American community women were always the teachers, the keepers of knowledge. They learned in secret in slavery, and they taught their kids when the schools wouldn't, during Reconstruction and Jim Crow times. They stayed in school when their brothers dropped out in the hard times of the 1970s, the 1980s. So you see I'm carrying on a tradition. I have to think that what I do, hard as it is, is no harder than what my great-grandmother, even her mother, did. But don't let anybody tell you it's easy. It isn't.

WOMEN'S HEALTH IN THE DEVELOPED WORLD

Though health care in the developed world could hardly be compared to the miserable conditions elsewhere, medical care had always been unevenly distributed between the sexes, and this predicament continued: men's afflictions were given priority over women's, men's health was better studied and more effectively treated than women's health, even for the same diseases, such as heart disease, HIV, and alcoholism. Reproductive health care, crucial to women, was, as it had ever been, slighted.

In the United States, continued tinkering with health schemes had led to wildly erratic health-care delivery, and hardest hit were poor women, who as a group suffered many of the disadvantages of Third World women. Drastic reorganizations of all health-care delivery as the old century ended and the new one opened had soon shown themselves to be nothing more than a shift in wealth from physicians to business executives who ran health-care organizations, with no advantage accruing to patients. New reforms were demanded and sometimes begun, but those health schemes serving the poorest and the most politically helpless were slowest to change. Disease, of course, was spread upward to the wealthy.

Moreover, shifting demographics also played a role. The rising incidence of women's diseases, such as cervical, ovarian, and breast cancer, had first puzzled public health officials in New Mexico, Texas, and Southern California at the end of the century. It took some work to unpack the numbers and discover that traditional Hispanic modesty, combined with husbandly machismo, kept women away from routine gynecological examinations, which would have detected each of these diseases early when they could be cured easily. It was the implacable rise in the proportion of Hispanic women that also meant an implacable rise in disease statistics. A similar pattern played out among Asian women, although second-generation Asian women were far more likely to take advantage of routine medical examinations than were either first-generation Asian women or any generation of Hispanic women.

Minority populations in other industrial countries also suffered disproportionately to majority populations when universal health-care schemes, considered too costly in the decade of the 1990s, were chipped away at, and women suffered most of all.

All this was an avoidable tragedy, because thanks to basic research in the 1980s and 1990s, combined with relentless cost cutting, medicine had changed dramatically in a few years. Long-term prevention now dominated over crisis intervention, which was not only cheaper, but more effective. When people did get ill, new noninvasive diagnostic procedures were available, and customized drugs—customized both to the disease and to the individual, with negligible side-effects—were commonplace and cheap.

Even before birth, an individual's health was open to scrutiny. Many disorders could be identified and some could be engineered out, even in utero. Thus diseases like diabetes, schizophrenia, and obesity were rare in the developed world by 2010. When prevention was impossible, behavior could be changed and therapies applied.

But this led to bitter arguments about the rights of the individual versus society's obligations to help, when the individual refused to change unhealthy behavior or take advantage of preventive care and therapies. Insurance companies argued that they ought not to be obliged to pay the high costs of caring for women who contracted breast cancer but then only presented themselves for treatment at the last minute, when the cancer was far advanced, instead of relying on early detection through routine mammograms, which these days were much cheaper and more reliable. A momentary scandal erupted when a woman with advanced tuberculosis was denied medical care because she had chosen to live in an unsafe habitation—a city housing project. That her alternative was the street seemed to make no difference. The courts nearly always supported this line of argument, favoring insurance company cutoffs when clients had not acted with due responsibility and care.

SUNSET IN THE WEST

In 2015, perhaps the most striking characteristic of the population in the Western and developed countries was its age—its dejuvenation, to use the technical term of demographers. Mortality reduction in old and middle age, especially among women, combined with fertility reduction, had meant that by 2015, about 20 percent of this population was aged sixty-five and older, a proportion twice that of the rest of the world, and for a variety of reasons, that proportion was expected to increase faster after 2015. Of this 20 percent, women outnumbered men more than 2 to 1. Though many of the elderly in 2015 had more assets than the elderly of the past, they also had fewer offspring and tended to live in households alone. However, as they neared the end of life, their needs rose dramatically, beyond any human assistance that their diminished and otherwise hard-pressed families could provide. The Western fetish for individual rights prevented many societies from coming to terms with natural death.

The effects of the Age Bulge were felt everywhere: in pension systems, in health and geriatric care, and in other facilities for the aged, all of which had increasingly become state responsibilities, and as we will see later, in the spending patterns for other social services and the patterns of merchandising and entertainment.

By the opening of the new century, dwindling resources and growing numbers of claimants had forced pension system reform in nearly every Western or developed country. In the United States, for example, late-twentieth-century projections of future Social Security revenues had been based on real wage gains that failed to materialize. Moreover, though the major killers—cancer, AIDS, and heart disease—had not yet been fully conquered, incremental improvements in health meant that men as well as women were living a year longer for every decade since 1975. The U.S. social security system was thus bankrupt after 2010 and had to be restructured, which meant that in a sluggish economy both income and outgo were minimal.

Elsewhere in the developed world, most pension systems raised the age at which pensions began; they became earnings-related instead of flat entitlements; and many reduced and even eliminated survivors' benefits, which had benefited mainly women, but which were now considered anachronistic. Some systems even offered differential payouts to men and women, arguing that since, in the aggregate, women outlived men by seven or more years, their payout must be reduced to account for this; but that lower payout often left individual women in difficult straits. Underpaid all their lives, Western women now found themselves joining Third World women in the ghetto of poverty. Other systems, recognizing that married women had been in the workforce most of their lives and were now part of two-pension households, tried to enforce a one-pension-per-household rule, but this proved so politically unpopular that authorities were forced to back down.

Overall health-care reform had begun in the 1990s, but accelerated at the turn of the century with the biggest changes affecting the elderly. Earlier studies had shown that between 30 and 50 percent of patient-days in acute care were devoted to people over sixty-five, and as their proportion in the general population increased, so did their proportion of patient-days, and other health-care requirements. This demand on the health-care system by those over sixty-five did not rise quite as quickly as it might have, thanks to better preventive medicine and more on-the-spot medicine (facilitated by intelligent technology). Nevertheless, small, medium-term care facilities and neighborhood day-clinics began to replace the large, acute-care hospitals that had dominated health care in the late twentieth century. Curiously enough, the numbers of old-age homes hardly increased at all, since most of the elderly preferred to return to their own homes from hospitals as soon as they could, where they called on other kinds of assistance instead, especially care and protection that low-paid Nomads—the young immigrants from the teeming population centers of the less-developed world—could give.

Significantly, this elder bloc was far more politically active than any other age group. As a consequence, they voted overwhelmingly for local and national politicians who pandered to them—who built prisons and subsidized pension and health systems, rather than the ones who built roads or subsidized education. With time to spare, the Age Bulgers dominated all levels of politics and made sure their special interests came first. Younger citizens grumbled that society's resources had shifted disproportionately into the hands of the elderly, but younger voters were too heterogeneous, distracted, and divided among themselves to be politically effective against the near monolithic voting power of the old. Thus it was that the young felt justified in evading what they saw as punitive taxes, as they moved steadily off the books, into the underground economy, until in some Western countries, the magnitude of the underground economy paralleled the official economy.

HOUSING AND ENTERTAINMENT
FOR THE ELDER BLOC

The Age Bulge also changed the housing market in the developed countries. In the suburbs, shrunken older two- and one-person families continued to occupy the large houses they'd needed when their children were growing, partly because they had got used to all the space and were loath to sacrifice it if they didn't have to, and partly because such properties glutted the market for lack of demand and could not be sold for what they'd fetched years ago. Sometimes unrelated elderly people set up co-housing in these larger houses, but it took dedication to learn to live with the habits of strangers, and few co-housing arrangements were stable. With more and more householders living on reduced incomes, those communities that had relied on property taxes to support services now had to find revenues elsewhere in ingenious taxes on retail sales and entertainment.

The only growth in housing was in the so-called three-stepper: the elderly could buy into plans where they moved first to a specially designed stand-alone unit and cared for themselves; then moved on to Step 2, where they still lived in the stand-alone unit but now ate in central dining facilities; and finally Step 3, where they remained in the same unit, now easily transformed into a quasi sickroom. This three-stepper existence not only seemed to solve the problem of professional care over the long run, but because the three-stepper communities were self-contained, they kept the elderly out of view of younger members of society, who were generally resentful of what they called society's unfair cash transfer to the old.

• • •

Entertainment had altered to attract those who had money—and spent it freely. After decades of pursuing the 18–49 age group audience, entertainers awakened to the fifty-pluses, who not only had the most money, the most leisure, and the most significant growth in numbers, but who were spendthrifts, at least compared to that age group in the past. This group of fifty-pluses had outgrown its desires for tangibles and wanted memorable experiences instead. Whether those memorable experiences were real or virtual depended on the nature of the experience, but a whole new entertainment industry was growing up to cater to them.

In the 1990s, one pioneer had been Space Camp, where clients were invited to explore space—virtually—for a week in the company of a few others. Inside space simulators, they learned to pilot spacecraft, went through a mini-basic training that culminated in a simulated space journey, and became at least temporarily enmeshed in the lives of strangers. Space Camp's three major components, thrills, education, and companionship, were duplicated by dozens and then hundreds of other such simulations in the coming decades.

There were programs that simulated, for example, undersea exploration, a trip along the Silk Route, a tour of the Antarctic, and even a journey to the center of the earth. You could be a (virtual) brain surgeon for a few days, or the Renaissance painter of your choice. In one case, your "patient" expired, or rose and thanked you gratefully, depending on your skill. In the other, your "patron" accepted your painting or cut off your allowance, depending on your skill—and the patron's whim. You could become a character in your favorite book—Captain Aubrey in the Napoleonic Wars, for example—or you could rewrite the book entirely.

This kind of entertainment was computationally intensive, expensive to produce, and expensive to buy. Cheap versions existed in malls and game arcades and were beamed into homes, where the less affluent younger members of society could enjoy a taste of the same recreations, but those experiences were vastly inferior to the large-scale, attentive-to-detail simulations offered older and wealthier clients.

The young immigrant Nomads, without the income (or the appearance) to frequent malls and arcades, absorbed a steady diet of international satellite TV, coarse, violent, and shallow.

THE WORLDWIDE PATTERN OF INEQUALITY

As soon as the United Nations began collecting statistics about women in the mid-1970s, it conducted studies that revealed a worldwide disparity between the way nations treated men and women. Though many countries could congratulate themselves on their rate of development at the end of the twentieth century, no country did as well for its women as it did for its men. Some did notably worse than others: Japan, ranked first on the general human development index, dropped to number seventeen when gender disparity was taken into account; Switzerland dropped from number four to fourteen. In the developed world, this usually meant differentials in employment and wages; in developing countries, the differences included not only work, but access to nutrition, health care, and education. In some places, it meant maternal mortality and female infanticide. In South and East Asia, where two thirds of the developing world's population lived, the GNP growth averaged between 7 and 10 percent a year in the last two decades of the century, but women did not share this equally with men, and when growth slowed at the opening of the new century, women got even less.

• • •

The single biggest obstacle to women's equality was, as it had ever been, social and psychological expectations shared by women and men alike. All over the world, women were assumed to be the primary caretakers of children. Women were also primarily responsible for the household. In the developed world, this meant one set of responsibilities, burdensome enough on top of a full-time job, the so-called second shift. In the developing countries, however, it meant another set: work in the informal economy (unwaged, uncounted, but utterly essential to livelihood) as well as hauling water or fuel (sometimes for miles) and farming for the entire family's subsistence. Notwithstanding a spate of laws aimed at equality, it was all women's work, and men disdained it. Women themselves often discounted it.

As more women worked outside the home everywhere, they could not help sensing an increasing anxiety among men. Fearful that men would translate their anxieties about equality into resisting it, many women felt obliged to help men through the transformation by changing their own language (from empowerment talk to talk of autonomy, which seemed to frighten men less), and by adopting the most traditional of roles while at home, including shouldering the "second shift" without asking for help. In many ways, it was as if women were waiting for men's permission to assume equality. Even women who had achieved high executive and professional positions perceived one another as "capping" their ambitions, perhaps because the top posts did not seem available, or perhaps because once women had finally achieved a high-level post, they were averse to taking risks.

With mixed feelings, women watched some of their own advocates move into the mainstream from the nongovernmental organizations where they had begun and subtly disassociate themselves from their roots to gain legitimacy in more conservative eyes. As a result, women's programs and special offices, whether governmental or corporate, were quietly and slowly starved to death.

Beneath it all was an almost universal assumption that women existed only for men—their benefit, their convenience, their pleasure. A Western traveler's jaw might drop at the blatancy of the picture she sees: the hot sun beating down on a woman of the African desert, an infant strapped to her back, hoisting a mortar almost as tall as she is to crush grains for a meal; while the men lounge in the shade of a nearby tree; but that picture is only unusual in its blatancy. The same assumption—spoken and unspoken—has informed most of civilization and did not change with cheap, broadband worldwide communications, enlarged harvests, or newly improved disease prevention and control.

SILENT CONSENT OF THE GOVERNED

In 2015, women were still not permitted to vote in certain countries. Even where women had long had the vote—nearly a century in the United States, seven decades in Japan—they were underrepresented in their own governments. The famous fixed 10 percent of women representatives in national parliaments worldwide had actually tripled to 30 percent by 2015, but this suggested less a growing power on women's part than a waning power on the part of national governments.

An exception seemed to occur in South Asia in the 1980s and the 1990s, with an odd pattern of wives and daughters of former political leaders taking on the mantle of leadership in countries where the average woman was among the most politically oppressed in the world. Sri Lanka, Pakistan, India, and Bangladesh, for example, each had a widow or daughter who took on the luster of the husband or father who had preceded her. These women appeared at regional and even global summit meetings, looking fit and at ease, deflecting world inquiry into the real conditions of women in their countries. Far from being signs of equality, they embodied the medieval hierarchy of their nations—a woman from a top family was superior to any man from a lesser family—and succeeded only because their parties were too feeble to groom candidates to succeed assassinated leaders. By the 2010s, parties had matured somewhat, and this odd pattern receded into history, the daughters and widows were retired (or assassinated) to be replaced by waiting men.

A number of new national constitutions were written as the new millennium began, most of them guaranteeing equality between the sexes, as the final statement from the 1995 UN Fourth World Conference on Women had called for. But a legal right to equality is hardly the same thing as equality in fact, and most women were cynical about such laws. A Ugandan woman snorted at her country's constitution: "We continue to be second-rate citizens—no, third-rate, since our sons come before us. Even donkeys and tractors sometimes get better treatment."

In the poorest countries (sub-Saharan African, rural China and India, parts of Latin America, and the Philippines) the state had failed in its most fundamental responsibilities. As men moved off to the cities in search of work, the burden fell on women to provide what sanitation, education, and health care they and their families would ever know. They were exhausted, depleted; what demographers noted as a rise in premature deaths was in fact millions of exhausted individual women gladly laying down an impossible personal burden.

In the developed world, most nations professed themselves deeply concerned about low fertility rates. Government spokesmen announced targets for increased fertility and scolded women for not bearing more children. But few governments could make the obvious leap: that family and child allowances, maternity care, child care, and schools are social, not women's issues. Thus women continued to forgo having children rather than be penalized for fulfilling their biological role.

In short, women came to realize that the harder they played the political game, the more the game resisted accommodating them. Though they understood that this would only change if the very game itself were changed, both men and the token number of women who had achieved political power under the old rules had no incentive to transform those rules.

WOMEN'S PERSONAL SAFETY

At the end of the millennium, in no society were women treated as the equals of men. In no society were they secure. None of this changed very much as the new century unfolded. As the United Nations had reported in 1995, "In the household, [women] are the last to eat. At school, they are the last to be educated. At work, they are the last to be hired and the first to be fired. And from childhood through adulthood, they are abused because of their gender. . . . One-third of wives in developing countries are physically battered. One woman in 2,000 in the world is reported to have been raped: 40,000 in former Yugoslavia alone. In the United States, there were more than 150,000 reported rapes in 1993. Sexual harassment on the job is common. In India, women's groups claim that there are about 9,000 dowry-related deaths each year. For 1992, the government estimates that the figure was 5,000." Another UN study of domestic violence showed that in many developing countries, women would often stay in a violent relationship, because at least they knew who would rape and beat them. Without a man, such women would be fair game for violence from anyone.

As the planet seemed to transform itself with the marvels of enhanced agriculture; high-speed communication; new forms of transportation, science, and medicine; and the provision of goods undreamed of, men still threatened, menaced, and battered women in what statisticians could confirm were growing numbers. Some observers even argued that it was exactly these changes—the intrusion of the new into traditional cultures, raising new questions and uncertainties—that caused men to batter the women in their families, or to assault strangers who offered no more provocation than that they were female and they were there.

Women from rural parts of Asia often went knowingly but fearfully into the international sex trade, aware that whatever modest profits they themselves made, they ran enormous risks to their lives. Saddest of all, the most conservative estimates were that half a million children were prostitutes on the streets of Thailand, Sri Lanka, and the Philippines, with similar numbers on the streets of Latin America. These were the likeliest victims of all.

Women themselves were not without culpability. In Africa, where up to one half of households were headed by women, where women produced 90 percent of the food, 2 million girls underwent genital mutilation each year, subjected to this ritual by women in their own families. Women themselves had looked the other way when they saw their mothers, their daughters, their sisters bruised and suffering.

Yet it was women who had broken the silence, who had stood up and reported the violence visited upon them by the fathers, brothers, and husbands who were supposed to protect them. As years went by, that courageous witness had its modest effects, if only to show women that being battered was not something they must endure.

A TIDAL WAVE OF IMMIGRATION

As the general population boom concussed the planet (a boom that was the result of the sheer numbers of humans on the planet at reproductive age) international migration at the end of the twentieth century and the beginning of the twenty-first was unprecedented. Demographers estimated that more than 100 million people all over the world had left their homes to escape war or find a living. Part of the flow reflected the worldwide shift from small farm agriculture to large export farms: the usual immigrant's path led from the farm to the megacity and then from the megacity to the North or West. At the same time, the best educated and brightest, who had come to the developed countries for an education, realized that they were unemployable if they went home. They too stayed in the developed countries.

The huge population cohort once known as the Global Teenager of the 1990s had become the Nomad Generation of the new century. The Nomads, now in their twenties and thirties, rolled in great migratory waves from South to North, East to West, in a futile search for jobs, for housing, even for food. They flowed from Africa, South and East Asia, Eastern Europe, Latin America, and the Caribbean to North America, Western Europe, and Oceania (Australia and New Zealand). They were unwelcome everywhere they swarmed, but in the North, where population had ceased to grow and in some places was even falling, they took the jobs no one else would do, and by paying at least some taxes, the Nomads shouldered part of the burden of supporting, and often caring for, the sick and old, when insufficient numbers of native workers were available.

Migrants can be the source of tensions in their host countries, but in sufficient numbers, sufficiently desperate, they are downright destabilizing. Most migrant Nomads gathered in shantytowns outside the large Western cities, or in the city slums, where they squatted in abandoned buildings. They were rootless, stateless outlaws, belonging to nothing, belonging to no one, with no stake in their host country, and nothing to lose when they made trouble, which they regularly did. Since, in most Western countries, illegal immigrants were hunted and imprisoned, they soon saturated the prisons, crowding out real criminals and in some sense joining them, since they were recruited into more formal crime syndicates or built their own ethnically aligned criminal organizations. For legal immigrants or even the native-born who happened to share the intruders' accent, eye-folds, or skin tone, life became a series of petty harassments. Violence between the native-born and immigrants was commonplace and usually ended in fatalities.

Women and children were the most common victims of this violence. It was one of history's sad ironies that many of these women were fleeing regional wars wherein the arms had been supplied by the wealthiest nations. Driven out of their homes, they fled directly across the frontiers of the very nations—the United States, France, Germany—that had first armed the combatants at home.

"Prison-mania," the wholesale construction of prisons in the developed world, especially the United States, had many consequences. First, as fast as prisons were built, there could never be enough to house the staggering numbers of illegal immigrants that kept pressing in. Police, knowing how full the prisons were, left many alone in a paperless netherworld with no protection from exploitation and little opportunity to escape. Since public revenues were scarce, other public expenditures—for education, for public works—were reappropriated to pay for prisons. Thus in many developed nations, an increasingly aging infrastructure crumbled dangerously.

One way this tidal wave of immigrants differed from previous generations is that it comprised large numbers of women— women alone, or women with their small children—rather than single men. These women had picked up and left conditions that were not just harrowing momentarily; they were escaping a way of life that had traditionally debased women. They did not long for home, ever: they intended to make new homes instead. But women without education and not entitled to state help were a tremendous drain on private charities, which staggered under the burden of caring for the daily needs of the youngsters especially. The newcomers depleted resources that might have gone to the native-born needy.

In many places, the children of these immigrants were prevented from going to school or receiving medical care. By 2015, these illiterate and often malnourished youths constituted a dangerous criminal underclass, desperate, rootless, enraged, and usually armed.

THE ASIAN NEW MOON BOOM

In the opening years of the new millennium, Asia spent more on infrastructure than any other region in the world. Roads, subways, power grids, and dams were constructed; cities were refurbished. This so-called New Moon Boom was financed almost entirely by private sources, since governments could neither underwrite these projects, nor guarantee repayment: a debt crisis like the one that still bedeviled Latin America lurked in the background, making financiers uneasy. The intimate involvement of discredited dictators' children and grandchildren in these private/public works schemes added to the discomfort.

Nevertheless, these privately financed projects yielded new fortunes that made the American robber barons of the nineteenth century seem like they were on a stingy father's allowance. These fortunes were for the few, however; they were taxed barely at all and so hardly benefited most people. These wealthy few were exclusively male, though they were surrounded by collateral women: wives, mothers, daughters, and concubines. In South and East Asia, where two thirds of the developing world's population lived, the GNP growth had averaged between 7 and 10 percent a year in the last two decades of the century, but women did not share this equally. When GNP growth slowed somewhat in the opening decade and a half of the new century, women received even less.

• • •

The largest Asian nation, China, had attracted and then frightened off foreign capital again and again, as it dithered between its need to develop and its ancient suspicion of foreigners and foreign exploitation. China's obstinacy about complying with rudimentary contract law, and its unwillingness to recognize intellectual property rights, deterred even the most adventurous investors. Until well after the turn of the century, China was also plagued by serious inflation and nonconvertibility of currency, a result of refusing to dismember wasteful state enterprises and to control inflation. All this kept it more backward than its first investors had rosily foretold.

China's economic backwardness fell disproportionately upon its women. Since China had cheated its females at every stage, it was the millions of uneducated country girls, originally intended as factory workers, who took the brunt of a twofold change in manufacturing: worldwide factory automation and the rise of highly skilled workers in Latin America and the Caribbean who took such manufacturing jobs as there were. Now came China's first famines since the ill-conceived agrarian reforms of the 1950s.

Though the big cities grew even bigger, especially as the power of the central government waned, and peasants could no longer be forced to stay in the countryside, neither construction nor infrastructure could keep up. Chinese citizens lived without piped-in water and grew accustomed to power brownouts and blackouts. Visitors to the big cities, especially Beijing and Shanghai, were shocked to see that the buildings of the 1990s boom had become decrepit slums by 2005—the result of shoddy construction and official corruption. Diseases of the poor—cholera, plague, typhoid—broke out regularly.

Sheer numbers, however, were pushing China, along with India, Indonesia, and Korea, into the circle of the world's largest economies, where they would join the United States, Japan, and Germany. But all this new wealth hardly benefited women at all since by tradition and by law they were cut off from the largess.

India: The Big Tiger Awakens

When India began deregulating its economy in the 1990s, one of the first results was a nearly spontaneous wiring up of dwellings great and humble with satellite dishes. For the first time ever, ordinary Indians were given a window on a new world in the images that beamed down from Star TV and other satellite services. As these new images spilled into India—good and bad, high culture and low—within months, teenage girls were wearing jeans instead of saris, and cosmopolitan young couples were living together before marriage, in imitation of popular Western soap operas.

Unfortunately, what appeared to be new liberties, new choices, were only a different kind of subordination for women, just as exploitive in their own way as the homegrown kind. For now Indian women compared themselves and were compared by others to all the images common to Western pop culture—women as sex objects, women valued only as certain kinds of beauties, women valued for their passivity and mocked for their assertiveness.

Moreover, the alien images of Western satellite TV began to distort traditional Indian priorities. A society that had been relatively uninterested in material wealth suddenly became grasping, and the long Indian view of time, fundamental to the subcontinent's sense of itself, was overnight, it seemed, compacted and destroyed.

Though business regulation proceeded unevenly in India, it eventually brought about business restructuring, and by the first decade of the new century that restructuring was paying off, particularly in the western parts of India, which were already blessed with better infrastructure. Middle-class women married to executives benefited from this business expansion, but only because of their role as wives: women in business for themselves were nearly nonexistent. Poorer women and men found themselves left behind, or worse, bearing the brunt of environmental laissez-faire that poisoned the fields they farmed or within a decade stripped bare the forests they had worked for centuries.

Economic growth in India was also erratic because of state governments that, still worried about foreign exploitation, insisted on reviewing, amending, and even voiding foreign investment contracts that had been made by a previous government, making every such agreement uncertain. Mindful of the economic example, even the economic threat, of China, Indian financiers and entrepreneurs worked together to reduce import duties and the cost of borrowing. But like China, India was well known for its graft, which Western businesses simply had to factor into their costs of doing business there. Socialism still hung heavy: it was 2010 before the government stepped back from requiring that no worker could be fired, thereby permitting failing companies to close.

India had problems similar to China's, though somewhat less severe, in financing its new infrastructure. Its electronic stock market finally came to life in 2003, taking advantage of the laws and protections for investors that were already in place (laws and protections missing in China until much later), but weaning its businesses from subsidies and separating its bureaucrats from red tape proved politically difficult and continued to impede economic growth.

Though several plague outbreaks had been contained in Indian cities, governments seemed incapable of learning the lessons of ordinary hygiene, and as soon as a plague outbreak was contained and disappeared from the news, garbage ceased being collected and sewage was allowed to fester. Women and children were the most common victims of the plagues, and it was women and children who had to deal daily with the filth in the streets.

• • •

Overall, the experience of East Asia proved that an educated workforce was an economy's most important asset. In 2003, India's disproportionate investment in higher education (meant to benefit the Brahman caste) was reversed, and far greater resources went into primary and secondary education for more people, especially girls.

But this veneer of Western-style free enterprise overlay a hugely complicated society of insuperable differences—differences between castes, between languages, and above all, between men and women. Violence abounded and, except among the wealthiest, kept women in their ever-subordinate place. The one third of rural households that had been woman-headed at the end of the twentieth century rose to nearly 40 percent in 2005 and to 50 percent in 2010, as men deserted the Indian countryside to seek their fortunes in the cities. Poverty in India had become distinctly feminized.

Sunny Kim, 45, poet, Seoul, Korea

Democracy and individual rights have been a joke in Korea forever. For a long time it didn't bother me: I always saw myself as a poet, an outsider, which is why I never joined any particular women's movement. No matter which one, I could see its drawbacks. If you worked inside the system, waiting politely like a good Confucian woman for the crumbs to be handed out by the men, you'd wait forever—and in the end all you'd get would be crumbs. If you joined the radicals, you'd get your skull knocked in. As it was, I spent three years in jail, 2000 to 2003, presumably for "illegal associations," whatever those are, but in reality for a book of poems about women's lives in Korea. The title poem is "I First Heard My Name," and the speaker is a woman who first hears her name—not her name as *wife of*, or *mother of*, but her own first name—at a gathering of women.

If I publish my next collection, *Illegal Associations*, I'll go back to jail. If they catch me. *Illegal Associations* is circulating electronically, of course. Anonymously. There's a poem about women as lawyers—that's one illegal association! There's a poem about women as members of the National Assembly. That's another illegal association! We're told that there are so few women in the National Assembly because running for office costs money, women are incorruptible, and therefore not a good investment! Isn't that wonderful? I offered myself up to be corrupted, but nobody took me up on it. For twenty-five years women in this country have been arguing for quota systems so that women will be proportionately represented in politics. But nobody can agree how those quotas should be achieved.

In that sense, all women are poets—we always see the problems without seeing the way to fix things. We've never been able to vote as a bloc to improve things for women—that would be another illegal association! Really, sometimes I think we deserve our subordination. Here we are, nearly half the labor force for decades, citizens of one of the wealthiest economies in the world, and we're still outsiders, perpetual poets. We ought to replace that yin-yang symbol on our flag with a phallus. This is still the Republic of Korean Men.

WOMEN'S HEALTH IN THE DEVELOPING COUNTRIES

Worldwide, women continued to be valued—or devalued—for their wombs alone, but nowhere was this more evident than in the developing countries. Both tribal and traditional religious cultures focused on women as if procreation were their only purpose (though in many tribal cultures women also did everything else: "*L'homme c'est le roi*" said an unabashed man to a UN refugee worker who wanted to know why women were doing all the lifting and carrying of water and heavy grain sacks in a 1990s Rwandan refugee camp; while the men sat idly by, assault weapons and machetes in hand, waiting to be fed).

Matters were exacerbated by a well-intended UN impulse, articulated in the mid-1990s, to promote grass-roots involvement in development as people's direct participation—through community organizations, trade unions, or political parties. Since these groups had traditionally excluded women, there was no one to represent women's interests. Thus the UN policy, like that of the World Bank and other development agencies earlier, had the unintended consequences of preserving, even amplifying, the misogyny that was already part of the local culture.

Though the UN Cairo Conference in 1994 had resolved to promote women's health in all its aspects, not merely reproduction, money to begin and sustain women's community health centers was slow to be allocated, even slower to be spent; funds were often diverted to men and boys who were considered "more valuable" to the local culture.

At the time of the Cairo conference, half a million women worldwide were dying from pregnancy, childbirth, the effects of chronic malnutrition, and unsafe, unhygienic abortions every year. As the population of the developing world grew, the numbers of premature deaths among women also rose: by 2015 maternal mortality had reached nearly a million women per year. Confronted with these numbers, religious groups that liked to prate about the sanctity of life, shrugged and laid it all to God's will. They were no worse than the academic accountants in the developed world who quietly welcomed these appalling statistics: being dead, a million women each year could no longer reproduce.

Indeed, the population control establishment—largely male, largely white, largely Western—continued to issue scholarly reports about women as if they were mere wombs, no more than the deadly delivery system for the dreaded population bomb, perversely reproducing all by themselves, and irresponsibly threatening to explode the world with humans. In the megacities of the developing world, it did seem as if a human explosion had taken place. In Mexico, in India, in the Philippines, in North and South America, and in Africa, desperate bands of street children roamed the megacities, orphaned or effectively cut off from their families. They were living emblems of social and economic failure. But when women suggested that men also take some responsibility for contraception, the reasons why this could not happen were intense with conviction, baroque with elaboration, and endless.

At the most basic level, then, the health of women and girls in developing countries continued to be neglected. In countries where males outnumbered females, demographers could track the probable numbers of first, sex-choice abortions, and then, when it became available in 2007, preconception sex choices among the wealthy, and female infanticides among the poor. They could track the premature deaths of girls and women owing to malnutrition, ignorance, forced exposure to AIDS and other sexually transmitted diseases by polygamous mates, and maternal mortality, fifteen times higher than in the industrial countries. In the mid-1990s all these had amounted to 100 million "missing" women in Asia alone, and the numbers grew there and in Africa.

EDUCATION IN THE DEVELOPING COUNTRIES

• • •

Women in Kenya have talent also. They try to discourage women. But I wanted to show them. In a country where only men are encouraged, you have to encourage yourself.

—*Tegla Loroupe, winner of the women's division of the New York City Marathon, 1994 and 1995*

. . .

Though the percentage of girls enrolled in primary school worldwide had risen (over a third of eligible girls were in school at the turn of the century, and that proportion edged toward 40 percent by 2015) the legacy of female illiteracy and the vulnerability that this imposed weighed heavily upon women: in 2015, two thirds of the illiterates worldwide were female. In Southeast Asia, women's literacy rates were only half those of men's, and in many countries the situation was worse. This proportion began to improve slightly, thanks to a combination of UN initiatives and certain technological innovations that were introduced, but the years between 2000 and 2015 were transitional years, and only the future would show whether literacy changed women's lives. With a world economy based on information rushing forward, it was hard to see how women lacking the most basic literacy skills could ever catch up and be integrated into a global structure.

It was true that less developed countries had seized educational technology; whereas the developed countries had resisted it. The developed countries had originally led the way in the so-called third wave, or third revolution (the first and second being the agricultural and the industrial revolutions). But as developing countries saw themselves falling inexorably behind in the new world, struggling to find livelihoods for millions of uneducated and unskilled young people; as they saw the developed countries seize more and more of the world's wealth, building on the head start in education and technology they already enjoyed, certain visionaries in the developing countries began to stir. They argued that their countries could not—nor should they—replicate the history of the developed countries. Even if it were financially feasible, the poorer countries lacked the luxury of time to educate a generation of teachers who would then educate a new generation of young people in conventional schools and classrooms. If the developing countries with their staggering rates of illiteracy were ever to join the global economy, they must do it now, and they must do it differently.

Thus electronic forms of education, using new technologies—intelligent, broadband, cheap—took hold in some places in the developing world in a way they did not in the developed world. Impelled by necessity, these visionary developing countries bought satellite time when they could not buy satellites, bought and distributed masses of cheap, solar-powered receivers, manufactured in their own or other developing countries, and above all, bought or contracted for software. With no choice, developing nations and states were free to experiment with what it meant to teach and learn in the new century; what it meant to be an educated person in the new knowledge society. Not all these experiments worked, and in any case, they were too late for the great population bulge of people born before world population stabilized, who were now in their twenties and thirties. But the experiments that worked offered hope.

Even in those countries that recognized the problem and tried to solve it, however, the quality of schools varied immensely. Some, like Pakistan, had never provided decent state education, and, at one point, the government took over the few decent missionary schools. Underfunded and paralyzed by provincial bureaucracies, these old schools had failed to educate. As a consequence, private schools flourished, from the very expensive to the shantytown schools run by women in the slums. Many of the poor, men and women alike, simply taught themselves as best they could, with a constant stream of satellite TV accompanying them as they worked, teaching them haphazardly.

Elsewhere, when governments had failed to provide schools, religious groups often moved into the vacuum. Sectarian schools were largely misogynistic, and the education given girls was deliberately restricted compared to that given boys. Thus even if an eight-year-old girl was enrolled in school, she was not learning what an eight-year-old boy in the next classroom was learning, nor did she have the same supplies. But some religious schools were at the frontiers of the best education: for example, in certain parts of Central America, Jesuit-run schools took seriously the recent Jesuit commitment to sexual equality and were training girls in large numbers.

The picture was most mixed in higher education. Females who fought to get to school most often stayed in school, unlike their brothers, who dropped out steadily. In many places in the developing world, women's persistence at school actually meant that by the time they got to college, their numbers nearly matched those of men. In other places, the picture was less rosy. In sub-Saharan Africa, for example, where women were outnumbered by men in higher education 3 to 1, they faced unapologetic discrimination in the workforce if they managed to get past education hurdles. Worse, though higher education was often presumed to be a solution to employment problems in the information age, in many developing countries of Africa and Asia unemployment rates among their well-educated citizens were higher than among their ignorant. This, combined with discrimination against women, meant that educated women were at a double disadvantage. Like their American and European sisters more than half a century earlier, these well-educated women married into self-imposed and premature retirement, the contributions their education might have made now confined behind walls of privilege.

In those countries where indigenous women existed side by side with a late-arriving and dominant population, the indigenous women suffered disproportionately. Before the turn of the century, Maori women in New Zealand, for example, had nearly converged with non-Maori women in terms of the numbers of children they bore. This looked as if Maori women were gradually progressing. But in fact Maori women had those children much earlier than non-Maori New Zealand women, and relatively high numbers of them bore their children outside marriage. This meant they had less education and continued to depend on state welfare, which was more and more grudgingly supplied. The contrast between the majority of well-off, well-cared-for children and the disadvantaged Maori children continued as they aged, pushing them further apart in income, achievements, health, and general well-being, a picture that repeated itself in many places with mixed populations.

NUR SADHANA, 25, FARMER AND POET, BANGLADESH

When I was a girl, I learned to read in the Women in Development center near my home. It was a tremendous thing for me. I couldn't go to school. Even my brothers couldn't go. But I went to the center at night, and I learned. I had such an unbearable hunger to learn. I didn't care about anything else, not how tired I was, not how hungry I was. People talk about drugs. For me, reading was a drug, I think.

In 1997 they burned the center down. Who? Who do you think? Those men who saw that if women learned to read . . . everything was lost. I was so enraged I ran into the burning building. That's when I got these scars. I was very badly burned. Now I know I'm very ugly to look at. But the funny thing is, my scars saved me from having to get married. I helped my mother farming, and when she died, I just kept on. I fed myself, I was ugly; nobody worried about me. It gave me relative freedom, you see.

I got help later on, and then I got a solar computer. But in 2007, ten years to the day the center had burned, an intelligent agent traced a posting on the Net to me. The purity squad arrived at my house and arrested me. No, no one in my country was quite clever enough to program intelligent agents. My government bought this software from a technologically sophisticated country, maybe the same one it buys arms from. What had been developed, they tell me, for seeking information throughout the world, in thousands of locations, was used to find people like me.

I can tell you, that software had bugs in it. I hadn't posted the message I was accused of posting. I told the court this. I told them that if I was going to post something illegal in this country, I could have reposted it anonymously through one of the Western countries so that it couldn't be traced. That made them even more furious, that I would know I could do this. Not that it mattered. While I was under arrest, my little house was broken into and my computer was stolen. I pray that it went to somebody who knows how to use it, and actually does use it. But my deep fear is that it was just vandalism—somebody hated the idea that I had something he didn't have.

There was a period when I logged onto the Net to speak honestly, speak in a way I couldn't anywhere else. Nobody knew I was ugly. Nobody cared. I met women from all over the world—well, I thought they were women, though I personally had no way of verifying this; the interface on a solar is pretty bad. They were talking about their lives. Even their sex lives! That was amazing to me. Frankly, I had nothing to share along those lines. No, I talked about being a prisoner—a prisoner in my culture, in my town, a prisoner of expectations. My country has adopted individual rights in principle, but as far as it goes, it means men, not women. It was vital to me that I know women somewhere lived differently, freely. And then I began to think, why not me too? Why not the women I saw all around me, working from before dawn to dark? But I want to stress, I only thought these thoughts, I never said anything to anybody else. I couldn't. But they arrested me anyway.

I'm here to tell you all this because my international friends on the Net began spamming the government computers. A clerk would sit down at his terminal to check on currency exchange rates, or an airplane schedule, or business permits, or the electrical grid load, or whatever, and suddenly a pulsing message would come on: *Nur Is Innocent! Free Nur!* It was a terrible nuisance to them; they couldn't get anything done. They couldn't protect themselves because—well, my friends and supporters are very clever. The government knew if it killed me, my friends abroad would bring the entire electronic infrastructure down. It was really much easier to just let this silly, insignificant woman out of jail! They saved face by the fact that over 40,000 people sent messages to the prime minister claiming to have originated the great fatal message. Forty thousand confessions! A despot of the old days would have been delirious with joy.

So I am out of jail. This is not the same thing as being free, but it's an improvement. Friends tell me they will get another solar computer to me somehow. I hope so. There's nothing for me here. My real life is in cyberspace.

SMALL POTATOES: WOMEN'S WORK AND EARNINGS IN THE DEVELOPING COUNTRIES

Small farmers, entrepreneurs in the informal sector of national economies, and women have traditionally been unable to get credit. But like their sisters in the developed countries, women in developing countries at the turn of the century were eager entrepreneurs, starting new enterprises in record numbers. In Latin America, a third of small new enterprises were begun and staffed by women—in some places (rural Honduras, for example) they were a majority. In developing countries generally, nearly a fifth of small new enterprises were begun by women.

But because they were small, because they were woman-owned and run, they seldom could get credit or capital. When they could, the interest rates were far higher than those for large enterprises. In reality, many small woman-run enterprises were forced to go to money-lenders, who charged them killing rates of 70 and 80 percent. Under these circumstances, many of them failed. But women refused to be daunted and hope triumphed over reality. In those few countries that recognized the jobs created by small companies, and so encouraged friendly credit policies that moved these enterprises from the informal to the formal sector, jobs continued to be created.

Late in the twentieth century in many places in Latin America, women began to bootstrap themselves by taking the jobs their husbands had long disdained—menial, unpleasant, often arduous. Nevertheless, this gave them cash, for many the first steady cash they had seen, and their new incomes were a new source of pride and self-esteem. Equally important, unlike men, women tended to spend their money on their families instead of on themselves, and by 2015, this simple, homegrown self-improvement program yielded happy results across the continent. Better-fed and better-educated children had grown into young adults who could move confidently into full citizenship.

Worldwide, however, women were the poorest class, pushed to the economic (and often the biological) margins. The news from the 1995 UN Fourth World Conference on Women in Beijing was that over the time—some thirty years—that statistics had been collected on the world's women, it was clear that they weren't just losing ground; they were going backward. By the UN Fifth World Conference on Women in 2005, women's status was still sliding, thanks to the sluggish world economy. They were significantly overrepresented in the underground economy, where they were prey to exploitation. In other situations, they had neither opportunity nor incentive to move away from economic dependency on a man or a government, which had many implications for their motivation and personal pride.

> ### ANONYMOUS THAI WOMAN, 42, DIRECTOR OF A WOMAN'S HOSPICE, BANGKOK

Prostitution has a long history in Southeast Asia, but its real growth began when the sex trade became the sex industry, during the Indochina conflict in the 1960s and 1970s. Thailand was then a place where American soldiers could come for what was known as R and R—rest and recreation. The recreation, of course, was sex. Thousands of bars and brothels were established here in Bangkok for the GIs.

Girls came in from the countryside. They came for many reasons. Some fled to Bangkok because they felt in genuine danger from the war, or because the war had utterly disrupted their traditional lives, and it was a matter of survival. Some were driven here because of forced urbanization. It's a fact that many Asian women feel a cultural obligation to take on responsibility for the family's finances, so in some sense, some were volunteers. But many women were sold by their families into the brothels. Fathers and brothers collected a fee, and there was one less mouth to feed, one less young woman to find a suitable husband for. Very few young women went into the sex trade out of real choice. I want to make this distinction, because I think there are places in the world where women choose the sex trade because they enjoy it. But here, in those days, it was mainly a matter of survival.

While they could work, those girls earned enormous amounts of money. Not for themselves, but for their male pimps and brothel owners. The inflow of foreign money was incalculable. There are no firm statistics—prostitution was nominally a criminal activity, so the income was mostly tax-free too. But fairly reliable estimates say that the sex trade in those days was perhaps the largest source of foreign capital for our country.

As early as 1975, women pleaded for help and protection from exploitation in the sex trade. Nobody listened, at least in the government. The contribution that the sex trade made to the balance of payments far outweighed the misery of individual women. Every so often, the police would raid a house or bar, but who was arrested? The women—not the men who were either spending the money or pocketing it.

These women charged both the state and society with sheer hypocrisy: the houses paid fines and protection money; the state levied taxes on the "entertainment industry" knowing perfectly well what the entertainment was. Everybody benefited except the women upon whose backs, most literally, this industry was built. They suffered as they worked—many of them turned to drugs to make life bearable, which was terrible, because it made them all the more vulnerable. They suffered when they were arrested, and they suffered after they grew sick or were too old to work. If they survived long enough to be released from the trade, they were outcasts. With the exception of this hospice I run here in the Patpong District, no care, no social security, no old-age homes exist for former prostitutes.

I have studied prostitution worldwide, and I understand that in addition to women who enter the sex trade because they enjoy it, there are also women who believe they can make some kind of political statement: they are practitioners of the erotic arts, defying a patriarchal morality (which is nothing more than property rights), and empowering themselves financially, and so forth. I have no particular quarrel with this, but I want to say it was not the case here in Thailand. Here it was the worst kind of exploitation.

Okay. The Indochina war winds down in the mid-1970s. Sex here is an industry, used to running at top speed, but suddenly the customers disappear, along with all that crucial hard currency. Governments all over Southeast Asia face a crisis. What to do? You look for other customers, of course. You go to the IMF, the World Bank, and tell them your sad story. Some genius says: promote tourism. Bring those dollars back that way.

As it happens, the genuine reindustrialization of Southeast Asia blooms out of the debris of war, and all those technicians and businessmen who are bringing it about need sex. Sex tours arrive from Japan. Foreign workers are flown in from the Middle East oil fields every two weeks—the Arabs are very careful to keep their women protected from foreign workers. Consultants come in from America and Europe. There's something for every taste: the live-in temporary wife for the businessman; casual sex for laborers. As economies improve, bride-prices rise. Therefore men remain bachelors longer, but still must be serviced by the sex trade.

With this model of industrial production, sex must always be available to customers—the just-in-time view. This means that violence increases in order to locate and control sexual labor. The girls—and boys—are ever younger; less and less willing; more and more often forced into a kind of slavery.

Then comes AIDS. By the early 1990s, 2.5 million people in Southeast Asia are infected; by 2000, that number has climbed to 7 million. In Thailand, this means about a third of the prostitutes, nearly half the drug users. It's only a matter of time until AIDS leaps out into the general population.

Fifteen years later, we see the consequences of all that. I live day in and day out with the human costs and can no longer talk rationally about them. Forgive me. Instead, let me take a more dispassionate point of view: Thailand's economic growth has been crippled by this terrible disease. We can prevent AIDS, ameliorate it, but such a complicated disease—we can't cure it. We can't cure its consequences, either. We can only wait and help each other and watch this dreadful plague spread.

SEXUALITY DENIED

As international agencies noted, the rise in adolescent sexuality (apparent since the early 1980s and accelerating in the first part of the new century) actually grew from positive causes. Improved nutrition and health care meant that puberty was beginning earlier. In the developing world, more girls and boys were going to school and staying there longer. The average age at marriage was rising in most developing countries. These were all healthy social signs. But they also implied a longer period between the onset of sexual maturity and marriage. Thus there was increased sexual activity before marriage.

Women's sexuality continued to be fraught with the confusion and contradictions that had surrounded it for centuries. That sexuality was fundamental to human beings had been implicit in advertising, marketing, and entertainment across the developed world, a presumption that subtly or brazenly invaded the developing world as twenty-four-hour satellites began broadcasting Western-style entertainment to millions of new viewers and competed with each other by offering ever more titillating material. But to a greater or lesser extent, depending on local circumstances, women's sexuality was somehow denied— or at best, expected to be hidden and private, in a way that men's was not.

As usual, this hypocrisy was hardest on the poor. A UNICEF observer said, "We've avoided the issue of values, thinking it is a sensitive area, best left to the parents and schools. But the schools can't do it, and in most poor families, mere survival is all they can manage, never mind imparting values."

Thus a fundamental aspect of humanity was compromised and denied to women by means of old moral strictures, taboos, and a double standard most graphically expressed in fundamentalist religions, and especially in the fundamentalist Islamic countries, where in the early 1990s a traditional punishment was revived: women accused of adultery (which included women unlucky enough to be raped) were routinely stoned to death; while adulterous males were let off. By 2015, the charge of adultery had become a convenient way of silencing women who protested anything.

People with this same religious mind-set (by no means confined to Islam) continued to deny adolescents access to contraceptives by denying that adolescents wanted sex. If they did, it was wrong and must be prevented, or at least discouraged. Few countries adopted Sweden's early 1990s policy of subsidizing the price of the Pill for girls, because this involved acknowledging that girls were sexually active with boys, an official acknowledgment many governments could not bring themselves to make.

The conspiracy of silence about teenage sexuality had many results. One worker reported how young women in her Latin American clinic seemed to feel guiltier about asking for contraceptives, especially the morning-after pill, than about getting pregnant. Though half of girls had their first sexual intercourse before age twenty in Latin America, contraceptive use remained in the single-digit percentages even as the new century opened. The abortion rate in these largely Catholic countries was about the same as in countries where abortion was legal—except that illegal abortion carried many more risks for young women. The morning-after pill, widely available in Asia and North America, was too expensive for wide distribution in Africa, and in 2002, whatever guilt Latin American women might once have suffered by using it was lifted from them when a combination of religious pressures and worries about protecting the emerging Latin American pharmaceutical industry led to the pill's being officially banned there.

With relatively wide distribution—both legal and illegal—of the morning-after pill, the actual numbers of abortions worldwide had dropped, but contraceptives had not much improved in fifty years. Thus by 2015, abortion clients were no longer mainly young, unmarried women, but instead married women whose regular contraception had failed.

In spite of the morning-after pill, the numbers of babies born to single mothers, some 35 percent of them under twenty, continued to climb, most dramatically in the United States, but also elsewhere in the developed countries (except Japan) almost independent of national attitudes about illegitimate birth. In the

1990s, France, with its more relaxed attitudes toward sex, had the same rate of illegitimate births as England (approximately a third of all babies). This proportion grew slowly in the opening part of the century, leveled off at half of all babies between 2005 and 2010, but showed no sign of falling.

Some sociologists argued that this growth was most dramatic in the countries where the gap between the haves and have-nots had also widened without precedent—the United States, Australia, and the United Kingdom—but others argued that it was the result of women's new economic independence. However frail that independence might be—and it was frail—it was now a fact, and if women could no longer depend on a man for economic support, at least half of them seemed to feel they might as well have babies by themselves too.

GOD REMAINS A MAN, MAN REMAINS A GOD

As the new century opened, women had made token gains toward equality with men before their official gods. The Protestant denominations had long ago admitted women to their clergy, though it was still true that few women occupied important pulpits: the stained-glass ceiling. Anglican congregations still made news when they converted en masse to Roman Catholicism rather than accept a woman priest. (Many Anglican congregations converted in 2000, when Queen Elizabeth II of England abdicated her secular power in favor of her son, Charles, but continued to hold her powers as head of the Church of England, which the divorced Charles could not. This unprecedented separation of secular and ecclesiastical power was insupportable for deeply devout Anglicans.)

Fundamentalist Christian sects consolidated their political power in the United States, the United Kingdom, Australia, the Netherlands, Korea, Singapore, and Taiwan, a power that grew in proportion to the economic and social uncertainties of times in the developed countries. Thinly disguised by the same phrases they had used for decades—"family values," "natural law"—their political ambitions were impeded only by their deep suspicion of one another, which kept the fundamentalist sects from being an even more effective political bloc than they were.

The Roman Catholic Church, for its part, continued to bar women from the priesthood, though a combination of demographics and internal dissension caused the Church of Rome to follow the American example elsewhere, permitting girls to serve as altar attendants and allowing lay and religious women some voice in local church policy. This was too little too late for many Catholics, who slid quietly away from a church that had grown ever more irrelevant to their lives. Each woman had her own reason for leaving—the beatification in 1998 of Filipinas who were martyred by domestic violence and exhausting childbirth turned more than a few thoughtful Filipinas away from their church—but the church stood firm in its dogmatism.

Jewish congregations continued to permit women rabbis in the more liberal branches of the establishment (though like their Protestant sisters, few occupied important posts in big cities), but women rabbis were absolutely forbidden in the more conservative branches. With peace in the Middle East, however uneasy it was, Orthodox religious leaders had begun to lose their Israeli power base, and in the opening years of the twenty-first century, many of them traveled elsewhere, especially to the former Soviet bloc and the United States. Here in the new diaspora, they created a fundamentalist fever, exhorting Jews to return to the true faith of their fathers, a faith that systematically devalued and subordinated women.

No woman imam or mullah could be found anywhere in Islam, though by 2015 the fundamentalist excesses that shocked the world at the end of the century had abated, largely owing to worldwide revulsion and the persistent efforts of moderate women of Islam to denounce these practices as un-Islamic.

Though Buddhism was widely regarded as being gender-neutral, in fact many forms of Buddhism declared that to be born a woman was the result of imperfect karma; women must be born again as men before they could reach Nirvana. The attitude underlying this doctrine was one circumstance that permitted the sex trade to thrive in Thailand, India, and other parts of Southeast Asia. In any case, the Dalai Lama continued his life surrounded entirely by men.

In short, twenty-first-century women were as excluded from the official divine as twentieth-century women had been, though male clerics assured them that obedience and resignation in this life would bring rewards in the hereafter. Small numbers of women, and men too, withdrew from official religions and went in search of the divine their own way, especially through Goddess worship, but they had no influence beyond themselves and their small circles.

Separate—and Doing Fine, Thanks!

I broke into a world of men where I wasn't wanted or understood. A woman like myself is often alone with her solitude. I admire my life and respect it. I know now that I must have been a rebel among rebels.

> —Mavis Alvarez, a woman of peasant origin, mixed race, and Catholic upbringing, trained as an agronomist, who participated, heart and soul, in the Cuban revolution and lived to see it betray women

In this scenario (which we call Separate—and Doing Fine, Thanks!) group priorities, mores, and values tend to prevail over the Western notion of individual rights in a globally integrated, growth economy that allows absorption of the international baby boom of the 1990s and its echo. Outside the Western democracies, which prove durable, governments of new nations and newly liberated states have resumed relatively authoritarian ways to force social order and achieve the stability necessary for economic growth on the Singapore model. This decision has often limited individual rights in those countries. Even the Western democracies have realigned the balance between the individual and society slightly more in favor of society than the individual, a reaction to what was perceived as individuality run amok since the 1970s. In both the new nations and the Western democracies, much of life is lived below the radar: closed electronic networks and other kinds of discreet behavior are permitted so long as they aren't flaunted. The governments of nation-states often profess to run themselves along ideological lines, religious or political, but it is no secret that those at the top are mainly captive to self-interest, which usually translates to accumulating personal wealth.

Under the circumstances, the rights of women especially are deemed unimportant and in some places are sacrificed. "For their own protection," women are treated as less than equals, though sanctions do exist against the worst excesses of misogyny. Women are generally educated, but excluded from the top levels of decision making and power. Their frustration and impatience with intractable bias pushes many of them into de facto separatism, sometimes clandestinely. The international network of experienced women activists, established in the last few decades of the twentieth century, though not illegal, functions invisibly through nongovernmental organizations (NGOs), special interest groups, and the equivalent of church groups.

MAJOR TRENDS

For anybody alert to trends, it was no real surprise that "separate" cultures began to dominate the global landscape in the first years of the twenty-first century. The late twentieth-century resurgence of tribalism—the independence movements of Turkish Kurds, the Zulus, the Mexican indigenous people, and the fragmentation of the Balkans—had already led to the dissolution of several nation-states, themselves often only fossil remnants of colonialism. Now smaller, ethnic-based states emerged, sometimes loosely confederated with neighbors whose history they shared, sometimes fiercely independent, though each was inextricably tied to the global economy, an economy that had to operate with the challenges of countless local values, rather than one international hegemony. Many cultures experienced profound stress, trying to choose between what they thought they wanted from the West, and what they thought they could, they must, resist in order to maintain cultural integrity, a stress that showed itself in inconsistent laws and the brutal suppression of internal dissent.

While women acknowledged these new loyalties to ethnic or tribal identities and their new political expressions as states—an appealing sign of this was contemporary adaptations of ethnic dress for men and women alike, adding happy variety to international gatherings—they also recognized that their own individual rights were being overlooked, often sacrificed, as new political entities struggled to survive. In national or tribal "liberation" movements, women's rights continued to be, as they had always been, secondary, or even an irritating diversion from what men considered the real issues.

But the relative stability of governments new and old had created many opportunities for prosperity, and if women did not have all the political and social rights they deserved, they had sufficient economic success to consider other solutions to their problems. For one thing, they built on and created yet more separate, woman-only organizations. These organizations existed in parallel to ethnic and state institutions, and the groups often transcended national borders, finding common cause with women elsewhere. They were intimately connected by an active worldwide electronic network, encrypted where necessary.

If male-female separatism characterized the first decade of the new century, it was separatism of a very distinct flavor. In most places around the world, women still associated with men daily, as colleagues, friends, and lovers, even as marriage partners (although throughout the developed world, the numbers of formal marriages continued to drop, following the pattern of the late 1980s and 1990s toward paperless living). But when growing numbers of women got up in the morning, they chose to go to school with girls and women; they chose to work at women-owned and -dominated shops and firms; they voted women-oriented tickets; if they were ill, they consulted women health workers; when they yearned for spiritual guidance, they turned to women.

It began to seem as if women had psychologically checked out: out of the economy, out of the day-to-day issues of politics, even out of traditional worship and the arts. Their energies went into women's versions of these structures, and the adventure and risk of living separately gave them unique zest.

Some pointed out that women in the Western democracies had awakened in the early 1800s to demand an end to the de facto separatism they had always been forced into: they awakened to demand legal equality with men, and then the vote, equal access to schools and colleges, to jobs, to everything they saw men doing. It had taken two centuries to achieve such equality. Now that they'd achieved it (at least on paper), why were they starting to withdraw? The psychological answer was the simple difference between choice and no choice. Women wanted the choice of going to any school they were intellectually qualified for; they wanted the choice of doing any job they were qualified to do. The answer was also the persistent gap between paper rights and reality—a gap many women had wearied of trying to bridge, so they had made other arrangements.

Individually, women continued to establish their own households in growing numbers, a trend whose beginning could be traced all the way back to the 1970s. This trend had been masked by children of both sexes who lingered longer in the family nest than their parents and grandparents had, postponing setting up households of their own. They lingered because they and their parents were seldom in conflict about values as parents and children in the 1960s had been, and because they could live a relatively independent adult life inside the family home, with more luxury and disposable income than would have been possible had they lived on their own. Protracted education and the demands made by beginning a career also kept young people at home. When they did eventually move out, they tended to begin one-person households instead of marrying or forming consensual unions, even in places where this had never happened before, for example, India.

For women in particular, the incentives to marry were few. The artificial womb, perfected in 2007 (over theological objections, but as usual, economics dominated ethics) meant that women did not even need to bear their own children; they could enjoy complete physical and economic freedom with an artificial pregnancy. In fact, sophisticated women sometimes chose to bear their first child, but seldom if ever bio-bore any further children.

Despite the arguments of many Western experts, that marriage and a nuclear family were the best way to bring up children (which ignored the varieties of ways children had been raised all over the world), polls showed that most women saw the combination of children and a husband as problematic. Most men still did not understand how to share either power or responsibility. Most men still thought in terms of who ruled or headed the family, who managed it, who was boss. "We are light years ahead of them," said an exasperated Delhi information specialist, one of tens of thousands of Indian women who chose to remain single.

Thus, by 2015, about two thirds of all mothers worldwide ignored the experts and elected to have a child outside of marriage. Expert wisdom was subverted by a generation of whole and wholesome human beings who had already grown up with only a mother to rear them—a mother who was financially secure.

But inside marriage or out, bio-carriers or arti-carriers, mothers were getting rarer: children were very labor-intensive and they had a distinct impact on one's life and career path. Women in the developed world had set the pace; and as women in the less developed world were offered alternatives, their patterns of childbirth began to follow the developed world's patterns. In cultures where taking on a husband and children also meant subordinating oneself to a mother-in-law, the drop in marriage and childbearing was especially dramatic.

Women were not only earning more all over the world, thus giving them significant financial independence (which led nearly everywhere to a growth in personal independence) but, as demographers noted, there were more of them, and they lived longer. In the developed world, women earned and then inherited a growing proportion of private wealth, a fact that would have important consequences for the world economy, even though in the less developed world, most wealth still remained under the control of men.

· · ·

The kind of male-female separatism that prevailed in 2015 had been prefigured in the late 1980s and early 1990s. As the century moved into its last decade, many older women in the West sensed that they had wasted some twenty years waiting patiently for credible reforms toward sexual equality that would never come—not in the government, not in business, not in education, not in private life. They looked at their few years left and, instead of continuing to fight, chose a separate life.

At the same time, younger Western women, who had taken their social equality for granted, were unpleasantly surprised when they left the relatively egalitarian milieu of the classroom. They found that their male colleagues might support equality in principle, but when faced with the reality of giving up male entitlements, men declined to act upon their convictions. Perhaps this also underlay the continued rise in one-person households and one-parent families (mostly mothers). In sum, all over the world, the numbers of households increased, and a majority of them were feminine: young women increasingly divorced or never married, and older women simply outlived their mates.

Since women routinely expected that they must earn their own livings—and if they had a child, would undoubtedly have to support it without help—they planned their lives more realistically and scrutinized their options. When it became obvious that those professions where women had made significant gains—the law and medicine, for example—had come to be considered "feminized" and their prestige and rewards fell sharply, women were forced to face the hypocrisy of mainstream cultures.

Many women opted out. Their withdrawal had precedents, in American history at least. When American women took the lead in fighting for emancipation of the slaves in the early nineteenth century, they were enraged to realize that the rights they were fighting for would not be extended to them, so American feminism was born. More than a century later, they learned this lesson all over again during the Vietnam War protests—an awakening that provoked the so-called Second Wave of Feminism. But by 2015 there was less rage than weariness with the same old game. Women were unwilling to be men in skirts in order to succeed. They simply stopped fighting and formed their own organizations with their own rules.

A DIFFERENT APPROACH IN THE DEVELOPED WORLD

By the turn of the new century, women of the developed world had generally taken up a different approach to achieving equality. Without abandoning individual appeals to justice (in the United States, once the Supreme Court effectively undid affirmative action laws, individual appeal was their only legal choice), they often regrouped and allied to create special women-only organizations. Backed by such organizations, they returned to mainstream institutions with the aim of achieving genuine reform. They meant to accomplish this with all the sophistication they'd acquired in more than thirty years of waiting and playing by the rules they'd been told mattered.

But the rules they played by also included the unspoken ones that really governed male-dominated institutions, those that still controlled much wealth and power. Though a number of hard-core separatists believed that reform was impossible and that only radical restructuring would permit women into social, political, and business institutions on an equal footing with men, the majority of women played in two games, the women's and the mixed. When they entered the mixed world, they arrived backed by women-only groups, expecting to play by the same old rules, explicit and implicit, and prepared to bend institutions to be friendlier to half the population.

Usually these women-only groups aimed to persuade, not force. When persuasion failed (as at first it often did) women no longer flinched from using their new organizations as forceful thumbs on social pressure points: boycotts, demonstrations, strikes. Pressure was applied with cool precision: women had discovered that to sidestep male dominance was to avoid destructive rage.

Even so, a world that had been male-dominated for thousands of years was very slow to change. If the world was going to understand and act upon a new egalitarian approach, that understanding and action was yet to come in any profound way. The organizations women formed to bring about equality were just as often havens from intractable, institutionalized misogyny. But significantly, they were not only havens. They were also places to learn, to meet women of like mind, places to fashion networks that these women would use throughout their lives.

DISTANT EARLY WARNINGS OF SOCIAL SEPARATISM

A mid-1990s poll of American teenagers had already suggested a big difference between the way boys and girls saw the future. It was a difference that was going to play out dramatically as these young people came of age. Boys were described as "substantially more traditional than girls in their expectations about the family life they will have as adults." Boys still believed strongly in a 1950s-style marriage, in which the wife stays at home, rears the children, cleans the house, and does the cooking; while the husband is responsible for making the money and mowing the lawn. However, only 20 percent of them really expected their wives to stay home, and nearly 60 percent of them thought that they couldn't prevent their wives from working.

In follow-up surveys, boys declared that although their own mothers worked, they were often "stressed out," an inconvenience to the family. Anyway, who would do the housework if women didn't?

Girls, on the contrary, were overwhelmingly committed to a full life, which meant having a career, and far less committed to making and maintaining a marriage. Eighty-six percent of them expected to work outside the home, and nearly three quarters of girls declared they thought they could have a happy life if they did not marry; the same number said they would consider being a single parent. In follow-up surveys, girls reported that their mothers had encouraged them to be self-sufficient. Many cited their own families or families they knew, where mothers worked, but then had to come home and do housework too, as unfair and unacceptable.

A majority of the boys said most of the boys they knew considered themselves better than girls. But girls said they saw themselves and boys as equals. Theirs was an unquestioned assumption: it gave the girls a qualitatively different kind of self-confidence that women who had been forced to fight for equality could never have.

Surveyed at the same time, nearly 60 percent of women aged eighteen to twenty-nine said that they would rather have an emotionally rewarding job than a boyfriend; 55 percent would rather have $5,000 than a boyfriend; 54 percent would rather have a great body than a boyfriend.

With these major differences between them in the 1990s, it was no wonder that most young men and women in the first decades of the twenty-first century found themselves in sharp disagreement about values and worldview. Nor were these attitudes confined to the United States. Well-educated European, Latin American, African, and even Asian women held approximately the same beliefs.

As time passed, many young men seemed to change their minds and concede that perhaps they would share the housework; perhaps ruling or heading the family was the wrong model; but young women remained skeptical. To the consternation of an older generation, and certainly to many clerics, most men and women all over the world had paperless liaisons and then went their separate ways.

At the same time, marriages between newly arrived immigrant women and native-born men in Europe and America rose, especially where such women had missed the chance of an education. This was plainly an economic transaction on both sides, and though affection could certainly grow in such relationships, nobody pretended that love had much to do with it.

EARLY SIGNS OF SEPARATISM IN INTERNATIONAL BUSINESS

Had they paid attention, business executives would have seen early signs of separatism in the corporate world itself. For several decades, women executives had been frustrated by what was known as the glass ceiling, that limit above which no woman (or minority member) was permitted to go in the corporate world, regardless of her accomplishments.

For the first few decades that women had been in the corporate world, they had been counseled to be patient: even though 99 percent of senior executives were men, women would eventually earn their right to excel. Twenty years after women first entered corporate America in large numbers, 95 percent of senior executives were still male. Women who dropped out temporarily to rear children found themselves professionally penalized for the rest of their lives. Thus, by the time top American executives had taken to calling the white male exclusivity that they still felt entitled to their "comfort zone," women had already long understood that it was the same old discrimination, the arbitrary, invisible rules that kept women away from power and money.

Though a few women pursued legal remedies (with elusive success) many corporate women took matters into their own hands. Rather than wait for the glass ceiling to crack, much less shatter, they moved out laterally and started their own businesses, often as vendors to or even in direct competition with the companies that had originally trained them. Despite a difficult economic climate in the United States during the famous late-century downsizing, the number of women-owned businesses grew so lustily in the late 1980s and early 1990s that by 1992, women-owned businesses provided the American economy with more total jobs than the Fortune 500 companies. As the U.S. economy strengthened, the numbers of women-owned corporations continued to grow until no one could remember when such corporations were a novelty: by the turn of the century, half of all American companies were woman-owned.

The changing nature of the corporation speeded this along. Where companies had once been forced to lease office and manufacturing space to house all their workers, the new, smaller companies now were often virtual, with focused work groups meeting

face-to-face only weekly perhaps, in some temporary, central location; they outsourced many tasks; leased workers from other
companies (or hired their own employees on a one- or two-year
contract); and coupled all corporate functions together loosely by
means of electronics and shareware. New management designs
had eliminated the need for face time supervision. This meant
flexible hours and more time at home, which eased the problems
of parents. Women spoke to other women about good vendors,
suppliers, subcontractors, and they tended to favor companies in
their own image.

> ### RAIMUNDA HERRERO, 40, SCIENTIST AND INVENTOR, THE PHILIPPINES

Pope John Paul II, the worst of the last of the male su-
premacists, happened to make his final visit to the
Philippines when I was twenty. This is the Pope who used
to say: "There, there, dear; you're wonderful. But not so
wonderful that you can be equal before God, of course.
God wishes only people with penises to address Him (so
long as they don't get caught stuffing those penises in
places they shouldn't). Your job is to serve the people
with penises and have their children until you drop from
exhaustion."

I'd been a convent student who wanted to be a priest,
so maybe that's why I couldn't take this old guy and his
nonsense too seriously. I mention this visit because I was
a university student at the time and it was to be pivotal
for me. At first it enraged me; then it made me very sad
to watch the millions of people who gathered to hear
him, to see him, to see how the people venerated him.
Those crowds in the streets, seeing them on TV screaming their lungs out, adoring this impossible bigot. He

came to the university, and we were supposed to sing a folk song in Tagalog. We made up different words:

> Do you see my little brown feet
> When you kneel to kiss the ground?
> They do not have satin slippers.
> They face the wall when a man
>   climbs on top of me.
> If I do not cry out I get ice cream.
> If I have the baby I go to heaven.
> Do you see my little brown feet
> When you kneel to kiss the ground?

An epiphany: the assumptions I'd made about my life needed to be reexamined.

I come from a good and loving family. My mother had her own clothing boutique; my father was in import-export; we were comfortable though not rich. I had a typical education, beginning with an all-girls parochial school, though I went on from there to the Philippine Science High School in Manila which is very competitive. I was third in my graduating class—another girl and boy were ahead of me—so I had my pick of specialties at the University of the Philippines.

I was one of those lucky ones who loves everything she takes up—mathematics, biology, physics. It was all wonderful to me. I was drawn to the women on the faculty, especially in astrophysics. It took the Pope's visit to open my eyes to the fact that these very bright women, whom I admired and wanted to emulate, were in the public sector because the private sector was closed to them. Their first love might have been engineering or applied science, but no industrial firm would hire them no matter how bright they were. Many of our indigenous tribal cultures were originally quite egalitarian, but the Philippines adopted wholesale that stifling machismo from the Spanish conquerors and American liberators, which means women are assumed to be weaker, stupider, etc. And since women were expected to be the childbearers, that also reduced our marketability to the corporations, of course. I thank the Pope for clarifying that for me when I was still twenty. It might have taken me years to discover it the hard way.

Once my rage and my sadness died down, I began to keep score. In my two fields—eventually I chose a self-designed dual specialty, biology and solid-state physics—I had the highest grades of anyone in my classes. But several of the men were offered research assistantships before I was, and they were promoted out of those jobs sooner, though my work was at least the equal of theirs. Better, frankly. When I complained to the department chairman, he said—just as if he'd learned his little speech from the Pope—that though I was one of the students they were proudest of, it was such a pity I was only a woman, because my ideas of commingling biology and solid-state physics were brilliant. Brilliant or not, I must reconcile myself to the idea that I would never reach the top. *It isn't for you, dear.* No, I should take pleasure in my children instead. I told him I fully expected to take pleasure in my children, but I also expected to receive what I'd earned.

My research meanwhile was going wonderfully. It was going so well that while I could see the implications very clearly, luckily nobody around me could. I telephoned an old friend of mine from high school and we went out to lunch. I told her I had the possibility of making a serious technological, even scientific breakthrough, but I needed some backing.

She couldn't provide me with anything like the backing I'd need to manufacture what turned out to be the biochip, but she did the next best thing. She put me in touch with a superb patent lawyer in the States. Once we'd filed patents, she put me in touch with a small woman-run company in the southwestern United States, which by that time was the center of wetware development. The rest is history.

The royalties for the biochip could have been shared by the Philippine government, by the University of the Philippines, and earned by a start-up in Manila. But this isn't how history turned out. Apart from my share, my considerable share, everything stays in the United States. I often see that old boy who told me, "It isn't for you, dear." I smile. He knows what I'm thinking: *It isn't for you, dear.*

> GABRIELLA BLAKE, 47, PRESIDENT, ASSOCIATION OF AFRICAN AMERICAN WOMEN ENTREPRENEURS, UNITED STATES

African American women are among the most successful segments of U.S. business executives, any way you measure. And we did it all ourselves. Julianne Malveaux, an African American economist, once wrote that white majority women had better watch what happened to African American women, because twenty years later they'd be facing the same economic problems. At the time she had in mind the rise of woman-headed families, and the entry of women into the labor force, a change among the white majority that echoed the same patterns in African American families twenty years earlier. Well, whaddya know. She was right.

But, hey, the pattern played out in other, more positive ways too. No access to capital, but African American women are forceful entrepreneurs. Here it is, fifteen years into the new century, and as a group we lead in per capita profits despite our well-known triple strikes: we're women, we're black, and we cope with the economic implications of the unequal treatment of black men. You could argue that entrepreneurship was forced on us, but African American women turned necessity into a virtue. I like to think we called on the centuries of experience of our foremothers, who ran the farms and markets of African village life, to lead the way. We networked—we made, I say without modesty, good use of our built-in networks of sororities, church, and professional groups. Unlike many African American men, we grabbed information technology as a tool. You didn't hear us saying it belonged to The Man and therefore was to be avoided. That kind of rhetoric is stupid and self-defeating. How many Chinese men do you see *not into computers* because white men invented them, huh? Is he worried it's compromising him? Is he worried it's going to dilute his Chinesemanhood? Right.

One smart thing these sisters did was lay down the burden of protecting the endangered black man. After years of hearing—sometimes believing—that this too was our responsibility, after years of patient understanding, we did a little audit and realized we'd got nothing in return but contempt and worse. What have I got to say to a man whose idea of manhood is the same old sexist patriarchy? How come he needs to dominate me to define his manhood? I, for one, don't even believe the black man learned that from the white man. I've seen enough about Africa to see how tribal cultures treated women. Oh well, they learned that from the white man too. Oh, really? When? In 1350? I don't think so. There are black men who live differently, and bless them, they don't need any saving by me. I know it, I'm married to one. He's someone to love, to have a family with. He's not A Problem. The rest of them? They're not my problem either.

My problem—and it's something the Association of African American Women takes very seriously—is teaching the young. We'll teach anybody, male or female. We recruit them in schools, in churches, on the playgrounds. We're teaching them new ways of being in the world. We're experimenting. We're saying you can have hierarchies without authoritarianism. We're saying, you write better poetry if you work inside the forms. The law is your strength. We'll have some failures. That's okay. We've survived bigger catastrophes.

SIGNIFICANT DIFFERENCES IN STYLE

That a quickly growing segment of the private sector in the West was woman-owned was novel enough; that such firms offered a quite different atmosphere for employees to work in was noteworthy. Against all evidence, many Western male-dominated corporations still held tenaciously to the idea that it was not the business of business to worry about families; that "normal" employees had wives at home who could take care of them and their households; that children were the responsibility of parents, whose role was somehow divorced from employment. The same belief had been eagerly adopted by the new firms in Eastern Europe and even in the new market economies of formerly communist countries in Southeast Asia.

Women-owned firms showed again and again that family-friendly policies were good business: good for employees, good for the company, and good for society in the long run. They operated under the assumption that there could be no real division between family and work, that the two overlapped endlessly. They permitted work teams to solve their own problems—not only business goals, but personal problems too, which led to a joyous creativity in problem solving. The key factor that accounted for the success of women-owned and -run firms in the West by 2010 was their better fit with the realities of the new global economy.

Women brought a different sensibility to their enterprises: they were more inclined to global, long-range vision. Women not only tended to set up relatively informal, lateral operations and structures, which were friendlier to those executives who didn't necessarily conform to home-country expectations, but they also set up operations and structures that were far more sensitive to stakeholders in every country where their firms operated. Women's companies were built for flexibility and fast response, crucial to the new business environment. Whether by nature or by nurture, women were skilled at building alliances, and, by 2015, women in business worldwide had constructed a complex network of partnerships, information exchanges, and cooperative ventures that synergized their various enterprises in unprecedented ways.

MARIE-CLAIRE MARRON, 51, BUSINESSWOMAN, PARIS

I was on the fast-track in a multinational I'd rather not name. This company had offices in all the French-speaking countries, as well as much of the English-speaking world. I was on planes or e-mail around the clock, seven days a week. In my twenties, it was very exciting. I had the feeling I was making a difference. I performed. I was rated tops. Nothing could stop me. Nothing that is, except turning thirty. On my thirtieth birthday, I was stuck on a very long flight from Singapore to Paris. I remember that I decided to look at my own job as a business problem. I began to wonder what the odds really were that my skills would get me to the peak of the pyramid. The men in my corporation—would they ever permit me to share real power? A dangerous question, because now you begin to notice the very subtle condescension. You yourself are no longer satisfied with being the bright, pretty young thing, hmm? You want to be taken seriously. But you can see that you're not.

Your colleagues look at your performance; that goes without saying. But to them, you're also the eternal feminine, somebody whose sex appeal they're entitled to judge, too. Since you're a woman you're expected to be gracious even when you've been crammed on a plane for nine hours and have crossed six or seven time zones; even when an incompetent employee has lost an account you've been trying to get for months. If you're not gracious, you're a bitch. They wouldn't expect such things of a male colleague.

Then a more dangerous question: is this really the life you imagined for yourself? I personally was never interested in raising a family, but it would be utterly impossible in such a milieu. I arrived at Charles de Gaulle airport in a very thoughtful frame of mind.

Around that time, my father died. This was 1995. In some ways he had been both my model and my mentor. Now I saw that he was completely expendable as far as his own corporation was concerned. Most of his work was done just as well by expert systems. For all the energy and long hours he had dedicated to that company and its growth, his death meant nothing to them. Why should it? If he'd nevertheless had a marvelous time during his life, you could say that's sufficient justification for enduring what he put himself through. But for the last ten or fifteen years of his life he was very frightened that the corporation would let him go in corporate downsizing—and then where would he be?

So: is this the future you want for yourself? It slowly came to me that all the training I had, my wonderful contacts in the field, all this could be transformed into a business of my own. I saw the opportunity, and I took it.

My father had left me a little money. I had intended to invest it for my old age, but then I thought no, better to use it to give birth to my new business. It wasn't quite enough; like many women who start businesses, I was undercapitalized. I went virtual out of necessity—I couldn't afford to rent an office—but it worked out better in the long run. These days my little company would go brain-dead without its electronic nerve net. I discovered outsourcing, which my old company hadn't (though they finally did much later), and I contracted with friends for specific tasks, not indefinitely, not for a lifetime. I worked hard, very hard; I was a little bit lucky. Within a two-year period I could start drawing on business earnings. I was thirty-three. And very proud of myself, hmm?

I've never gone to the banks. In my country to this very day they would still only try to humiliate me. I do have one significant loan outstanding now, but that banker came to me. The banks may be biased, but they're not stupid. They saw what a good investment my company was. Though employees share in the profits in the sense that they get bonuses at the end of their contract period, my company is still privately held, and I'm undecided whether it will remain that way.

At the outset I intended my company to be different—better—than the company I left. In the first place, I understand that people are my contractors, not my slaves. They have lives. They need some flexibility. We have flextime and job sharing, paid and unpaid personal leave. Our work hours are adaptable—why not? Most of us work from home anyway. Plus, I expect flexibility from my employees: they'll seize technological innovation, give away as fast as possible to the *ordinateur* anything the *ordinateur* can do. So they're free to concentrate on the things only humans (so far) can do. They're reinventing themselves every couple of years. Time clocks don't make sense for people like that. Anyway, we're an international company, and action is always under way somewhere on the globe.

France has long been forward-looking about child-care, so that wasn't my problem as an employer. When we set up our first branch office in the States, it suddenly became my problem. I didn't want to get into the child-care business, so I offered parents—not just mothers— help with child-care expenses, paid parental leave. At first we got a little bit of static from nonparents. Why weren't they getting something special too? I pointed out that I wasn't a parent either, but I was interested in human welfare generally. People knew I meant that. We're careful to get such space as we need in buildings where there are small health clubs or gyms, and we pay part—not all—of our people's health club dues. Not all. I don't believe in socialism.

Cooperation is more than just a phrase around here. It includes not only my employees, but my suppliers and my customers. All the people in my company are good at forming special bonds with suppliers and customers. *That's* something only humans can do, let me tell you! It also makes life pleasanter, no? Practical reasons to be close to our customers exist too, of course. For one thing, it gives us early feedback about their changing needs. Our customers trust us, they want us to succeed. If the competition has something better, they tell us. They want us to have it too, so we can continue our good relationship.

Above all, I was determined to give my employees, my contractors, what I once wanted as an employee—a real say in how things are run. A real expectation that an opinion will be respected, make a difference. I'm a good listener, and it has always paid off for me. My company's fast response to change is my strongest competitive advantage, so I'm always trying to nose out what form change might take. Change, for certain, is a constant. I feel best when we leap ahead, cause the change ourselves. I've always been partial to electronic communications, so messages are always waiting for me—people know I'll look at them, that is, if they're brief.

Yes, we're almost all women. I never thought I'd live to hear myself saying it, but the truth is, I have more things in common with women in India and Senegal, where many of my suppliers are, than I do with men in France. I *know* these women; I know that they're as concerned about their country's general welfare, especially the women and children there, as they are about their own bottom line. I've had suppliers say to me: I can't give it to you at that price without violating the water pollution laws. I say fine, we'll all share the costs. We're women: we know if we make a mess, we're going to have to clean it up sooner or later! I'm afraid you can't make most men see that, even now.

I'm still not married, though I'm in a long-term relationship. I finally have time for that. My lover is so keen on my way of operating that he'd like to join me as a business partner. No, thanks! Did I add that I'm personally earning more than twice as much as the senior executives at the old company?

IT'S CALLED CLOUT

One consequence of women's new wealth was their determination to control its relatively more equitable distribution worldwide. As the plan for action that emerged from the UN Fourth World Conference on Women at Beijing had declared in 1995, the growing economic inequality among nations and within nations was harshest on women. Women took on the fight against inequality out of self-interest.

Therefore, no institution escaped scrutiny. In the mid-1990s, Norwegian women had been instrumental in keeping Norway out of the European Common Market, because they perceived that the EEC was more backward than their own nation in granting equal rights for women. Other international bodies, such as the UN General Assembly and Secretariat, the World Bank, and multinational corporations, were just as likely to find themselves confronting demands for radical reform. Courts of law and the professions, long-established religious institutions such as Islam, Roman Catholicism, and the Eastern Orthodox Church, educational and artistic institutions, all found themselves targets of increasingly strong criticism. The threat was that if reform failed, one of their liveliest, most intelligent, and often wealthiest constituencies would withdraw. Since this worldwide eruption of women's disaffection and impatience coincided with fractionalizing tribalism all over the globe, the combination disrupted and often destroyed brittle organizations.

This was nowhere more apparent than in pension funds. The United States had offered its citizens various private pension fund schemes for many years, but for Europeans in the 1990s, they were an innovation, made necessary by the inevitable graying of populations and the impossibility that pay-as-you-go state pension funds could provide for them. These private funds offered tax incentives coupled with strong growth, since to a certain extent, funds were invested in domestic and international equities.

In some countries, such as the Netherlands and Britain, these funds became so large that they matched the country's annual GDP.

Though the funds were managed by professionals, they were accountable to stockholders, that is, pensioners, of whom two out of three were women. By 2010, women pensioners in both the United States and Europe were sophisticated and well educated. They not only demanded strong returns, but they took a very active interest in their governments' economic policies (inflation, for example, was bad news for people on pensions, and women brought great pressure to bear on their governments to follow conservative practices).

But women took an equally active interest in the policies of the firms where their funds were invested. Both corporate and pension fund managers might rail against nosy amateurs and make bitter remarks about "granny governors," but clout was clout. When women didn't like what they saw, they organized and demanded change. They followed the news bulletins of such groups as Good for Women and formed their own watchdog groups. To say they felt no loyalty to the firms that had discriminated against them during their working years was to put it mildly: many women made it clear that they were going to balance the books and wring from those firms what had been withheld from them as workers. But self-interest wasn't all that motivated these granny governors. As young women, many of them had learned their organizing skills in grass-roots environmental organizations, in civil rights groups, and in other improvement groups. To these causes they had enormous loyalty, and they saw no reason why profits—which they fully expected to receive—should be incompatible with good corporate citizenship.

THE NORWEGIAN START-UP FUND

American women in general were assiduous networkers and urged European women (who had been slower to come into the corporate world) to follow them into business for themselves. Until the turn of the century, the proportion of women-owned businesses in Europe lagged far behind the United States, and the numbers, though growing, were small in most of Asia and Latin America.

Along with the usual discriminatory practices, one major obstacle European women faced was obtaining start-up capital from sources that were traditionally antiwoman. No solution was apparent. Then in 2005, the profoundly egalitarian Norwegian government set up a revolving loan fund for women entrepreneurs of any nation. Loans were made at market rates—European women faced discrimination, not lack of ability—and the fund flourished along with an ever-growing number of new, women-owned companies, not only in Europe but in Asia, Latin America, and, to some extent, Africa.

The success of this revolving entrepreneurs' fund inspired the Norwegians to broaden its beneficiaries. As it grew fatter, the fund was expanded to include women in agricultural countries who wanted to buy their own land (either as individuals or in women's agricultural cooperatives). More than once, a Norwegian man would pose as a dummy front to buy land in countries where women were not permitted to own property. One explained: "I'm glad to lend my name to this deception. When I was much younger, I inherited land that should have gone to my sister, but in those days, Norwegian law did not permit women to inherit farmland. It sounds silly now, but it was a very emotionally divisive issue in Norway for several years."

In 1996, we opened a modest Internet bulletin board here in Amsterdam where we named multinational corporations (and their products) charged with being woman-unfriendly. Maybe the firms exploited women employees or relied on child labor. Oh, it's an edifying thing to watch a graybeard in London defend the slave labor of a six-year-old in Pakistan. Maybe they refused to promote women beyond the glass ceiling; maybe the firms made inappropriate use of natural resources so that the health and livelihoods of women near local plants were threatened; or maybe the firm's products themselves were harmful to women. We posted these details, and we were very careful to corroborate them with information from many sources. Then we invited executives of the companies on-line to explain our findings.

The women who logged on to our conversations weren't told what to do with the information. But what followed was usually at least embarrassing for the firms, and quite often the disclosures provoked international action. Individual decisions to boycott would have had a limited effect, but women on the Internet were politically sophisticated, some of them veterans of the South African anti-apartheid efforts, and they formed alliances to press their retail chains, their municipalities, their states, and even their national governments to join the boycott too. For many companies, this proved significant, and at least five large corporations explicitly blamed their subsequent bankruptcies on Good for Women. This was rather flattering, hmm? Other corporations caught on fast.

There were governments who didn't like what we

had to say either, and of course tried to censor it, at least in their own countries. But as folklore will tell you, the Net treats censorship like an obstacle to go around. Censorship can't really be successful on the Net.

I didn't win any popularity contests. I couldn't admit my real name publicly for the better part of a decade; instead I had to use a nom-de-Net, *duivelin*, she-devil.

We spent our second five-year period on a campaign we called "Enough Is Enough." Its target was international funding agencies and their clients. By the end of the century, for a variety of reasons, foreign aid clients were no longer national governments receiving lump sums to spend on large, flashy, economically marginal, even frankly destructive, projects. Fifty years of that nonsense was enough. Instead, clients had become small local groups doing small, local things. Good for Women insisted that funding agencies be publicly accountable for ensuring that women got an equal share of these funds, and often (in the case of certain religious groups, for example) we were able to have funds withheld because such groups systematically discriminated against women.

Good for Women welcomed—it still welcomes—support and information from men, but it remains a woman-only group. We're still here in the Netherlands; most of us live close by one another, kind of like the medieval Beguines, but we have representatives all over the world who report and monitor via the Internet.

No question in my mind that the effectiveness of Good for Women was largely due to the fast, easy communications provided by electronic networks. As costs dropped, and satellites and wireless made expensive infrastructure beside the point, more and more women around the world could join the network.

As I'm sure you know, the Good for Women movement had at least one unintended side-effect. When women in donor countries such as Japan began putting political pressure on their governments on behalf of women elsewhere, it dawned on them that it made no sense to demand equality abroad for foreign aid clients when genuine equality was so elusive at home. That's how Good for Women stimulated change in unexpected places. Call me *duivelin!*

INEZ MATURÍN, 27, BUSINESS EXECUTIVE, BOGOTÁ, COLOMBIA

I was born in 1983 in a small city outside the capital, and my mother brought me here when I was small so she could work. Hers was the first generation of Colombian women who were mostly single. Unlike my generation, she'd actually once been married. But before I was born, my father died in some kind of drug-related brawl. We all lived in a world without men in those days—my uncles died too, they ran off, who knows? Who cares? You could say I am entirely the product of a woman's world, a responsible, *working* woman's world—when she went to work, my mother dropped me off at a child-care center that was also run by a working woman, a wage earner. I took earning a living for granted, and so did all the girls of my generation, whether they were city girls, like me, or country girls.

Our mothers were relentless self-improvers—they were always taking classes, learning how to do what they did better, learning new technology. It was all women there too, since that generation of men disdained education as "not macho." The women set an excellent example for us, so, naturally, as we grew up we overwhelmed the colleges and universities. The government tried quotas to keep us out, but we wouldn't stand for it. Anyway, women were moving into government, so they were our allies. I think the few old men who blocked us finally caved in because they knew we could probably run the country better anyway!

Just after I entered secondary school, the Colombian government declared financial amnesty. That was the first tidal wave of drug money into the legitimate economy, though it had always seeped in in smaller ways. So, about 1998, we had the equivalent of $80 billion dollars looking to wash itself clean with the detergent of good works. One thing they did with this money flood was build new universities with big endowments. So I went to university in a fine place, learning from—why not say it—the best minds that money could buy. Now I keep up electronically. I never stop learning. I love it; but even if I didn't, in my business I have no choice.

Probably it was my mother's influence, but I'd always been interested in business, and by the time I got to work on my M.B.A., women students outnumbered men 2 to 1. My mother hadn't had my advantages, but she was smart enough to rely on a wonderful network of other women for business advice. She knew all the women-run, women-friendly banks to borrow from, and she impressed on me the importance of reliably repaying your debts. All these influences were crucial to me as I started my own business. I went to some of those same women for venture capital for my first production—I run my own fused-media production house—and now as my business matures, I'm beginning to talk to their daughters. Business is women's work here.

Bogotá is often called the Renaissance Florence of the Spanish-speaking world. But it's more than that. It's the world's cultural capital. It's what Paris was in the nineteenth century, New York was in the twentieth century. We produce the best fused-media on the planet, and you don't have to be Spanish-speaking to appreciate it—our sales are tremendous throughout Asia, for example. You don't even have to be female, though it's female-produced and intended for women. But men everywhere love it too. That's why we're a world cultural capital, not just the capital of the Spanish-speaking world. We're the best. I say that with no false modesty. We have the money, we have the taste; it brings artists to us from all over. Who attract other artists. The law of increasing returns. Art follows money, always has.

Yes, it's originally drug money. For decades, the drug lords have been sitting on top of mountains of money that they couldn't spend at all, let alone wisely. I'll leave it to the head-doctors to ask why plunderers start getting worried at the end of life about sanctifying themselves, but they always do—from Lorenzo the Magnificent to Andrew Carnegie. Anyway, finally they began putting it into foundations and appointing women like me to help spend it. Look around you. Isn't this a fine, livable, handsome city? This one we really did right, if I say so myself.

What else can I say? My colleagues and I wish the drug madness of the last century hadn't happened—without getting into issues of how much they brought on themselves, I'm well aware of what drug madness cost the civilized world, and it nearly destroyed our country too. But that's history; it's done. We're pragmatists. We can't give the money back. We're obliged to spend it wisely instead. We can set an example. The men don't know how to spend money. They were originally thugs and their sons are still thugs. When they don't think in terms of money, they think in terms of toys; they think in terms of personal glory. We women, on the other hand, think in terms of the future. We support art, we fund education, we fund health research and health care, spiritual development—which yes, takes money. We began by making our cities beautiful, livable, and now the cities work. This is what accounts for Bogotá as the new Firenze.

Everybody knows that the (exclusively male) drug economy still runs in parallel to the official Colombian economy, but everybody also knows its revenues are falling and will never recover, owing to a variety of global circumstances. The official Colombian economy is growing robustly, and I don't deny that drug money is still priming the pump, finding its way into legitimate channels such as real estate, information start-ups, and so on. All we can do is invest and spend it well. Self-serving as I'm sure it sounds, I believe we're doing exactly that.

Myself? As you notice, I still have only one surname, my mother's. I'm thinking I might have a child, but it would be an engineered job from beginning to end. I can't imagine carrying and bearing it myself. I don't have the time, for one thing.

EASTERN EUROPE: WOMEN WITHDRAW

In the East under communism, women had enjoyed at least a paper equality, though in practice it usually gave women the right to work like men and then come home to domestic chores, without any help from men. Nevertheless, after the fall of communism, even that paper equality was overtly threatened with the rise of the Orthodox and Roman Catholic churches, both deeply patriarchal and, as a consequence, deeply antagonistic to women. Worse, it was no secret that many Orthodox leaders had been strong allies of the KGB, the Soviet secret police, during the palmier days of communism. After the fall, these alliances continued, and both parties had strong interests in subordinating women.

Economic chaos of the first period of freedom nearly destroyed education and social services that had been taken for granted. Though a small number jumped in as early successful capitalists, most Eastern European women found themselves forced to band together to hold on to what little equality and social security they could claim.

Overcoming a legacy of secrecy and mistrust, Eastern European women not only banded together; they withdrew. The first evidence of women's wholesale withdrawal from the dominant culture was the startling drop in birth rates in the former Soviet Union and eastern Germany in the mid-1990s, a trend that continued well into the first decade of the twenty-first century. Though experts attributed this to uncertainty about the future, it also suggested the psychological shock that Eastern European women had suffered when, exposed for the first time to big doses of Western-style popular culture, they were astonished and revolted to find women represented solely as sex objects, a situation harder to fight than the groping and crude remarks of the old-style comrades.

Eastern European governments were the first to adopt on a large scale the artificial womb, developed in Japan in 2007. While they couldn't compel women to bear children, they could compel them to "donate" their eggs, which were then "scientifically matched" to male sperm and used to incubate babies who would belong to, and be reared by, state child farms. (Although the artificial womb had been developed in Japan, which was also suffering from an imbalance between the many old and the few young, partly a result of young women's unwillingness to marry and bear children, conservative cultural forces in Japan continued to resist the idea of state baby farms.)

At the same time, the violence of Eastern European sub-economies at the turn of the century, dominated by organized crime that operated with impunity, forced many women to flee into their own informal if primitive economies, often based on barter rather than cash exchange, since cash only attracted male predators. A woman without the support of other women found herself trapped by crime syndicates into prostitution, pornography, and drug trafficking.

By 2015, Russia maintained one of the most distinctly separate women's cultures on the planet. Through strength and tough perseverance, Russian women had transformed themselves from victims into the one consistently civilized element in their region. They were the objects of intense study, and not a little envy, but they told visitors that under the circumstances, they had no alternatives. For the widespread rise in violence after 1989, especially homicides, combined with alcoholism, infectious diseases, malnutrition, and stress, had taken its largest toll on young men. Thus Russian and Eastern European women found themselves in the same position their great-grandmothers had been in during World War II, living in a world without men, a world without children, a world that wanted everything except the gratuitous and pervasive violence it had. Their withdrawal, their separatism, was, they said, a sane response to an insane world.

POOR WOMEN AS BANKERS AND ENTREPRENEURS

Women's microbanks, an idea begun by the Women's World Bank in the early 1970s, then developed further in Bangladesh by the Grameen Bank, spread to Central and South America, sweeping across the Caribbean Islands and into West Africa where, by the 1990s, they were thriving. Launched with small foreign aid loans, they were more often loan societies than banks, revolving funds that permitted poor women to borrow a small start-up sum for self-employment. Profits from these small businesses were reinvested in the borrower's business, used to enhance the family's welfare, with the balance going to pay off the weekly installment on the loan. These were extremely successful for several reasons. Women had shown themselves far more reliable than men as responsible borrowers and bank leaders—paybacks were 99.99 percent, a rate Western banks only dream of—and many ingenious schemes were produced to get around the inflation that beset the currencies of poor countries. Women themselves learned and prospered by weekly contact with each other as they came together to make their formal installment payments.

This scheme launched enterprises with dramatic results, instead of doling out aid to passive clients. It had immediate economic payoffs for the women and their households, of course, and raised their self-esteem as they took charge of their own lives. By 2010, when the children of the first women's bank pioneers had grown up, that psychological difference was embodied in a generation of entrepreneurs with dozens of enterprises no longer necessarily woman-run (some sons had taken over the family enterprises) but that were, in various languages, known as "Mama's Brickworks," "Mama's Weaving Factory," "Mama's Pottery," and even "Mama's Specialty Steel Works."

Some of these women took grave risks to start their businesses and faced even more danger when they succeeded. Envious village elders would instigate whispering campaigns against them, or accuse them directly of witchcraft. It took a strong, dedicated, and energetic woman to stand up to all the problems she encountered.

Her children usually divided the family work: some stayed with the enterprise, some began their own enterprises in a healthy capitalistic chain reaction, and some ran for political office. These second-generation entrepreneurs not only contributed to their national economies, but were far less tolerant of the corruption that had formerly characterized their various governments—they knew how hard you had to work to make the money that government drones had routinely appropriated as their private allowance.

To be known as a "village bank kid" was as valuable in some cultures for winning political office as a university education was in other cultures. It was such a badge of honor that it protected young women especially from charges that they were being un-feminine—that is, insufficiently reticent, passive, and self-effacing by traditional cultural standards. Everybody understood that young women who had taken over from their mothers the jobs of dealing with wholesalers, retailers, suppliers, truckers, and em-ployees had no girlish reticence to shed, either in business or in seeking political office.

GOVERNANCE AND POLITICS IN THE NEW MILLENNIUM

For all its difficulties, business was well ahead of governance and politics in adjusting to new conditions. In the mid-1990s, a young American president and several of his European counterparts had undergone relentless criticism by the press and other experts for exhibiting a lack of leadership. In fact, he and others like him represented the uncertain beginnings of a new model of nonau-thoritarian consensus leadership. As the new century got under way, although the prevailing winds were away from the rights of the individual, some political groups were learning from business that the world no longer needed national leaders who were father surrogates. On the contrary, a leader must now understand how to share power, how to facilitate action, how to keep an open mind that could be changed as quickly as conditions changed.

In the United States, for example, the slow pace of electoral change had driven women to create their own political organiza-tions in the 1980s, such as EMILY's List. Independent of major party structures, this fund-raising group supported and helped elect a record number of women to office in federal and state elections beginning in 1992. Though the proportion fluctuated, it inevitably climbed, and by 2015, women occupied at least a third of elective offices at every level, and in the cities they occupied closer to two thirds of elective offices.

In 2004, a small independent women's political party called Common Sense had been founded, with the goals of promoting individual and family security. It began as a response to the prevailing turn-of-the-century disillusionment with what was disparaged as "failed liberalism." Common Sense argued that though liberalism had suffered some failures, it hadn't failed. The party wore the liberal label proudly, but the members began to redefine it. Fundamental to Common Sense was the belief that real progress took place only when equality of opportunity and Social Security were legislated, funded, and enforced. Though Common Sense was simply not viable as an independent party, it was powerful enough to be taken seriously by the major parties; Common Sense aligned itself with them whenever they agreed to pursue the goals and policies that Common Sense promoted, thus bringing a kind of parliamentary dynamic to the two-party system of the United States.

In Europe, a well-planned campaign by women to mandate a fifty-fifty representation in the European Parliament in Strasbourg was eventually successful, but it would take another generation before men actually regarded women as equal partners. Therefore, one-sex caucuses prevailed, and though they sometimes cooperated, they were often at odds. Stalemates were common, and women yielded more often than men to bring issues to closure.

• • •

In India, women had already become a sizable voting bloc by the 1990s, and their political power was amplified by an Indian law mandating that 33 percent of elective positions be reserved for women. What women wanted was distinctive: food grain, education for their children, and dignity. They listened to political rhetoric with skeptical ears: never mind all the lofty nonsense, they said, give us things that will have an impact on our lives. Political parties soon recognized that they must deliver.

Women's skepticism with government expressed itself in countless self-help groups that grew up all over India, each grounded in a let's-do-it-ourselves attitude. Simultaneously, a new generation of Indian women leaders had emerged, and between 2000 and 2015, they moved swiftly into politics, taking not only their so-called reserved seats but many other seats besides. Unlike earlier generations, where female politicians had been connected to great families, this generation was full of independent, self-made women, from sophisticated city dwellers to rural women who were not necessarily formally literate. What all these women shared in common was their experience in grassroots political movements—the southern antiliquor effort, the antidowry initiative, the myriad environmental protection movements. They ran on platforms that stressed options: tradition and modernity together, in a context of art, of habitat, of reappropriated tradition.

But then all over India as the old century waned and the new century opened, a fresh wind seemed to be blowing. Women seized the initiative everywhere. When religious riots rocked Bombay in the mid-1990s, Indian women told each other that obviously they could not depend on either the government or the police to keep the peace. They formed multireligious women's unions, with the idea of transcending the old enmities and learning to live together peacefully. This was the seed of the famous Bombay Women's Cooperative, founded in 2000, one part craft market, one part schooling center with the latest technology, one part think-tank, where Indian women evolved their own kind of feminism, somewhat different from the Western model, a feminism that took into account the extended Indian family, with both its advantages and its disadvantages for women.

Even India's implacable dispute with Pakistan seemed closer to resolution in 2015 than it had for decades, when the two heads of state met to begin talks, flanked by women who had been trained in successful conflict resolution in the bloody fields of what was now New Yugoslavia.

ANNA MARSHALL-LOPEZ, 43, MAYOR OF NEW YORK CITY

I was elected on a platform of making the city woman-friendly for the first time in its history. I can't say we've succeeded beyond my wildest dreams, but we've certainly changed things. It was obvious early on that American cities were getting blacker, browner, more female, and poorer than the rest of the country. We've got a lemon, I thought; let's make lemonade.

Myself? Hispanic-Afro-Irish. They say there's a Native American on both sides but, hey, who knows? American. Plain New American. You'll see me marching in everything from the Caribbean Day parade to the St. Patrick's Day parade: any excuse to party, okay?

Women elected me, and I don't forget it for a moment. I ran on a platform of turning this city into a woman-friendly place, something completely new in its history. In a way. But in a way not. Little-known fact: there were 200,000 single working women here before the end of the nineteenth century. When the whole population of New York was, oh hell, under 2 million.

I always thought of Manhattan as one of the few places where a woman could live like a man—the level of personal services here: hey, you don't have a wife, you have food delivery, okay? The dry cleaner delivers, mobile clinics come to you. We've instituted the Big Apple builders, municipal handyfolk, the volunteers who work either for minimum wage or none at all to rehab, to do repairs. They come to you too. In the 1970s and 1980s, the municipal codes were so hopelessly complicated, and getting approval was so slow that it definitely discouraged people from fixing their places up. On top of that, the building industry was very corrupt. If you wanted to install a new toilet, let's say, you had to pay five times what anybody else in the country paid. So most people, landlords included, said forget it. A few brave folks did it, remodeled the bathroom or something, but they did it quietly, no plans filed, nothing. A lot of that was dangerously below code, but you could hardly blame people. The housing stock got worse and worse.

Junior year of college, I got a grant to go to Paris—this was 1994—and here are all these old buildings, and I go, hey these are older than anything in New York and they look great. I saw it could be done, you know? There was nothing to stop us from streamlining the permit process. It used to take months to get permits. We do it on-line in less than half an hour now, and if you've got a problem, the system can instantly offer alternative designs that fit the codes.

Housing. The first thing we did was offer to sell public housing to the people who lived in it. Nobody had ever done that in New York City. Privatization? This is the best kind of privatization, people owning their own homes, having a stake in where they live. We had a lot of opposition, of course. There was, there still is, much invested in keeping people helpless, keeping them as clients. Used to be a whole industry for that. But nobody could argue that things were terrific as they were. They argued that things would get even worse. We said, maybe, but this is worth trying.

Child care. If they'd followed all the rules, the Father, the Son, and the Holy Ghost in partnership couldn't have run a child-care center in New York City. We regularized what people were really doing—the grandmas and aunties in the neighborhoods. That's how our Big Apple Abuelitas program began. We didn't run up a thousand rules and regulations or get those kids out of there—like there's someplace else they can go? We figure: you want to be a community grandma, an Abuelita? Okay. We'll put in a decent kitchen and an air conditioner and fix up the plumbing in your apartment; we'll fix up the hallway. We did low-cost loans, no outright grants. If you're spry enough to take care of little kids, you're spry enough to pay back a loan. It's a revolving fund: the paybacks go to make other loans; everybody knows that.

Each little pot is controlled by the neighborhood. All the accounting is right up front, very public. If you default, everybody knows it. Someone has light fingers, everybody knows it. It puts a certain amount of pressure on people to be responsible citizens, but that's okay. We got a few lawsuits at first: you know, people's feelings are going to be hurt if the world sees they can't pay the loan back. But that seemed crazy to me. Community shame is a great motivator, has been for thousands of years in the history of the human race. One thing that disappeared in the last half of the last century was community shame—people weren't ashamed in front of their neighbors that they weren't taking responsibility for themselves. I'm not talking about a few bad breaks, I'm talking about responsibility for yourself. No more, we said. So sue us. They did—and they lost. Hah! People were just up to here with it all, you know what I'm saying?

The moms pay. It isn't a tremendous amount, but it covers costs, gives the Abuelitas enough to pay back their loans, a little profit. First they pay back the improvements, then we talk about them owning their own places. It's a great incentive. The moms have to work. It's cool. Moms have always worked, but it was a big secret left out of the history books.

Now the Abuelitas have been expanded to serve the elderly who need help at home. Basically, these are jobs for the unskilled, including the new immigrants coming in. It's a nice program, and I'm real proud of it. I wish I'd had something like that when my kids were small. I'm looking forward to it being around when I'm old.

To make a city woman-friendly doesn't mean we don't like men. Somebody is making all those babies, right? With all due respect to the archbishop, the human race isn't into immaculate conception here. But a lot of men have been in a kind of social default for the last few decades.

Look at school enrollments. In the 1990s, between two thirds and three quarters of the students in the New York City community colleges were women. Not necessarily young women, either. A lot of them were over thirty, kids of their own. This is where our leadership came from. Where were the men? Murdered on the street, strung out, a very bad scene. But women took responsibility for their lives, you know? It wasn't easy. But it was personal responsibility.

So—men. The ones who want to take genuine responsibility, great. Glad to have you here. I like male energy myself. The others? Find someplace else for your arrested development, okay? Take your whining and stuff it. We've borrowed a lot of ideas from the femmunes, but we aren't separatists. People say, get rid of the men, you get rid of the crime. Not quite. We aren't rid of crime.

We have plenty of men. But let's say I can see why they say that.

GENDER POLITICS RESHAPES PARTY POLITICS

* * *

Women have their own ceremonies in Ojibway, and the men have their own ceremonies in their Sun Dance. Then, when they break their fast, the men serve the women.

It's the opposite way around with the Sioux. You'd never catch a Sioux man dead serving a woman.

Used to with the Sioux, the woman would walk two steps behind the man. The only reason I'd walk two steps behind a man is to kick his goddamn ass.

—*Betty Laverdure, Ojibway tribal elder, 1994*

* * *

As the millennium turned, each of the major American parties, Republican and Democratic, had both women and men as active members, but this disguised an enormous advantage that the Democratic party enjoyed beginning in 2000, an advantage owing partly to its closer attention to what were traditionally called women's issues. As late as 2010, the Republican party was still trying to recover from what turned out to be an ill-advised infatuation with the Far Right, which had shaped party policy in the presidential elections of 1996 and 2000. Misreading not only the American public's mood, but also the times, Republican strategists had permitted their party's platform to be shaped by vociferous, wealthy, but numerically small paternalistic and antiwoman groups campaigning under the tattered banner of "family values."

Between a dose of electoral reality and the inevitable passing of men who couldn't understand why paternalism repelled voters, the Republican party had begun to recover somewhat during the presidential elections of 2004 and 2008. The recovery was mainly due to a small team of Republican women who had worked together quietly for years, who had learned to use information technology strategically, and who finally seized control of the party themselves, forcing it not only to open up to women's issues, but to go well beyond Democratic policies.

This Republican coup recapitulated a pattern that had been in operation since the beginning of the 1990s. Politically experienced women would band together quietly, bide their time, meanwhile working diligently to gather allies. They would wait until just the right moment to pressure, or even take control of, mainstream organizations to insist that they address so-called women's issues. In a limited way, this had happened at the UN Conference on the Environment at Rio in 1992; it had happened more effectively at the UN Conference on Human Rights in Vienna in 1993. Most conspicuously it happened at the UN Conference on Population and Development in Cairo in 1994, when, despite an alliance with fundamentalist Muslim groups, the Vatican suffered its first—and as it emerged, deeply significant—political defeat in modern times. By the time women met in Beijing for the UN Fourth World Conference on Women in 1995, they had learned that political effectiveness meant putting aside the issues that divided them and focusing on those that united them.

Political observers described themselves as pleasantly puzzled by what they called women's "radical moderation." Somehow activist women were passing resolutions and even enacting legislation far more radical and inclusive than anything that had gone before, yet they accomplished this in an atmosphere of cooperation, reasonableness, and relative good will. Part of the reason for their success was their primary identification as tribal people, or citizens of the developing world, or Muslims, or environmentalists, or educational or health specialists, a primary identification that obscured the fact that they were also all women. In the hallways of international conference centers, male legislators and activists who had been accustomed to being in charge gazed with wonder and not a little envy at women who, strangers a moment before, would find near instant rapport with each other, comparing snapshots of children and grandchildren, admiring each other's apparel and jewelry, even as they planned the next day's political agenda. What most men (and many women) had long criticized as stereotyped triviality turned out to be a means to easy and unself-conscious mutuality.

NYASHA NDOKE, 35, FARMER, BUNYORO (FORMERLY UGANDA)

First my father and then my mother died of AIDS, which meant I was orphaned at age ten. This was 1990. My village was in what was then called Uganda, which had maybe the highest rate of AIDS then known. The country had been completely looted by that monster of all history, Idi Amin, so it was no wonder all the plagues found no resistance.

At ten I was alone. I didn't believe in my village, in my tribe, and I didn't believe in my country—that least of all. I only believed in myself. If I wanted to survive, I had no choice.

My auntie, who was older than me, had gone to Kampala earlier, but now she came back to be with me. I never asked her what she did in the city. Women don't need to ask those questions. I simply prayed—if I believed in any gods then, and I'm not sure I did; maybe I was praying to myself—I *willed* her, with every ounce of my ten-year-old's strength to stay well and stay with me. As things turned out, she did. We went back to our little farm and we began farming the way our great-grandmother, our grand-mother, even our mother had farmed.

But you know what? It was easy. There were only the two of us at first. We worked very hard, we had some hard times, but we loved it. There was nobody telling us what to do; nobody sitting around drinking palm wine and de-manding dinner. Pretty soon a cousin came to join us, and she fit in very well. Her sister came too, but she didn't like it—no men—so she left. That was fine. We didn't think everybody wanted to live like us. At night we sang and told stories. My auntie taught me how to read and write French. I surpassed her very quickly—I loved read-ing and writing. When we went to the market, I bartered the food I'd grown for more books. They were terrible old books; you never knew if you were going to get French or English or something else. Sometimes they were very stu-pid things—agriculture reports with lots of numbers. I didn't care. I taught myself to read and write English. When we got a little ahead and got a TV—that was a great moment for us—then I knew how the language sounded.

Other women joined us. Some of them were related to us; some of them were only members of our tribe. They were all without men. Some of them had already con-tracted AIDS, and those we nursed as they died. That was very sad, very hard. When you saw a woman die like that, you didn't have any trouble saying no to the occa-sional man who came by and wanted to make love. You could say it with a knife or a gun in your hand if you needed to.

Babies? There were enough orphans so that we didn't miss the men for that—we had plenty of little ones to look after. That's how I got my daughter. Maybe they weren't ours biologically, but they were ours in the more important spiritual sense. We found our sexual comfort in each other. Much has been made about that by the outside world, but it was only necessity, a fact. Then it stopped being necessity and became a choice. Before the plague, women in my tribe had shared a husband. They had looked after each other's children. Well, now we shared everything—but without the husband. It worked out much better.

We didn't know it, of course, but groups of women like us were forming all over Central Africa. We were practicing the same agriculture our mothers had practiced for centuries. It didn't make you rich, but you ate. You were healthy. That meant a lot. We had to buy some guns. There were bands of bad men, eager to take from us. We protected ourselves without a qualm. When you've worked that hard for something, you can kill without remorse. It was as easy as killing a hyena. I myself have killed six men. Does that shock you? It was very simple: me or them. I long ago chose myself. The word got around, and we weren't bothered very much after a while. It helped that our village was remote. I've heard of women who weren't so lucky, and those bad men, they just laid a village waste despite the resistance. What did that get them? They had a piece of the same old Africa they'd had before. Wonderful.

In the market I heard about the women's loan society. It was very simple. Everybody contributed something, and then we agreed to loan the money out to various members. The members were very scrupulous about repaying their loans, with interest. We got the TV with one of those loans. Then we got bigger ideas and bought our truck. We've been able to pay that one off too. We were able to afford some solar-powered computers, which makes all the difference: now we know other women like us; we farm more efficiently—all right, we play games on them too.

Sometimes the men hang about, especially around the younger women. The younger women know that if they want to be with men, they have to leave us. We don't banish them forever. They can come back and visit; they can come back if they change their minds. They just can't live with us and have a man too. Some have gone away; some have come back. Some bring their children home to stay. We like that. They just can't bring men. Maybe the next generation will change this, but we don't make rules for the future; we make rules for now.

My auntie is getting older. She's been more than a mother could be to me. Now it's my turn to mother her, so to speak, to make sure her old age is peaceful, the way she tried to make my childhood peaceful. The women in my village—we call it a village now—have had their differences. It hasn't been all tranquillity. I wanted to go to a formal school, and that wasn't possible for me. I have a young daughter, and she's already started school. I read with her every night. I'm learning alongside her. In my heart, I know school will separate us. She doesn't know that yet, luckily. When she gets lazy (all children get lazy) I have to be very careful not to pressure her with my sadness about my own life, my envy of her opportunities. I was born during hard times, that's all.

Is the next generation of men better? Only time will tell. I hear arguments that by being so strong, we have somehow emasculated our men. I laugh. It isn't as if we had a choice. If you ask me, women like us, we are saving Africa. So let the men be as strong as we are, not stronger, not weaker.

THE ISLAMIC WORLD: THE SLAUGHTER
OF THE INNOCENTS

When the Slaughter of the Innocents flashed across the TV screens of the world in 2004, showing hundreds of Alexandrian women and girls being gunned down in a public square for refusing the demands of the new religious Egyptian government that they veil themselves and remain sequestered, it was a reenactment of a scene that had already taken place in Bosnia, in Pakistan, in Rwanda, in Thailand, and in dozens of refugee camps throughout the world. But in this case, the fundamentalist Egyptian government was so confident that no one would complain, television cameras were permitted to record the entire outrage. When these pictures were broadcast live across international television screens, it was obvious that the issue was misogyny, not theology.

The video was captured and stored on the Internet, where it could be seen as often as women around the world could stand to look at it. But one small group enhanced those images electronically, studied them avidly, and painstakingly identified each of the perpetrators. One by one, the perpetrators met gruesome, unspeakable deaths at the hands of a group known only as the Daughters of Scheherazade.

The Slaughter of the Innocents marked the beginning of Islamic women's general withdrawal into women-only groups. Some women withdrew for their own protection; some withdrew with the intention of reshaping Islam to be the basis of a civil society. Now began Islamic women-sponsored schools and health centers, intended to bypass the traditional Islamic institutions that had been compromised, even corrupted, by cooperating with fundamentalists. As these women-sponsored schools and clinics spread across the Islamic world, cultural tensions mounted, putting more pressure on Islamic women to live separately from men.

The Slaughter of the Innocents had one good outcome: its sheer baldness would eventually provoke responsible Muslim leaders of both sexes to restudy and reinterpret the *shari'ia* so that it could provide a plausible moral guide for new times.

MIRANDA SWIRA, 38, FORMER FACTORY WORKER, MALAY STATES

In 1993, when I was sixteen, I left my village to work in one of the semiconductor factories established in our country by Western multinationals. As workers we were considered ideal: well educated, very docile, and cheap. The labor recruiter, a Muslim woman like me, assured my parents that I would be very well taken care of, very well protected, everything Muslim parents could want for a daughter. When I was ready to be married, she said, I would have a wonderful dowry that I would have earned myself.

In some sense, all this was true. We were well educated and we worked hard. We made better money than we could make in our villages. We were certainly protected—factory girls were required to stay in company dormitories. We were practically prisoners. Some girls ran away. But I was very good, very obedient, and did what I was told.

Where dreams and reality parted company was about marriage and the dowry. At those wages, I couldn't earn enough for a dowry by the time I was ready to be married, two years later. I couldn't save enough: I was sending too much home for my family. So I thought I'd stay another two years. Those two years became four. By the time I was twenty-five, I'd not only sent a great deal of money back to my family in my village, but I finally had enough for a dowry too. Of course, at twenty-five, I was far too old to be married!

I was also a little more sophisticated by then. A group of us in the same position decided to stay in the city, keep on working, and invest our dowries. The company told us we would not be permitted to work there unless we lived in the dormitories. With sixteen-year-olds! It was quite impossible. We tried to form a union. We got some help from international labor organizations. First of all, we called it a mutual aid society. We made it sound as if we were giving sewing lessons after hours. We had computer classes; we had reading circles. In the beginning—we showed the mullahs the poetry we were reading—very religious, and they approved of that. We learned English, that subversive tongue!

Meanwhile, we downloaded wonderful books from the West that came across the Internet, books about the history of religions, the history of the oppression of women. We began to read the books by Muslim women that had been unknown to us. These also came from the Internet. We spread them all over the city. The mullahs didn't understand where these new books were coming from. They were sure the customs inspectors were being bribed. It was very strange that they didn't understand how information flows; it's harder to contain than the air. They certainly didn't understand that women—well, some women—who work in a semiconductor factory are going to be curious about computers and learn more. Much more. Some of us even joined in the discussions on the Net, those of us who could write English. That was *very* educational, believe me.

So: forced by international labor organizations, and with a big boost from the boycott organized by Good for Women, the factory agreed that it could not require us to live in its dormitories. We'd won that one.

Here we are, you see, women of modest but independent means, living together, but without male attachments. We live apart from our families, no families of our own. You can imagine the provocation this is to fundamentalists. Even if we live as pure as nuns, we defy the patriarchal order just by existing. We cannot go back to our villages now. My own village, for instance, is all but destroyed. A multinational came in and stripped the forests within four years. The officials they'd bribed left with the last tree. The situation here is precarious, quite unstable.

Sometimes I feel enormously strong: this is what we have accomplished. God is just. Women all over the world know about us; they stand by us. We're in constant electronic contact with them, and we take great heart from other women who are in the same position as us. In fact, there are women worse off, and we can give them courage.

Then sometimes I feel terribly fragile: we live at the sufferance of the mullahs, the government. I sometimes fear that when they realize what we represent, they will destroy us without a second thought, and nothing the women of the world can say will make a difference. Who can forget the Slaughter of the Innocents in Alexandria? Who paid for that? In this world, nobody. In the next world—well, let us hope. I cannot take pride in these so-called Daughters of Scheherazade. They're just terrorists. Though I would be only human if . . . well, never mind. Brutalities against Muslim women all over the world, in the refugee camps, the horrible war in Bosnia in the 1990s. And not just Muslim women, no. Where were the priests when the Filipinas of Mandago were slain so pitifully? Where was the Pope? Nobody has paid, nobody.

We live day to day and pray to Allah to protect us, his faithful. *Inshallah*.

TOWNS OF WOMEN: THE FEMMUNES

A small but notable minority of women formed all-female towns. In addition to the all-women villages of Africa, these single-sex settlements could be found in Latin and North America, Northern Europe, several Islamic cultures, certain areas in Southeast Asia, and in Japan. Their genesis varied from place to place, and their actual populations were minuscule, but their influence was far out of proportion to their numbers. For example, the founders of the Good for Women movement in the Netherlands were a women-only group, and it was women's groups reclaiming the inner cities of North America that began to transform those cities into vital places to live once more. At a minimum, these femunicipalities or femmunes provided women with physical safety in a world where violence against them had been the unremarkable norm. For women outside their walls, the femmunes set examples, raised questions, monitored compliance with law and common decency, and offered intellectual leadership and spiritual support.

In countries with a Christian heritage, these women consciously modeled themselves on the Beguines of the European Middle Ages, a powerful lay movement of women that had thrived for a century or more in the Low Countries and the Rhineland until it was crushed by the Catholic Church, and the Beguines were all but destroyed as heretical.

As a rule, the women's towns were secular though they usually drew women of like mind together (some Islamic femmunes were founded with the express purpose of restudying the Koran to purge it of the misogynistic interpretations that various cultures had attached to it over the years). Women came to a femmune for brief periods or for a lifetime. Like the Beguines, the femmunes welcomed young women as temporary residents before they went into partnership (or marriage) with a man; they welcomed older women who had dissolved partnerships or were widowed; they welcomed women who never planned to have a long-term relationship with any man. Though each femmune had its own standards for admission, the emphasis was on flexibility: their governing bodies were ad hoc and light-handed.

The only universally and rigidly enforced rule was that men were prohibited inside the femmune's boundaries. Beyond the boundaries, any arrangement a woman wanted to make was her own business. Most women had at least occasional liaisons, and some even bore children while they lived in a femmune; most found it a congenial place to be a single mother, with friendly help on every side. Typically, boys over age twelve were not permitted to live in the femmunes, and mothers would sometimes send their male children to the children's fathers, or, more commonly, would themselves leave the femmune with the boys. Since, apart from the women-only covenants, private property was respected, and since there was often a waiting list for the femmunes, a dwelling sold inside a femmune was usually a profitable transaction. It was not unusual for a woman to hold on to her property and rent it to other women while she temporarily left the femmune, with the anticipation that she would eventually return.

What threatened femmunes was not the church, as in medieval times, but legal and economic forces: several U.S. women's towns underwent protracted legal attack for violating equal access laws. They prevailed only because of clever readings of the equal access laws, citing as precedent the gated communities of the rich that had proliferated in the North American suburbs during the last part of the century. They cited the need for common safety and the right to congregate. Having at least temporarily beat back the legal threats to their existence, the economic threats were more difficult to counter.

In the United States, for example, women's towns were often towns-within-towns, where women had reclaimed formerly derelict inner-city ghettos. At first the femmunes were neither interesting nor attractive to anyone else. Women had only taken over what nobody else wanted. But cleaned up and repaired, the unlivable was transformed into the highly desirable, and real estate interests often made irresistible offers. A number of femmunes dissolved as a result of this.

• • •

Most Asian femmunes had a sadder beginning than North American and European femmunes. They often grew on the sites, indeed out of the debris, of old refugee camps. They were less communities of choice than communities of last resort. Camps on the Thai border between Laos and what was again called Burma offer an example whose details are particular, but whose outcome is typical.

The tribal, ethnic, and political wars that had ravaged Southeast Asia in the last part of the twentieth century continued, though to a lesser degree, in the early part of the twenty-first century, producing a second and even third generation of refugee camp dwellers. These camp dwellers were mainly minorities who resisted repatriation in a homeland that no longer recognized their right to traditional existence, though a significant minority were intellectuals who had fled to avoid death from brutal regimes.

As a consequence of their long stays in the camps, refugees were cut off from their old ways, yet confused by the contradictory teachings of Western refugee agencies (often the adjuncts of religious groups that dogmatically promoted Western practices and culture). Unsurprisingly, refugees often fell into a torpid dependency, which did not bode well for the future. Health conditions had never been good in either the villages or the camps;

toward the end of the twentieth century, they got steadily worse. For women, conditions had been particularly bad: they were chronically undernourished, bore many children quickly, suffered more than their share of disease, and died early.

These social and health conditions appalled two remarkable physicians who had fled their Burmese homeland when intellectuals were being persecuted and killed. Each woman organized general medical services inside several of the camps, but their particular interest was the health of women and children. Indefatigably they began training young women as nurses, midwives, technologists, and other paraprofessionals to work in camps for women and children only. A steady stream of children arrived at these special camps, mainly bewildered and damaged victims of the Asian sex trade.

The two doctors' efforts were amplified by visiting medical groups and support from international agencies. When the resolutions of the 1994 Cairo Conference began to be implemented by UN agencies, these two women were able to leverage generally meager resources to accomplish an astonishing amount.

The physicians themselves were married with children, but they came from an elite class that acknowledged women's multiple roles. Their growing team of newly trained women health workers were from the village peasant classes, however. These young women foresaw that if they married, not only would they have to give up the work they were dedicated to, but they must return to a life of traditional deference to men. Nurses' housing in the refugee camps was the first step toward what would soon become women-only villages.

. . .

Other femmunes in Southeast Asia began when Vietnamese women, who had fought (and faced death) side by side with men in wartime found themselves suddenly pushed to the margins in a postwar world, their maternal leaves and child care eliminated as "too costly" for the new market economy. Women formed the first femmunes in India when their livelihoods (and lives) were threatened by multinationals cutting down southern forests.

Japan, however, owed its first femmunes to its vestigial tea-house culture. When groups of young Japanese women turned away in disgust from the endemic political corruption of major political parties, when they turned away in disgust from the endemic misogyny of corporate and political Japan, they took as their model the old tea-house all-woman culture. The geishas were Japan's first independent woman entrepreneurs.

• • •

In the Arab world, a distinction must be drawn between a small number of Islamic femmunes, founded with the specific aim of studying the Koran to reframe the misogynistic interpretations of law, or *shari'ia*, which had accumulated over the years by various cultures, and secular Arab world femmunes. But the connection between Islamic femmunes and secular Arab communes was deep and nourishing: each gave the other models and ideas.

Misogyny—sometimes subtle, sometimes overt—had characterized many Arab cultures for centuries, and so it wasn't until the end of the twentieth century that Arab women began to be literate in large numbers. That burgeoning literacy, as well as a general exposure to the West through the media, provoked dramatic change in the lives of many women, a change their mothers and aunts (and certainly Arab men) did not always understand. Secular femmunes were one answer to a transformation that Arab women felt compelled to make, but which their cultures weren't yet ready for. Ironically, the femmunes claimed their heritage from one of the most misogynistic of institutions, the traditional harem, where Arab women had been isolated for centuries. They acknowledged this heritage proudly: women had been emotionally self-sufficient in the harems, and now they would be economically self-sufficient in femmunes.

Once the cold war was over, neither my parents nor my children knew what to call me. Since my college days, when I supported Jack Kennedy for president, my parents had been praying for my soul. Mom in particular remained quite sure that only divine intervention could save me from the Communist Conspiracy that was presenting itself in the form of liberal politics.

It was then, during my college days, that Mom started lighting candles after Sunday mass (daily during Lent) for the salvation of my soul against communist incursion. She continued until she died, quite sure that my "liberal" bent was associated with something not good for America or the Pope. I think she never forgave me for organizing my friends against wearing hats to mass in 1965.

Every time I did something true to the letter of what I'd been raised to believe in, it was turned into a Communist Conspiracy. This was especially true during my activities in the civil rights movement. "Isn't there enough to do in Boston, what with your new job and all, that you don't have to welcome those Negroes off the buses from Mississippi, dear? They really should stay with their own people. And so should you, dear. Now why don't you just come home to Connecticut?"

I argued a-plenty that the Negroes were just like my own immigrant grandparents. They were a minority who deserved no less than what we had been taught was right at catechism, in civics lessons at the new suburban school, not to mention the liberal arts college my family struggled to send me to. Another candle flickered for me in the front of the church.

It all came to a head, as you might imagine, when my career officer Air Force brother was running bombing raids over Vietnam and I was chaining myself to the White House fence in protest of the war. Marching against the war in Vietnam while Nixon's White House was surrounded by Metro buses for protection against potential violence was not Mom's idea of what a very pregnant mother should do with her three-year-old on a weekend. Another candle.

And then my darling sons, who had marched with me, grew up to suspect that all the other kids' parents were right. That handing out leaflets against Wonder Bread at suburban shopping centers because the parent corporation made antipersonnel weapons was not an "American" thing to do. Profits and consciousness raising were entirely separate things!

Moreover, nice ladies don't have their picture in the local paper with fists of defiance raised against uniformed Pentagon generals. And they certainly don't host endless women's organizing meetings and fund-raisers with I. F. Stone speaking. The men in the black cars parked at the corner who watched the house during these events made my sons and their friends nervous. And when the D.C. police came to break up a party for Izzy Stone as "an event without a permit," both the boys had nightmares for weeks. They told my mother. Another candle.

The Civil Rights Act became law. The war ended. Nobel Peace Prizes were awarded. The Equal Rights Amendment was defeated. The kids played soccer, got chicken pox, sang in school plays, mastered foreign languages, new math, and science. They went on to college. It was the "went on to college" that got me a candle of thanks one week.

Then came the 1980s and the flowering of Generation X. I knew there would be quarreling at holiday reunions before my grandmother's prophecy, that the apple never falls far from the tree, was fulfilled. The moment of truth arrived with the second letter home from my out-of-state-tuition college son. It contained a registration card for the Republican party and a membership card to the National Rifle Association. I lit a candle.

With the cold war over, I became an embarrassment to my parents and a joke to my kids. The enemy is gone. Can't I stop talking about all of this equality stuff? Didn't the fall of communism teach me anything? This peace, freedom, and justice stuff just doesn't work. "Couldn't you just worry about the environment, dear?" Are Sunday candles bad for the ozone hole, I wonder, to no one in particular.

They all consider me a sixties leftover, whatever that is. I never smoked pot. Never wore miniskirts. But they are sure that being arrested for principle instead of insider trading is foolishness. Not even my occasional corporate consulting was good enough cover for my unrelenting commitment.

I kept explaining that they could call me a radical or a fallen-away Catholic pacifist. They stared back at me unblinking. I can see my mother imagining the candle stand at church. Maybe it would help if I stopped yelling back at the TV during the nightly news. Maybe not.

So here I am at election time again. A never-was communist, an unreconstructed radical in post-post-modernity, lighting candles of my own, and praying to the Goddess for the future.

CHANGING BEHAVIOR

Gender roles—those behaviors assigned by culture rather than wired in—had changed dramatically in many places around the globe by 2015. In the megacities of Latin America and Asia, in the inner cities of North America (and even its comfortable suburbs), in the relatively civil cities of Western Europe, women fifty years earlier would have been hard-pressed to recognize women's behavior in 2015 as feminine. Economic independence, coupled with nearly universal education and health care, had given women a new spring in their step, a new sense of their own possibilities. Earn your own money and you need defer to no one. Space your children, eat sufficient food, and you're healthy yourself, you have healthy children; above all, you have a different outlook.

Perhaps nowhere was the change as dramatic as it was in sexual matters. For the first time since patriarchy had spread over the planet thousands of years ago, women began to acknowledge their own sexuality and sexual needs, without having to bind those needs to some particular man, especially a breadwinner or the father of their children. Anyone listening to popular music in the last decade of the twentieth century might have seen it coming: young women sang bluntly about the importance of their own sexual desires, the joy they took in sex for its own sake, all very different from the love lyrics women sang earlier in the century. And these new songs expressed the feelings of a large, appreciative female audience. But it took many by surprise, those who still imagined that women only loved; whereas men lusted.

Women's lust was certainly unexpected given the medical intractability of sexually transmitted diseases, especially AIDS. But like adobe as a building material, say, flesh-sex had become common only among the very rich and the very poor. Thanks to dramatic advances in electronic sex, known as e-sex, most young people preferred the wider variety and sustained sensations of sensory on-line games over their unaided senses. E-sex was nearly undetectable officially, since its electronic signals were encrypted. Though women were often forbidden by their national or state governments from moving into certain areas of the Net, an underground movement of hackers, male and female, cheerfully broke the law to bring in young women who couldn't hack their own way in. In Western European countries that took a pragmatic view of sexual activity, e-sex was a welcome conduit for strong fundamental urges, a conduit with no lasting consequences, whether disease, unwanted pregnancy, or criminal activity. In the United States, where pockets of Puritanism still existed, e-sex was out of sight, and therefore put out of mind, though every year or so, a politician or cleric would decide to make an issue of e-sex, heedless of the futile efforts of politicians or clerics who had gone before.

For certain classes of teenage women, e-sex was a startling change from the passive and pregnant roles of their mothers and grandmothers. A complicated set of circumstances was responsible for the new sex, including the violence associated with traditional sex, and the opportunities that unprotected sex foreclosed, but probably the most decisive event was the invention and widespread use of the artificial womb, which rendered childbearing highly unfashionable. Successful minority businesswomen moved into the ghettos to organize, proselytize, and set examples. They succeeded where generations of social workers had failed.

MEGAN ROYCE, 43, BUSINESS EXECUTIVE, LONDON

I've no idea when the first sex resorts were established. As you know, they cater to women who can afford the best; they're staffed by attractive men and women of all ages, races, and sexual orientations. Like the Japanese geishas of old, the staff are accomplished in conversation, acting, dancing, and sports. The sex resorts I've patronized offer everything from brief virtual reality encounters to long-running play scenes that can last for months, with a cast of half a dozen players or more, sumptuous costumes, and sets. Their main business, however, is a two- or three-day stay intended as a full experience: sex, fine meals, wine, music, outings, sports, massages, and so on. On the outskirts of cities where most executive women work, which is to say North America and Western Europe (though Johannesburg, Shanghai, and Tokyo also have their share) there are villas where you can go for an hour's or an afternoon's refreshment. There's no bother from the police or the fundamentalists. Wealthy people have never been their target.

You might ask, why would anyone pay for a sex resort when, as a rule, sex is so readily at hand? Easy. First, I appreciate the anonymity of it. At work, I might encounter a man who eventually becomes my lover, either briefly or not so briefly, but that always involves—well, entanglements. That's fine. I like romance as much as the next woman. But sometimes—maybe even at the same time—you just want to get laid, then leave. No sweet little messages afterwards, please. In other words, we've cut away all the false sentimentality that surrounded sex in the patriarchal age.

Next, I like the professionalism of a resort. It isn't just that the staff are well educated and trained to be entertaining, though that's very nice indeed. At a sex resort, nobody's going to ruin my only getaway in six weeks by developing a sudden case of hurt feelings and sulking, or having regrettable attacks of wilting weenie, or coming down with a last-minute case of the flu. And speaking of health matters, the kind of resort I go to is absolutely scrupulous about safety and hygiene. If I want the added stimulation of electronics or chemicals, they're available, of course. I can rest assured that everything is going to be perfect: that's what I'm paying for, isn't it?

Also, I've never found it easy to share my fantasies with a partner I know in real life, so to speak. If this is my weekend to get into a Daddy's Girl scene, then it just is, and I don't want to have to explain it or justify it, or hear somebody cluck over my mental health. It's a fantasy, that's all. I've done a Carmen scene and even a Queen Elizabeth I scene once or twice—with an absolutely glorious young Essex, I might add—but in most of my scenes I'm passive. Look, at work I'm in charge and making decisions all day, all week, all year. When I play, I want fantasies where things are the opposite from real life, like Naughty Maid or Harem Girl, my favorite lesbian scene. Outside the resort, I'm straight, but at the resort, anything goes, and I've thoroughly enjoyed gay scenes there.

But don't you see, my passivity there is all pretend. I choose to go to the resorts, and the money I've earned makes it possible; I choose the scene I'm going to have; I choose the mix of flesh, chemistry, and electronics; I've even started to script my own scenes with professional actors. It's all just one more little game, though I must say it's one of the pleasantest ones.

SEXUAL BEHAVIOR OF THE MAJORITY OF WESTERN WOMEN

For women without significant financial means, widespread anonymous sex had become available, though on a more modest scale. Brothels for women operated discreetly, attracting attention from neither syndicated crime nor the police. In many cases, no money changed hands: sex was for mutual stimulation and pleasure, a co-op exchange rather than a transaction. Such arrangements could be found everywhere in Europe, in the bigger cities of the Americas, and in China, India, and Japan.

"Brothel" suggests a fixed location, but in fact sex co-ops floated from place to place, part of the time in the real world, part of the time in cyberspace. The middle class had long ago claimed cyberspace as its playground, and it was only natural that sex was a big part of its play. Even at a real world session, invitations and responses were typically arranged electronically. The host of a real world session usually received a small fee from each participant to cover costs. Often, potential partners met once in a real life session and then continued to meet remotely in cyberspace, employing a combination of sensors, virtual reality, and chemicals, the latter enhanced by temporary or permanently implanted biochips. Thus a woman could fine-tune her own libido depending on opportunity and whim.

Though nothing was quite illegal about such arrangements, encrypted communications were used to deflect nosy authorities and to eliminate undesirable participants in the groups: the diseased, the disruptive, the hygienically careless.

• • •

For poor women both in the West and elsewhere, the situation wasn't vastly different from what it had been thirty years earlier. If their more fortunate sisters had turned away from men on ideological grounds to build their own separate organizations and societies, poor women had effectively been deserted by men for many years, across many cultures. Harassed by poverty, by the sheer struggle of keeping body and soul together, they hardly had time to give much thought to their own sexual gratification, nor did its fulfillment have the same ideological meanings it had for better-off women. Again, across many cultures, poor women were prim when they spoke of sex, but matter-of-fact as they practiced it: they separated sex and fertility and used sex to lure men for temporary companionship, or to coax them to solve a small problem.

Side by side with the kinds of independent new social organizations Nyasha Ndoke describes, another pattern also emerged in many cultures where poor women formed all-women "families," burlesquing the roles of female submission and male domi-

nance. In these families, respect was demanded, disrespect punished (often physically). The submissive females offered sex and
domestic service and put all their financial resources into the
family; the dominant females neither worked nor offered financial help to their "families," but instead lived off the submissives,
demanding monogamy but not practicing it; spending any money
available only on themselves. A number of women in these situations even took up a kind of prostitution, offering sex for money
or favors from dominants; they were generally scorned by women
in established families—still, the dominants used the prostitutes,
scorn notwithstanding. Sociologists who studied these pseudo-
families often pointed out how grotesquely they parodied the traditional patriarchal family; how oddly they mirrored the situation
of turn-of-the-century women's jails.

> ### BECKY DRUCKER, 83, FOUNDING MEMBER, THE WHITE WIDOW SPIDERS, CALIFORNIA

In the 1990s, you got a feeling that top to bottom, things
had gone terribly wrong in California, and a catastrophic
future loomed ahead. But nobody knew how to take the
next step. The usual groups whose brief was the environment, or education, or government reform, they'd all lost
their effectiveness. They had only themselves to blame:
they were shrill, you could see they'd succumbed to
media posturing; their all-or-nothing demands and declarations put everybody off. You just got to thinking that
everybody was a special interest, in it for the money, period.

As this malaise seemed to grip our beautiful state, a
small group of us got together. We were mostly old
friends, and we wondered whether we could do something about the problems everybody could see and nobody could solve. We were all a bit too old to have been

part of the feminist movement of the 1970s. We thought of ourselves as that nearly extinct species called the traditional housewife: we'd raised our families, done PTA duty, worked in the League of Women Voters, and one of us even picketed for racial equality once in 1958. At our age, it was our last shot to make a difference.

Since we were all widows, all white, all economically secure, as a kind of joke, we called ourselves the White Widow Spiders. Our task, as we concluded after a few weeks of discussion, was first, to bite the hand that fed us, the very society that had left us secure: shake it up, clean it out. Why, you ask? Maybe because we saw that what had given us security was just good luck for us, bad luck for others, and it was time to even things out a bit. Maybe because we wanted to give something back— that happens at a certain stage in life. I do know that it wouldn't have occurred to any of us if our husbands had been living. Maybe the problem was because we'd been nice girls for a lifetime and it was getting tiresome. Anyway, it beats sitting around talking about your aches and pains.

Having bitten the hand that fed us, we knew we wanted to spin connective webs among all kinds of different people. Both these tasks were intended to shape a society that would be responsible for all its citizens and to make all citizens take responsibility for their society.

Rather optimistically, by the reckoning of some, we thought the commonalties among women across cultures would be the basis for mutual interest and ad hoc collective action. Single-parent households in California had burgeoned, most of them headed by women. We learned that from 2 million such households in the year 2000, they had grown to 3.5 million in 2010. The White Widows suspected that here lay our natural constituency: we guessed that women from ethnic groups where females had traditionally been passive and subordinate to males (both Asian and Hispanic) had sniffed the freedom enjoyed by their more independent sisters and cut themselves loose from those ethnic traditions that seemed particularly stifling, even when they risked losing the other benefits conferred by those traditions.

Well, using our old PTA telephone-tree skills, the White Widows began spreading the word of our concerns—and our meetings—to other women, and we soon made connections in the different ethnic groups that make up California now. You see, we could talk both to women who remained in the traditional roles of mothering and homemaking (we ourselves had done that), and yet we found much affinity with what newspapers would eventually dub the "Black-Eyed Susans" (in honor of feminist Susan B. Anthony), those Hispanic and Asian women who discovered that in America, traditional roles aren't the only ones open to women. In the black community, the White Widows found a well-organized set of formal and informal women's groups that were already energized and effective.

The Spiders came to include local branches of the American Association of Retired People, which were really stung (as well they might be) by the accusations that their only interests were selfish. We also attracted people who weren't white and people who weren't women. We and our allies weren't so much activists as we were facilitators.

In my opinion, the Spiders embodied womanly pragmatism: if it worked, fine; if it didn't, try something else. Goddess knows we were old enough to laugh at credit, hierarchy, and turf battles. Eleanor Roosevelt used to say that you can accomplish anything at all if you don't insist on taking credit for it. We insisted on common courtesy, and we were patient about results.

The Spiders, you see, were half a step ahead of the fastest-growing segment of the population: at the turn of the century, the sixty-pluses became the biggest single age group in America. This was thanks to the famous baby boomers (though I'm a decade older than most of them). These people were veterans of 1960s political activism, healthier, more active, and more experimental than any generation before them.

Among our other allies, maybe the most surprising were quite young women. I'm speaking of teenagers. I've observed that, both at the beginning and at the end of adult life, human beings seem more at ease, more honest, more able to talk frankly than they do in their preoccupied middle years. I think young people, trying out adult identities, were fascinated by us old people, women especially; we'd reinvented our lives several times over and were willing to talk about it. I think young women sensed that here might be models for living and reinventing a life in a continuously changing society.

Anyway, by the year 2015, nearly two thirds of California's student population was Hispanic and Asian, both cultures that traditionally honor older people in ways American culture never has. So the Spiders were delighted, and I might add more than somewhat surprised, to find ourselves treated respectfully by adolescents.

Our young allies disclosed that multiculturalism was already a given in their lives: they borrowed their music, their food, their language from the cultural currents around them, just as American culture always has. We Spiders in turn offered to young people a sense of American historical continuity, reminding them that bagels, stir-frying, and even hot dogs were once considered exotic. Since we Spiders were also getting slightly deaf, we could listen to the new music at the same volume the young people liked it.

With a sense of life as a cycle, or a set of different stages, the Spiders acted as informal cultural anthropologists. We discovered coming-of-age ceremonies and other rites of passage embedded in the new cultures that we thought could fill the ceremonial vacuum of everyday American life. It's thanks to us, I believe, that young women of utterly different backgrounds can be honored in a Ghanaian female coming-of-age ceremony, followed by a Hispanic *Seisaños*. It's a mixture of cultures and ceremonies that would floor purists, but it's being happily and eclectically embraced by ordinary people. Oh the purists! Do they think tradition was handed down from Mount Sinai?

At the same time we were acting as cultural emissaries, we were also cultural conservators. We pointed out gently to our young friends (who therefore learned it better than any civics lesson in school) that while it might seem that they and their families had arrived in California for economic opportunity, what made that possible was political opportunity, derived from the ideas of a few wild and crazy young guys of the late 1700s who couldn't stand the way things were and decided to invent a nation.

As I look back on what I've accomplished in my life, nothing gives me greater pleasure or gratification than the White Widow Spiders. We've really made a difference. If you'll pardon a bit of metaphor mixing here, the webs we've spun have been straw into gold. We've made the Golden State gold once more.

In Beijing the Future Is Hidden in Plain Sight

To report on the historic meeting in Beijing of 1995 in terms of the four scenarios we offer in this book is a reminder once more that real life is more complex than scenarios. Real events result from an intricate, subtle, and indirect web of cause-and-effect complexity that depends only partly on economics and political trends, the axes along which we have laid our four scenarios. (Even economists ask aloud which factors cause economies to grow, and which are by-products of economic growth.) Real events do not always fit neatly into coherent scenarios, nor do they necessarily evolve from the matrix we expect.

So we need to remind ourselves again: one of the main purposes of a scenario is to *illuminate the present*, not necessarily to *predict the future*. That said, we believe that inside the events of the Beijing meeting lies the future of women. The future is there, hidden in plain sight, if we are only wise enough to open our eyes to see it. Or make it happen.

• • •

The UN Fourth World Conference on Women did not begin auspiciously. The United Nations rotates its large meetings from region to region: the first such women's meeting had been held in Mexico City in 1975. Then, as 1975–1985 was declared the Decade of Women, a second, mid-decade meeting was held in Copenhagen in 1980; and a third meeting in Nairobi in 1985. For the grand September 1995 meeting, it was Asia's turn.

Unfortunately, no Asian nation wanted to host it.

Finally, the People's Republic of China, hoping to win the Olympics site for the year 2000, was persuaded that by taking on the UN Fourth World Conference on Women, it might convince the Olympics Committee that China was ready for more important responsibilities. In any case, it would give the Chinese practice in handling large numbers of temporary foreign visitors.

The Chinese gerontocracy had been stung and clearly puzzled by the world's reaction to the Tiananmen Square slaughter, an event broadcast in real time all over the world. Why such a fuss over two hundred deaths? they asked. What were two hundred— even two thousand—deaths in the long cavalcade of Chinese culture? The women's conference seemed to offer a way to disinfect, if not quite absolve, what the Chinese called "the events of June 1989."

As the time approached, however, and the Chinese lost their bid for the Olympics after all, they began to regret their haste in agreeing to hold a meeting whose main focus would be human rights, a topic of particular sensitivity along Beijing's corridors of power. The government now understood that the UN Fourth World Conference on Women actually consisted of two meetings—the official UN conference, and alongside it, the NGO (nongovernmental organizations) Forum, which had evolved into a kind of think-tank and goad for the more conventional and decorous official meeting. The NGO Forum in particular was home to the most radical kind of outspokenness.

With a series of internal struggles of their own, with a figurehead leader who was said to be dying (and rumored for months to be already dead) Chinese officials contemplated the idea of the world's most outspoken women debating and demonstrating under their noses in Beijing during this delicate time. Their nightmares apparently grew florid: AIDS might be spread by sluttish Western women, Dykes on Bikes might spin wheelies in Tiananmen Square. Taiwanese and Tibetan women might demand self-determination. It was decided to sever the two meetings.

Offering the implausible excuse that the original site for the NGO Forum, a sports pavilion, was structurally unsuitable, and anyway was essential for a volleyball tournament at the very moment the NGOs would be meeting, the Chinese announced in March, six months before the meeting was to take place, that the forum would be moved to Huairou, a small, sleepy resort city a journey of an hour or more from Beijing. In Huairou, the Chinese ruled, any demonstrations must be confined to a small—very small—official demonstration area, which the Chinese felt confident they could control. To further seal off the Chinese people from contamination by unsavory NGO behavior, the two-lane road between Beijing and Huairou was declared closed except to official buses that would convey delegates between the two sites. Finally, Chinese officials actively intervened in the visa process, withholding or even rescinding some ten thousand visas from women who had been certified by the forum but whom the Chinese deemed undesirable—especially Tibetans and Taiwanese, and especially the enemies of China's friends, such groups as Catholics for a Free Choice. All this was in clear violation of the agreements they had originally made when they undertook to host the meeting. Potential delegates asked each other whether any host nation would dare impose such conditions on a UN meeting of men. Or whether men would tolerate it.

In early summer of 1995, a crisis loomed. Many women predicted that the whole meeting, official conference and forum alike, would be canceled. Only collusion at the highest levels of the all-male UN hierarchy could have permitted the Chinese to flout the original agreements with such impunity. Women shook their heads: did the United Nations think it could get away with patronizing women and pushing them to the margins yet again?

From our point of view, the United Nations seemed to be in full embrace of the scenario Two Steps Forward, Two Steps Back. Yes, women could have their promised meeting—but on terms so restrictive they mocked the meeting's purposes. Knowledgeable women recognized this as UN business as usual: eloquent words about justice and equality for all, immediately contradicted by the United Nations' starkly sexist treatment of women in its own organization.

China's worry about the incendiary nature of the NGO Forum was reasonable from its standpoint. During the cold war the role of NGOs at the United Nations had been negligible. But UN meetings that had convened since the end of the cold war— in Rio on the Environment (1992), in Vienna on Human Rights (1993), and in Cairo on Population and Development (1994)— had seen the NGOs grow dramatically, both in numbers and influence. (Significantly, women too had been driving forces for the first time in all those post-cold-war meetings.) The NGOs were grass-roots organizations, springing up all over the world, the sign of a citizens' movement that had begun to take itself seriously and was demanding a voice in transnational governance.

No wonder denizens of both national and international bureaucracies who had obediently played by the rules—one rule was don't rock the boat—were vexed by the obstreperous NGOs and the awkward questions they raised. In some UN circles, China's forced removal of the NGO Forum to Huairou had the welcome effect, they hoped, of diminishing the influence of the NGOs on the formal conference.

But whether the United Nations likes the idea or not, it has lately emerged as a place where ordinary citizens believe they can have a say. Flawed as the UN mechanisms might be (and even that was arguable: at the Beijing conference, Iceland's president,

Vigdis Finnbogadottir, would say forcefully that the United Nations' original design had been distorted by the cold war; now, she said, the organization was for the first time ready to work as its founders intended), the United Nations is still seen as the only international body with the moral authority to press corrupt or oppressive national governments to render to citizens their human rights.

So for all the talk of canceling the UN Fourth World Conference on Women, the momentum from all the regional preparatory meetings that had already taken place all over the world in the winter and early spring was much too strong to resist. Women had identified a list of problems common to them *as* women no matter where they lived: they wanted autonomy over their own bodies, they wanted health and education, they wanted freedom from violence, and they wanted their share of political and economic power. Those common problems might have different priorities with different women, but there they were. Women were eager to meet and begin to tackle those problems.

Thus after a certain amount of brinkmanship and protracted negotiations between the forum administrators and the Chinese government, an agreement was struck (although its conditions were still never fully met by the Chinese). The meeting went on.

• • •

The UN Fourth World Conference on Women, unwelcome to its hosts, evoked mixed feelings in its sponsors. But the determination of those with the most at stake, the world's women, ensured that the conference indeed took place in Huairou and Beijing in September 1995. Women arrived in Huairou to be met by what the U.S. military might call a "kick-ass and take-names" attitude: delegates were menaced and harassed and never for a moment allowed to forget that the Chinese military was in charge. If the United Nations was marching along with Two Steps Forward,

Two Steps Back, the Chinese had decided to exercise Backlash with a vengeance.

The NGO Forum, scheduled to begin a week or so before the official conference, was held under nearly impossible conditions. After the March decision to move it from Beijing, some housing and meeting facilities had been hastily tacked together in Huairou, but the few dormitories and hotel rooms were nowhere near adequate for the 20,000 persons finally admitted by the Chinese, and toilet facilities were pushed beyond capacity. Electricity went off at 9:00 P.M. each evening in most of the buildings. Indoor meeting rooms were adequate, but most of the hundreds of sessions each day were held in open-sided tents at three different and far-flung sites on the forty-two acres.

Rain had greeted the first forum attendees and rain continued: routes between the muddy tent sites were paved with rough concrete squares that quickly crumbled into loose gravel from use. An early typhoon blew over tents and ruined supplies hauled by participants from around the globe. With a pause in the storms, women reset tents, slogged through the mud, and resumed.

For information, a delegate had to walk half a mile from the conference entrance to the "Global Pavilion," an ad hoc information center, which in a few days was all but taken over by African artisans selling their wares. Misprinted maps, misnamed buildings, even the vital Press and Electronic Information Center was misplaced—it was the farthest building from the entrance. The primitive communications within the forum meant that meetings were often canceled without notice. Volunteer Chinese guides knew little more than the delegates—and too often their only foreign language was English. Food service was difficult at the best of times and usually delayed in the rain. Delegates who did eat got cold, rain-soaked rice and vegetables three times a day. The Chinese tried but could not keep up with trash collection.

To add insult to injury, the Chinese had set up metal detectors and scanners, which delayed entry into the meeting places. Under strong pressure from the United Nations and from individual national delegations, those detectors and scanners were eventually turned off (just as eventually, taxis were permitted to make the trip between Beijing and Huairou), but military guards continued to stand by, an ever-present reminder that the Chinese authorities could force compliance whenever they wished. Chinese security intercepted, read, and censored incoming private e-mail to the forum members, and, we can infer, outgoing mail as well. At least one bus en route to Huairou during the first days of the forum was stopped by Chinese soldiers who demanded $25 from everybody aboard. The riders refused, and the bus took them back to Beijing. *Backlash* without apology.

• • •

Despite all the hardships, the spirit of the forum was steadily upbeat. If Mexico City had been giddy and hopeful, if Copenhagen had been disruptive and confrontational, if Nairobi had been notable for its local color (although women there had begun to get serious about their agenda), Beijing had a new feel. Call it maturity, focus, clarity of purpose. Veterans noted less hugging and kissing, more note taking, a new seriousness about how to implement the good ideas.

Women knew why they were in Huairou, and they went about it: teaching, learning, and sharing. They refused to be distracted by religious disputes, and they refused to permit the conference to be monopolized by debates about contraception and abortion. When a meeting was canceled, or a leader failed to show up, women spontaneously stood up and conducted the meeting themselves.

This do-it-yourself attitude was symbolic of the forum's mood. Whether new to the process or old-timers, whether young, in between, or old, women at the NGO Forum knew that no one would give them equality: they knew they would have to take it for themselves. Whether that taking would be painful or easy remained to be seen, but it would fall to women themselves, and they signaled that they were ready. In one way or another, every woman had seen it all before and knew she was there to work to make equality happen.

Western women had taken to heart one major lesson of Copenhagen, that they must listen more. In Nairobi they had tried. In Huairou and Beijing, nearly everybody listened. Nearly everybody learned. Typical was a delegation of women from a New York City Jewish women's group, exhilarated after their ten days of interaction with Palestinian and other Arab women. "Before," they said, "we just walked out on each other or yelled at each other."

Women who spoke at the sessions were experts. For some, their expertise was personal experience; for others, it was professional training. Neither was judged more valuable than the other. Each was understood to move things forward. Though sometimes women had to agree to disagree, by truly listening to each other—a sign between humans of respect among equals—in Huairou and Beijing women took the first steps toward a new way of living in the world, in what we have called in this book the scenario of A Golden Age of Equality. But it was clear that unless the world's men also joined women in listening to each other as respectful equals, these first steps at Huairou would in fact be toward the scenario Separate—and Doing Fine, Thanks!

Celebrated leaders spoke to the forum (with blunt, brave words that heartened the rain-soaked, hungry women), and Huairou was also a place of happy celebration. There were parties (much more modest, to be sure, than the parties that would characterize the official conference in Beijing), including a deeply moving celebration of Bella Abzug. (A few days earlier, she had been gratuitously sniped at by former President George Bush, himself in China at the same time, pocketing some millions as a spokesman for an organization financed by the Reverend Moon's religious cult.) Bella Abzug, who has become a worldwide icon for women, loves to tell of recently encountering a young Asian woman who told her brightly, "I'm known as the Bella Abzug of Inner Mongolia!"

But the forum's main purpose was not to hear celebrities talk, not to party. It even grew beyond its functions of think-tank and gadfly for the official conference. It became the school where ordinary women could share specific examples of action that had worked for them, actions that other ordinary women could adopt—the very practical techniques for claiming equality and justice.

Asian women workers reported, for example, on the special groups they had organized to make demands often overlooked by mainstream labor organizations, demands such as child care, maternity leave, flextime, and health and safety practices in high-tech industrial production. Women workers of Mexico talked about their efforts to increase production through the use of high technology without impacting negatively on women. Women of South America spelled out how they are fighting for parliamentary quotas for better women's representation in their governments.

The Working Women's Forum, a mass organization of 360,000 workers in southern India's informal economy, reported on how they had established grass-roots training, formed credit and savings banks, and distributed health information to their members, with the result that women are challenging local power structures and spearheading social action against wholesalers, exporters, middlemen, and landlords. African women reported their census of "femicide"—the killing of women specifically because they are women—and their protests against the lax justice systems that permit the killers to escape with impunity. Activist Islamic women (routinely described by the press as ultraconservative and shocked by Western women), focused in Huairou and

Beijing on teaching their sisters worldwide that although Islam has been used to justify the oppression of women, the reality of the Koran is basic equality and justice.

Were these steps toward a Golden Age of Equality? Or were they moving us into the scenario of Separate—and Doing Fine, Thanks? No one could be sure.

A frequent visitor to the Youth Tent, herself a middle-aged Western activist, expressed some doubts about the future. "I have the distinct impression that young people disdain the way we won what we have—what they have. They want to do it their way, as every generation must, and they want to do it one by one. But their problems, from work to home to relationships, are the same litany of problems women of my generation shared in consciousness-raising groups. Has it all changed less than we think?" In other words, Two Steps Forward, Two Steps Back?

What was crystal clear at Huairou, and later at the official conference in Beijing, was that the statistics collected by the United Nations since 1975 show that in most economic respects, things are getting worse, not better, for most women in the world. Should this trend continue into the future, we might think of it as a more subtle form of Backlash than the behavior of the Chinese militia, but Backlash all the same.

The UN Development Program administrator John Gustave Speth pointed out that "whenever women have made choices for themselves and for society, they have chosen peace over war and they have chosen development over deprivation." The unpaid work of women is not a marginal contribution, he continued. The value of women's unpaid work is estimated at $11 trillion—nearly half the global output, which is estimated at $23 trillion at present. But no accounting system records this, or gives women credit for it. Women do it on the second shift, often in addition to their other work: Two Steps Forward, Two Steps Back.

The forum's Electronic Information Center provided a particularly telling symbol of the several possible economic futures of women. Run by the Association for Progressive Communications, the center was staffed by women from twenty-five countries who spoke eighteen languages, from Arabic to Wolof. Upstairs were seventy-five Apple and Hewlett-Packard microcomputers: between September 1 and 7, 1995, they received or transmitted some 40,000 e-mail messages. Women thronged into this center, many of them encountering a computer for the first time, eager to learn how to get on-line. They also learned about scores of grass-roots electronic networks already up and in place all around the world, from Croatia to Colombia, from Sweden to Senegal. These were the beginnings of the nerve nets that would keep women in touch with each other as they seized their own futures. Separate—and Doing Fine, Thanks! They also learned that an unscrupulous government could interfere with electronic communication at least as easily as with any other kind: Backlash.

Downstairs, along one side of the room, were state-of-the-art computers and screens, all demonstrating programs that might be useful to small, activist networking organizations. An aisle bisected the room (not unlike the equator, thought a visitor), and across the aisle from the keyboards and laser printers were African women hawking their handmade artifacts. Was this mixture of high and low tech a sign of Two Steps Forward, Two Steps Back? Would African women ever be permitted to learn, to earn, to hold on to and inherit wealth (an important demand they raised at the conference) the same way their brothers do?

Step lively, and watch the closing doors! The distant chant of New York City subway conductors seemed to echo eerily around this room in China. The contrast between high technology and hand-carved artifacts said that if women didn't step lively and directly into the information age, the closing doors would leave them forever in Backlash. Mindful of the appalling literacy figures in developing countries, Western educational agencies were still talking in terms of slates and chalk, as if they were old-time Christian missionaries, collecting the clothes the rich wore last year for distribution to the heathen this year.

Microeconomics, a great sentimental favorite among international bankers and politicians just now, suggests that with a small amount of capital, women can succeed in their own businesses. Well, yes. But these are all old-fashioned businesses, these sandwich stands and brick-making shops. A woman from a developing country said angrily, "Why do they suggest I sew shirts? I can never make shirts as well or as cheap as the machines can, and I never will! I want a job for my future!" Shirt sewing, learning to be literate with a slate and chalk: better than nothing, surely. But for the electronic information future already here? Not much better than nothing. Backlash.

• • •

The official conference, which started in Beijing about a week after the Huairou forum had begun, seemed very distant from the lives of real women slogging it out in the mud and tents of Huairou—in the mud and tents of life. Well-behaved "suits" moved between glittering parties at Beijing's newest, shiniest joint-venture hotels. (Sadly typical of excesses that the system grants itself, the conference president Gertrude Mongella of Tanzania hosted—held court at—a Beijing reception of such garish splendor that the activist guests blushed with embarrassment. They couldn't help calculating how much of this precious money might have educated hundreds of Tanzanian girls.) The suits sat politely through listless opening ceremonies, through the droning speeches and elaborate platitudes that make international deliberative bodies so infamous.

But Prime Minister Benazir Bhutto of Pakistan brought things to life with a pointed, brave, and passionately delivered speech. Arresting in bright blue with a white head scarf that, significantly perhaps, kept slipping off her head, she spoke eloquently: "Muslim women have a special responsibility to help distinguish between Islamic teachings and social taboos spun by the traditions of a patriarchal society. This is a distinction that obscurantists would not like to see. For obscurantists believe in discrimination. Discrimination is the first step to dictatorship and the usurpation of power." We must remember, she went on, that Islam forbids injustice: against people, against nations, against women. It treats women as human beings in their own right, not as chattels. The Prophet himself married a working woman. And the first convert to Islam was a woman, Bibi Khadija.

"The cries of the girl child reach out to us to chart a course that can create a climate where the girl child is as welcomed and valued as a boy child, that the girl child is considered as worthy as a boy child." Bhutto went on to state that a woman cannot ultimately control her own life and make her own choices unless she has financial independence. A woman cannot have financial independence if she cannot work.

Bhutto spoke of the changes she had seen in her own life. Girls in her extended family had not been permitted to travel, marry outside the family (so wealth would remain concentrated), or be educated. She, however, had traveled, was educated, and married outside her family. She looked forward to seeing many more positive changes, flowing from the Universal Declaration of Human Rights. But women could not be expected to struggle alone against the forces of discrimination and exploitation. She quoted Dante: "The hottest place in Hell is reserved for those who remain neutral in times of moral crisis."

A few days later, President Alberto Fujimori of Peru made a surprise address to the conference. He began by admitting that in Peru, poverty has a female face, but he praised Peruvian women as agents of change, their central role fighting not only hyperinflation but physical terrorism. In 1994, Peru had the greatest economic growth in the world (13 percent), and he praised women as the true architects of the Peruvian economic miracle. It was time now, Fujimori said, to translate the economic miracle into a social miracle. This would be accomplished first by progressively allocating resources to women so that they would receive 50 percent of social expenditures of the national budget by the year 2000, and second by carrying out a program of family planning. He understood he was in conflict with the Catholic Church here, but he noted that "an open debate cannot be interpreted as a declaration of war." Rather than calling for "the power of darkness," as the church had characterized this initiative, he believed that the "torches of hope" were being lit. He outlined Peru's plans and invited other governments in South America to join Peru in a coalition to break the church's hold over South American population planning.

Women accustomed to complicity between church and state in most of Latin America, people everywhere who identified theocracies as the enemies of justice for women, were heartened by Benazir Bhutto, by Alberto Fujimori. A prime minister who has been under constant threat, even jailed by the enemies of women, and who still speaks out defiantly; a national president who has successfully faced down the terrorists of the Shining Path—these are significant allies. Did they, along with John Gustave Speth, signal the beginning of a Golden Age of Equality?

. . .

Yet an observer at the Beijing conference was also struck by how much of the official conference was redolent of the same old thing. Official delegates showed in their careful dress—tailored suits, not the panoply of costumes in Huairou—that they were insiders; they had won their place by living a double life: they were a handful of women who behaved no differently from the men who'd permitted them inside.

That handful often made good speeches, but would they have the courage to follow where the logic of their arguments led? Especially if it meant risking their power? These women held a few prominent positions. Could that small number make a difference? Or would things stagnate for another twenty years? Two Steps Forward, Two Steps Back?

Bella Abzug, the ebullient spiritual leader of the NGO Forum, cautioned the NGO women, who were deeply skeptical of the insiders. "We can't do this without each other, the downtown suits and the NGOs. The importance of that mutual respect has to be kept alive." She was really saying that there could be no separation between government and grass roots if we were to move on to the new paradigm, the Golden Age of Equality.

• • •

Eventually, a good draft platform of action emerged from Beijing. The bracketed clauses—the so-called holy brackets around statements that offended religious reactionaries—remained in the document, which suggests that in the terms of our scenarios, individual rights prevailed over the rights of the group. (With a duplicity that was, at the time, more comical than outrageous, representatives of the Vatican and Islamic reactionaries declared victory and decamped. Surely there were gullible reporters who believed them. Word on the street was that this pullback was a tactical response to a lustily growing movement to strip the Vatican of its official UN status, a status no other religious group enjoys.)

But the draft platform document wasn't the meeting's only achievement, nor even perhaps its best one. The Beijing meeting, in both of its aspects, forum and conference, was about feminism finding a second wind. Feminism once belonged almost exclusively to Western women, but women around the world have now seized it and made it their own. As a result, feminism is poised to become an international movement of stature and strength that can press the United Nations (and other international bodies, such as the World Bank) to push national governments to treat women justly.

In Beijing, women worldwide declared a common agenda and a deep resolve to achieve it. The issues on that agenda vary in priority by region, but every list called for personal sexual autonomy, education, health, equal opportunity in the workplace, power sharing in all decisions, and an end to all kinds of violence. Let's analyze these issues as they emerged at Beijing to see how they might play out in our four scenarios. Unsurprisingly, most of the issues are intimately connected with each other.

PERSONAL SEXUAL AUTONOMY

Women in Beijing said it plainly: religion is often a rationalization for oppressing them. They now call that oppression by its real name and will not give up either their civil and professional ambitions or their own faith and interior spiritual life to accommodate reactionaries. Despite their high confidence and strong efforts, religious reactionaries failed in Beijing to rescind language adopted (by the UN General Assembly) from previous conferences. Successfully preventing such unprecedented recisions was crucial to demonstrating the power women now have in the international arena. The Beijing conference moved beyond previous conferences and added women's right to say no to sex.

The separation of church and state was an explicit priority for women at Beijing, and—touching here on politics—support is solid for politicians ready to take this public. When Pakistan's Benazir Bhutto, and Peru's Alberto Fujimori traveled to the conference to make strong public statements against clerical interference, it was not only a historic first; it was also a sign that these two politicians have their constituents' backing. If the movement to separate church and state, declared at Beijing, is implemented, it could point to either a Golden Age of Equality or a Separate—and Doing Fine, Thanks! scenario, depending on other global and local circumstances. If, however, women are unsuccessful in forcing that separation, look out for Backlash.

VIOLENCE

Worldwide, violence against women is now acknowledged as a violation of human rights—at least by most women. Outing this violence has generated an emotional commitment to eradicate it. The singular momentum of this issue broadens the perspective and understanding of what inequality means daily for women and will doubtless broaden the definition of violence. Though a positive outcome to this issue would send us toward a Golden Age, we could just as well be pushed back into Backlash as men reclaim their ancient "cultural and religious rights" to violence.

EDUCATION

The Beijing conference vowed to eradicate illiteracy among the world's women and to ensure the completion of primary education by at least 80 percent of all children, with special emphasis on girls, by the year 2000. The women pledged to create an educational system that ensures equal education and training opportunities and to develop curricula, textbooks, and teaching aids free from sexual stereotypes for all levels of education. Until Beijing, the focus on female education had been mainly on older girls and women—catching up on basic skills or job training. There was reason for pride: the numbers of girls and women in school since the 1970s have increased at all levels. But that rate of increase is slow.

Thanks to the urging of certain African preparatory meetings, Beijing made the girl child a priority in education. As with violence against women, the girl child's plight became in Beijing not just an intellectual but an emotional awakening to what inequality means to girls for the rest of their lives. Thus basic education was declared a human right (or redeclared: the Universal Declaration of Human Rights signed some fifty years ago already says this). Every girl, every woman, is entitled to a basic education by virtue of being human. Pledges to the girl child were pledges to the reality of the future of women.

However, the Beijing declaration on education was short on detail, partly because much education has become hostage to local curriculum disputes. The dilemmas and tensions of religious, cultural, and social norms thrash through the international debate as surely as they thrash through debate at the local school board. Thus pledges toward education point at best to Two Steps Forward, Two Steps Back, at worst to Backlash, since the assumptions they are based on are mired in old-fashioned technology, with no understanding that computing is not just a faster way of doing the same old thing, not just vocational training for data entry and word-processing, but is a whole new thing itself, which brings with it new ways of thinking and approaching intellectual tasks. Women relegated to slate and chalk will be sentenced to another century of slavery.

HEALTH

The Draft Platform for Action proposed to provide women with access to affordable, high-quality primary health care; to eliminate coercive medical interventions and inform women of their options in medical treatment; to close the gender gap in morbidity and mortality and reduce infant and child mortality; and to enact legislation and eliminate environmental and occupational health hazards.

Statistics suggest that over the past twenty years, women's health situations have improved slightly. In Beijing, however, health issues were still captive to reproductive rights. This stands to reason, since in the developing world between one third and one half of women's morbidity and mortality is directly tied to pregnancy and childbirth. Eliminating unwanted pregnancies would improve women's health dramatically, and women in Beijing recognized this. The language of the Cairo declaration was not only upheld, but expanded: the new Beijing document is the first international paper to assert a woman's right to make sexual decisions free of coercion or violence—the right to say no to sex. Since the actual implementation of these tenets will be a nation-by-nation (not to say household-by-household) battle, this amounts at the moment to a mighty Two Steps Forward. We hope the Two Steps Back aren't inevitable.

EQUALITY IN THE WORKPLACE

A growing body of evidence from the World Bank and other international monetary institutions demonstrates that inequality for women is bad for economic development generally. In a world where there is increased attention given to economic priorities, this could be a new tool for organizing. International monetary institutions are studying the issue to design corrective programs in client nations. However, it would be sad indeed if, having finally recognized the importance of women's contributions to the economy, international agencies now get carried away by a love affair with microeconomics. Recall the developing world woman who protested the suggestion that she sew shirts: she's right. Women need jobs for the twenty-first century, not the nineteenth.

Certainly this economic attention is just in time, because unlike the statistics in health and education, which show modest improvement in women's lot, those for economic conditions indicate that conditions are growing worse for most of the world's women. Despite substantial growth in the world economy, fully 70 percent of the world's poor are women. If change is to occur, women believe they will have to do it for themselves and do it together.

The mood at Beijing seemed to say that women are prepared for this, and that they take strength from each other and from past progress. Women are not waiting for experts to find solutions to problems. Their confidence in themselves and the work they are doing is palpable. When outside counsel is sought, women look first to other women. Women at Beijing made it clear that they understand that no one will give them anything. They will have to battle for every step forward. Despite the talk about equality and the breakthroughs of individuals, equality for women is seldom achieved and always hard won.

Women's individual efforts and victories, no matter how impressive, have not and will not bring about systemic equality. The world's women are presently caught in the Two Steps Forward, Two Steps Back scenario. Without dramatic changes, including women's mutual support of each other, the "critical mass" necessary to implement full equality cannot be achieved. This is a particularly important message for do-it-yourself American women who are moving toward Separate—and Doing Fine, Thanks!

POWER SHARING IN ALL DECISIONS

One goal of the Beijing document is to include large numbers of women in all international peace negotiations. "We will be equal partners here," said women from former Yugoslavia who were at Beijing. At first this sounds like a utopian fantasy. But women and children are 80 percent of all war victims, and they are weary of men making war—pouring a nation's entire resources into war—and then making unjust peace afterward. If this representation in peace negotiations can only be achieved by quotas, then the world's women welcome quotas.

Experience demonstrates that established quotas, relentlessly enforced, are the best, perhaps the only, way to make substantial progress toward achieving women's proportional representation on peace negotiation teams, in electoral politics, or, for that matter, in the corporate board-room. Nordic nations have led in this, and other EC women admire their success. Developing nations are also adopting that method for making a breakthrough (for example, India ruled in 1994 that one third of all seats at the state level must be held by women).

Minimum quotas for women are endorsed by some powerful

men in the UN bureaucracy, such as the Development Program administrator Speth, who has a big purse to back him. Leaders like Speth have vowed to use their power to establish and enforce specific quotas for women, and they are not put off by the domestic debate in the United States on the issue of quotas. In many places, such as the United States, quotas are at present considered anathema and will not be supported: Two Steps Forward, Two Steps Back.

· · ·

Other political trends (another axis upon which we build our scenarios) apparent in Beijing deserve some general comment. The Beijing meeting embodied the reality that the cold war has ended and, along with it, the old balance of power politics. But the new pattern has yet to emerge. While, on the one hand, citizens spurn the vote, since they have lost faith that the old system will respond democratically; on the other hand, citizens clamor to participate in public political discourse through call-in shows and grass-roots activism. These new forms of democratic expression are only embryonic.

One such symbol of the embryonic form of citizen participation is the proliferation of NGOs. They are forcing their opinions and presence into formal meetings despite opposition by some national and UN representatives. Having learned UN rules and procedures, NGOs are demanding accountability and "transparency" (openness) in deliberations and decisions. With some strong official support from other national leaders, they are making their influence felt. One reason for this is that it is safer to challenge the international body than to raise awkward questions at home—where you might be jailed or shot.

But NGOs themselves have a problem. Danielle Bridel, a former head of Swiss Social Security and now chair of the NGO-Economic Commission for Europe's Working Group on Women in Geneva, says that just after the Beijing Conference she called all NGO representatives in Geneva to announce a briefing on events at Beijing. Interpreters were hired, a room rented. Many women attended the briefing from dozens of organizations. Exactly three men showed up. The fact is, even NGOs ghettoize "women's issues"—see them as a special (and, the implication is, less important) case of human rights, or poverty, or censorship, and unrelated to their mission or agenda, even though women make up the vast majority of the poor, the politically disenfranchised, and the culturally disinherited worldwide.

The significance of the NGO phenomenon may be that it offers a new model for democracy. Citizen access to international agencies and governing bodies makes citizens less willing to tolerate being shut out of their own national governments: a Golden Age of Equality. But—as has happened with some national governments, among them the United States, NGOs may also end up as just another bunch of hard-knuckled lobbyists and special interest groups. The sad history of environmental groups is cautionary here. We need to avoid taking Two Steps Forward, Two Steps Back.

If democratic forms of expression are in transition, so are the outlines of the nation-state. As historian Harlan Cleveland puts it, the nation-state is leaking upward to globalism and downward to tribalism but it is leaking—it isn't finished.

Into all this must be factored women's quiet resolve to keep going all the way to equality. They are not willing to stop part way. Is that trajectory toward a Golden Age of Equality or Separate—and Doing Fine, Thanks?

• • •

Other developments that emerged at Beijing are worth bearing in mind. Women's common resolve transcends, but does not eliminate, regional ethnic and interest caucuses. Women have confidence in networking. Despite differences, mutual trust and reliance is growing. Women understand that liking each other is less important than helping each other. Debates among women were respectful and geared toward mutual resolution.

An impressive group of women has assumed powerful positions within national and international organizations and governments. These women know and respect each other and, again, agree on their common agenda. They have worked together in the past and are committed to supporting each other in the future. Whether they can in fact model a new paradigm of cooperative work remains to be seen. They leave the conference with new organizations and networks to carry out this commitment, from the world's widows (usually the poorest of the poor) to the women parliamentarians' caucus.

A cooperative, though sometimes strained, relationship exists between generations of women. Part of the strain comes from two views of how to accomplish things. Veterans who have participated in other UN conferences believe that the go-it-alone method doesn't work. A new generation of women in their thirties, educated and experienced, good at what they do, are not yet convinced that go-it-alone doesn't work. Or perhaps they think it will work for them.

More than anything, the Beijing meeting epitomized "the time between." That the world is moving into something new seemed palpable under the sodden tents of Huairou and along the wide avenues of Beijing. Whether that transition will be slow or fast, good for the world's women or not so good, remains to be seen.

We feel confident that the Official Future, whether men's— or that sub-Official Future women secretly harbor—will not take place. We are less sanguine about predicting which of our scenarios might transpire. More realistically, certain parts of each scenario will probably occur.

Backlash? We hope not, but the evidence of history weighs heavily in its favor. Two Steps Forward, Two Steps Back? If it's only good for some of us some of the time, it's not so good after all. A Golden Age of Equality? Eminently worth working for, but willing it can't make it happen, and it won't be handed to any of us, men or women. Separate—and Doing Fine, Thanks? In our view, it's an unsatisfactory substitute for a Golden Age of Equality, but some women may feel that there's no better choice.

This entire book has been an invitation to choose and then move ahead. Let's talk it over.

BIBLIOGRAPHY

Abu-Lughod, Lila. *Writing Women's Worlds: Bedouin Stories*. Berkeley: University of California Press, 1993.

Aburdene, Patricia, and John Naisbitt. *Megatrends for Women*. New York: Villard Books, 1992.

Advancing Gender Equality: From Concept to Action. Washington, D.C.: International Bank for Reconstruction and Development/World Bank, August 1995.

Ahmed, Leila. *Women and Gender in Islam: Historical Roots of a Modern Debate*. New Haven: Yale University Press, 1992.

"A Look at U.S. Military Spending: More Than You Thought." *Timeline*, September–October 1994.

Ambah, Faiza S. "Saudi Girls Show Pen Is Mightier Than Their Lords." *Christian Science Monitor*, March 24, 1995.

Anderson, Sherry Ruth, and Patricia Hopkins. *The Feminine Face of God: The Unfolding of the Sacred in Women*. New York: Bantam Books, 1991.

Andrews, John. "Culture Wars." *Wired*, May 1995.

Angier, Natalie. "Males Called Weak Link of Species." *New York Times*, May 16, 1994.

Arthur, W. Brian. "Complexity in Economic and Financial Markets." *Complexity* 1, no. 1 (1995).

Ashley, Beth. "Women Are Still in Chains in Russia." *Marin Independent Journal*, January 27, 1994.

"Asian Finance: The Next Revolution." *Economist*, November 12, 1994.

Atkinson, Rick. "German Unification Lays Heavy Burden on Eastern Working Women." *Washington Post*, March 29, 1995.

————. "Illegal, But Not Punishable: Germany's Abortion Compromise Has All Sides Angry and Confused." *Washington Post*, August 21, 1995.

Bardash, Ann Louise. "Tearing Off the Veil." *Vanity Fair*, August 1993.

Barkhausen, Silvia, and Rita Niemann-Geiger. *Keine Angst vor dünner Luft: Chancen für Frauen in Politik, Wirtschaft, Wissenschaft, Medien.* Frankfurt/Main: Campus Verlag, 1994.

Basler, Barbara. "In Hong Kong, Fight to Inherit Land." *New York Times*, November 14, 1993.

Beaulieu, Carol. *Feminism Comes to Vietnam: Are Vietnamese Women Losing to Market Reforms?* Hanover, N.H.: Institute of Current World Affairs, CB-22, 1994.

Bergmann, Barbara R., and Heidi Hartmann. "A Program to Help Working Parents." *Nation*, May 1, 1995.

Bhutto, Benazir Mohtarma, "Address to the Fourth World Conference on Women." Beijing, September 4, 1995.

Bipartisan Commission on Entitlement and Tax Reform: Final Report to the President. Washington, D.C., Superintendent of Documents, January 1995.

Bolen, Jean Shinoda. *Crossing to Avalon.* San Francisco: Harper, 1994.

Brook, James. "Women in Colombia Move to Job Forefront." *New York Times*, July 15, 1994.

Brooks, Geraldine. "Teen-Age Infidels Hanging Out." *New York Times Magazine*, April 30, 1995.

Brown, David. "World Bank to Emphasize AIDS as Economic Threat." *Washington Post*, November 24, 1994.

Bucharest Statement on Change: Systems and People. New York: United Nations Development Program, 1992.

Burgos-Debray, Elizabeth (ed). *I, Rigoberta Menchú: An Indian Woman in Guatemala.* New York: Verso, 1984.

Burtless, Gary, and Timothy Smeeding. "America's Tide: Lifting the Yachts, Swamping the Rowboats." *Washington Post,* June 25, 1995.

Calafia, Pat. *Public Sex: The Culture of Radical Sex.* Pittsburgh: Cleis Press, 1994.

Carrington, Tom. "Gender Economics: In Developing World, International Lenders Are Targeting Women." *Wall Street Journal,* June 22, 1994.

Chang, Jung. *Wild Swans: Three Daughters of China.* New York: Anchor Books, Doubleday, 1991.

The Changing Nature of Telecommunications/Information Infrastructure. Computer Science and Telecommunications Board, National Research Council. Washington, D.C.: National Academy Press, 1995.

Changing Population Age Structures, 1990–2015: Demographic and Economic Consequences and Implications. Geneva: United Nations Economic Commission for Europe and the United Nations Population Fund, 1992.

"China in 1993: One More Year of Political Repression." *Asia Watch* 5, no. 20 (November 1993).

Clash of Civilizations: The Debate. A Foreign Affairs Reader. New York: Foreign Affairs, 1993.

Cleveland, Harlan. *Birth of a New World.* San Francisco: Jossey-Bass Publications, 1993.

———, ed. *New Strategies for a Restless World: Refugees in the 1990s.* Minneapolis: American Refugee Committee, 1993.

Cohen, Eliot A., and John Gooch. *Military Misfortunes.* New York: The Free Press, 1990.

Cohen, Richard. "Ethnic and Religious Conflicts Now Threaten Europe's Stability." *Washington Post,* November 26, 1994.

Colomina, Beatriz. *Sexuality & Space.* Princeton Papers on Architecture, vol. 1. New York: Princeton Architectural Press, 1992.

Coontz, Stephanie. *The Way We Never Were: American Families and the Nostalgia Trap.* New York: Basic Books, 1992.

Coupland, Douglas. *Generation X.* New York: St. Martin's Press, 1991.

Cowell, Alan. "Vatican Fights Plan to Bolster Role of Women." *New York Times,* June 15, 1994.

Creating Community: What Is It and How Do We Do It? Center for the Study of Community. Proceedings of a meeting at Sol y Sombra, Santa Fe, N.M., October 15–16, 1993.

Crispell, Diane. *The Insider's Guide to Demographic Know-How.* 3d ed. Ithaca, N.Y.: American Demographic Books, 1993.

Critchfield, Richard. *The Villagers.* New York: Anchor, 1994.

Crossette, Barbara. "A Woman Leader for a Land That Defies Islamic Stereotypes." *New York Times,* October 17, 1993.

———. "UN Study Finds a Free Eastern Europe Poorer and Less Healthy." *New York Times,* October 7, 1994.

———. "Worldwide Study Finds Decline in Election of Women to Offices." *New York Times,* August 27, 1995.

Dasgupta, Partha S. "Population, Poverty and the Local Environment." *Scientific American,* February 1995.

Day, Kathleen. "Laboring Toward Lilliput." *Washington Post,* June 22, 1991.

Decade of the Executive Woman. A Joint Study by Korn/Ferry International and UCLA Anderson Graduate School of Management. New York: Korn/Ferry International, 1993.

Dee, Catherine, ed. *50/50 by 2000: The Woman's Guide to Political Power.* Berkeley: EarthWorks Press, 1993.

Der Derian, James. "Cyber-Deterrence." *Wired,* September 1994.

deRosario, Louise. "Women in a Double Bind." *Far East Economic Review,* September 24, 1992.

deStoop, Chris. *Ze zijn zo lief, meneer: Over Vrouwenhandelaars, Meisjesballetten en de Bende van de Miljardair.* Leuven: Uitgverij Kritak, 1992.

de Waal, Frans B. M. "Bonobo Sex and Society." *Scientific American,* March 1995.

de Witt, Karen. "Job Bias Cited for Minorities and Women: The 'Glass Ceiling' Is Real, Panel Says." *New York Times,* November 23, 1995.

Doi, Ayako. "The Other Poison in Japan's Air." *Washington Post,* March 26, 1995.

Dowd, Maureen. "Playing 'Good Ol' Girl' Card Against Son of Ex-President." *New York Times,* November 2, 1994.

Drake, Joan Walters. *The Status of Women in the United States*, vol. 2. New York: Facts on File, 1992.

Drucker, Peter. *Post-Capitalist Society*. New York: Harper Business Books, 1993.

———. "The Age of Social Transformation." *Atlantic Monthly*, November 1994.

Eberstadt, Nicholas. "Marx and Mortality: A Mystery." *New York Times*, April 6, 1994.

Edsall, Thomas. "Masculinity on the Run." *Washington Post*, April 30, 1995.

"Energy in India: Decision Time." *Economist*, May 27, 1995.

Faison, Seth. "Women's Meeting Agrees on Right to Say No to Sex." *New York Times*, September 11, 1995.

Faludi, Susan. *Backlash*. New York: Anchor Books, Doubleday, 1991.

"Fast Tracks and the Risk of Running into Sidings." *Financial Times*, August 7, 1991.

Flaake, Karin, and Vera King, eds. *Weibliche Adoleszenz: Zur Sozialisation junger Frauen*. Frankfurt/Main: Campus Verlag, 1993.

Fleischman, Janet. "Zimbabwe's Disinherited Women and Children Rebel at Tradition." *Washington Post*, March 29, 1995.

Flower, Joe. "The Other Revolution in Health Care." *Wired*, January 1994.

Frank, Irene, and David Brownstone. *The Women's Desk Reference*. New York: Viking Press, 1993.

Fraser, Jill Andresky. "Desperately Seeking Capital." *Working Woman*, July 1993.

French, Howard W. "African Democracies Worry Aid Will Dry Up." *New York Times*, April 2, 1995.

Friedman, Thomas. "Havel's Paradoxical Plea: Help Soviets." *New York Times*, January 22, 1990.

Frymer-Kensky, Tikva. *In the Wake of the Goddesses: Women, Culture and the Biblical Transformation of a Pagan Myth*. New York: Fawcett-Columbine, 1992.

Fujimori, Alberto. "Speech Before the IV World Conference on Women," September 15, 1995. Translation from Spanish provided by Peruvian Embassy, Washington, D.C.

"The Future (Through the Glass Lightly)." *Science*, March 17, 1995.

"The Gene Exchange." Washington, D.C.: Union of Concerned Scientists, February 1994.

Geppert, Linda. "The Uphill Struggle: No Rose Garden for Women in Engineering." Institute of Electrical and Electronics Engineers, *IEEE Spectrum*, May 1995.

Global Campaign for Women's Human Rights: Making Women's Voices Heard. An Analysis of U.S. News Coverage of Women's Human Rights Issues. Washington, D.C.: The Communications Consortium, July 1993.

Greenwald, Jeff. "Wiring Africa." *Wired*, June 1994.

"Growth in the South: Latin America Takes Off." *NPQ* 10, no. 4 (1994).

"Half-empty or Half-full? A Survey of Brazil." *Economist*, April 29, 1995.

Hampden-Turner, Charles, and Alfons Trompenaars. *The Seven Cultures of Capitalism*. New York: Currency/Doubleday, 1993.

Haraway, Donna J. *Simians, Cyborgs, and Women: The Reinvention of Nature*. New York: Routledge, 1991.

Harding, Sandra. *Whose Science? Whose Knowledge?* Ithaca, N.Y.: Cornell University Press, 1991.

Heinzen, Barbara. "Flirting with Cassandra: Business Challenges of HIV/AIDS in Asia." Paper presented at the British Pacific Rim Seminar Series, Liverpool, England, May 26–28, 1993.

Helgesen, Sally. *The Female Advantage: Women's Ways of Leadership*. New York: Doubleday, 1990.

Hochschild, Arlie. *The Second Shift*. New York: Avon Books, 1989.

Hockstader, Lee. "Crime Atop Chaos." *Washington Post National Weekly Edition*, March 20–26, 1995.

Hoffman, Eva. *Exit into History: A Journey Through the New Eastern Europe*. New York: Penguin Books, 1994.

Holmes, Stephen. "In Fighting Racism, Is Sexism Ignored?" *New York Times*, September 11, 1994.

hooks, bell. *Ain't I a Woman? Black Women and Feminism*. Boston: South End Press, 1981.

————. *Black Looks: Race and Representation*. Boston: South End Press, 1992.

Horan, Deborah. "Palestine at the Crossroads: When Worlds Collide, Will Women Lose?" *On the Issues*, Summer 1995.

Howard, Robert. "Values Make the Company: An Interview with Robert Haas." *Harvard Business Review*, September–October 1990.

"How Does Your Economy Grow? Economists Know Surprisingly Little about the Causes of Economic Growth." *Economist*, September 30, 1995.

Huffaker, Julie S. "Village Banking Puts Trust in the Poor." *San Francisco Examiner*, July 10, 1994.

Human Development Report 1993. New York: Oxford University Press (for the United Nations Development Programme), 1993.

Human Development Report 1994. New York: Oxford University Press (for the United Nations Development Programme), 1994.

Human Rights for the Twenty-First Century: Perspectives from the Global South. Conference Proceedings, Center for the Study of the Global South, School of International Service, American University, Washington, D.C., April 1993.

"Human Rights in the APEC Region." *Asia Watch* 5, no. 19 (November 1993).

Ingrassia, Lawrence. "Sex and Power in the Office." *Wall Street Journal*, October 18, 1991.

International Business Woman. Premier Issue. Clearwater, Fla., 1994.

Investing for Social Gain. New York: Ford Foundation, 1993.

Iwata, Edward. "A Mother's Crusade Brings Her Employer Around to Day Care." *Washington Post*, November 27, 1994.

Jacobs, Deborah L. "Back from the Mommy Track." *New York Times*, October 9, 1994.

"Japan's Missing Children." *Economist*, November 12, 1994.

Johnson, Dirk. "White Communities: A Corporate Deterrent." *New York Times*, April 18, 1994.

Johnstone, Bob. "Wiring Japan." *Wired*, February 1994.

Kaminer, Wendy. "Feminism's Identity Crisis." *Atlantic Monthly*, October 1993.

Kaplan, Robert D. "The Coming Anarchy." *Atlantic Monthly*, February 1994.

Kapor, Mitchell. "Where Is the Digital Highway Really Heading?" *Wired*, July–August 1993.

Kauffman, Stuart. *At Home in the Universe*. New York: Oxford University Press, 1995.

Keller, Evelyn Fox. *Secrets of Life, Secrets of Death: Essays on Language, Gender and Science*. New York: Routledge, 1992.

Kelly, Kevin. *Out of Control*. Reading, Mass.: Addison-Wesley, 1994.

Kelly, Kevin, and Steven Levy. "An Interview with Alan Kay and Danny Hillis." *Wired*, January 1994.

Kennedy, Paul. *Preparing for the Twenty-First Century*. New York: Random House, 1993.

Kert, Bernice, and Abby Aldrich Rockefeller. *The Woman in the Family*. New York: Random House, 1993.

Kirdar, Uner, ed. *Change: Threat or Opportunity?* Vols. 1–4. New York: United Nations Press, 1992.

Kissling, Frances, and Denise Shannon. "A Nation Unto Himself." *New York Times*, September 30, 1995.

Kleiman, Carol. "Women Managers: A Foreign Notion?" *Chicago Tribune*, February 10, 1994.

Krebs, Nina Boyd. *Changing Woman, Changing Work*. Aspen, Colo.: MacMurray and Beck, 1993.

Kyte, Rachel. *Beyond Cairo*. Bolinas, Calif.: Common Knowledge Press, 1994.

Lafayette, Leslie. "Fair Play for the Childless Worker." *New York Times*, October 16, 1994.

Laland, Kevin N., Jochen Kumm, and Marcus W. Feldman. "Gene-Culture Co-evolutionary Theory: A Test Case." *Current Anthropology*, February 1995.

Lancaster, John, and Boyce Rensberger. "Cairo Delegates Come to Terms." *Washington Post*, September 12, 1994.

Laqueur, Thomas. *Making Sex: Body and Gender from the Greeks to Freud*. Cambridge, Mass.: Harvard University Press, 1990.

Lefkoff, Merle. "What Is Conflict Resolution?" *The Sante Fe New Mexican*, May 14, 1995.

Leo, John. "When Subtle Sexism Is a Con." *U.S. News and World Report*, February 7, 1994.

Levy, Steven. "E-Money (That's What I Want)." *Wired*, December 1994.

Lewin, Tamar. "Traditional Family Favored by Boys, Not Girls, Poll Says." *New York Times*, July 11, 1994.

———. "Men Whose Wives Work Earn Less, Studies Show." *New York Times*, October 12, 1994.

———. "Working Women Say Bias Persists." *New York Times*, October 15, 1994.

———. "The Decay of Families Is Global, Study Says." *New York Times*, May 30, 1995.

Lewis, Paul. "An Eclipse for the Group of Seven." *New York Times*, May 1, 1995.

McClintock, Anne, ed. *Social Text 37: The Sex Trade*. Durham, N.C.: Duke University Press, 1993.

McLeod, Ramon G. "Human Migration Enters New Era." *San Francisco Chronicle*, August 9, 1994.

Magnusson, Paul. "Social Security: Apocalypse Soon—Or Sooner." *Business Week*, May 1, 1995.

Malveaux, Julianne. "Diversity vs. Downsizing." *San Francisco Examiner*, January 2, 1994.

Margolick, David. "Conversations, Roberta Cooper Ramo." *New York Times*, February 6, 1994.

Markoff, John. "Reprogramming the Hacker Elite." *New York Times*, January 2, 1994.

Maslin, Janet. "Sex and Terror: The Male View of the She Boss." *New York Times*, January 14, 1994.

Mathews, Jay. "Survey Finds Gender Gap in Entrepreneurial Paths." *Washington Post*, July 19, 1994.

"Measuring Crime: A Shadow on Society." *Economist*, October 15, 1994.

Mernissi, Fatima. *Beyond the Veil: Male-Female Dynamics in Modern Muslim Society*. Bloomington: University of Indiana Press, 1987.

———. *Islam and Democracy: Fear of the Modern World*. Trans. Mary Jo Lakeland. Reading, Mass.: Addison-Wesley, 1992.

———. *Dreams of Trespass: Tales of a Harem Girlhood*. Reading, Mass.: Addison-Wesley, 1994.

Minai, Naila. *Women in Islam: Tradition and Transition in the Middle East*. London: John Murray, 1981.

Mincer, Jillian. "Boys Get Called On." *New York Times*, January 8, 1994.

Montalbano, William D. "Italy's Lack of Bambini." *San Francisco Chronicle*, July 10, 1994.

Moore, Molly. "Paths to Power for Asian, Latin Women." *Washington Post*, November 13, 1991.

———. "Consumerism Fuels Dowry-Death Wave." *Washington Post*, March 17, 1995.

Morgan, Robin, ed. *Sisterhood Is Global: The International Women's Movement Anthology*. New York: Anchor Books, Doubleday, 1984.

Morin, Richard, and Barbara Vobejda. "94 May Be the Year of the Man: GOP Is Powered by Male Support." *Washington Post*, November 10, 1994.

Morrow, Lance. "Men, Are They Really That Bad?" *Time*, February 14, 1994.

"Name Calling and Its Perils." *Economist*, May 6, 1995.

Nasar, Sylvia. "Statistics Reveal Bulk of New Jobs Pay over Average." *New York Times*, October 17, 1994.

———. "Older Americans Cited in Studies of National Savings Rate Slump." *New York Times*, February 21, 1995.

Nelson, Barbara J., and Najma Chowdhury. *Women and Politics Worldwide*. New Haven, Conn.: Yale University Press, 1994.

Nelson, Sharon. "Negotiating: The Womanly Art of the Deal." *Nation's Business*, January 1993.

"New Faces of America: How Immigrants Are Shaping the World's First Multicultural Society." Special Issue. *Time*, Fall 1993.

Nguyen, Minh Chau. "Gender Dimensions of Development." Paper Representing World Bank, Global South Meeting, Washington, D.C., April 1995.

Noble, Barbara Presley. "A Few Thousand Women, Networking." *New York Times*, March 27, 1994.

———. "She Always Said Feminism and Economics Can Mix." *New York Times*, July 10, 1994.

———. "Now He's Stressed, She's Stressed." *New York Times*, October 9, 1994.

Noble, David F. *A World Without Women: The Christian Clerical Culture of Western Science*. New York: Oxford University Press, 1992.

Noddings, Nel. *Women and Evil*. Berkeley: University of California Press, 1989.

Nollinger, Mark. "Surrender or We'll Slime You." *Wired*, February 1995.

"Nordic Countries: Heading South." *Economist*, November 5, 1994.

Ostrom, Elinor. *Governing the Commons: The Evolution of Institutions for Collective Action*. Cambridge, England: Cambridge University Press, 1991.

Pacific Economic Outlook, 1993–1994. San Francisco: U.S. National Committee for Pacific Economic Cooperation, 1993.

Pacific Economic Outlook, 1994–1995. San Francisco: U.S. National Committee for Pacific Economic Cooperation, 1994.

Perelman, Lewis J. "School's Out: Public Education Obstructs the Future." *Wired*, 1993.

Perlez, Jane. "A Painful Case Tests Poland's Abortion Ban." *New York Times*, April 2, 1995.

Plevin, Nancy. "Hope amid Hate." Series of eight articles on women in former Yugoslavia. *Santa Fe New Mexican*, May 14, 15, 16, 1995.

Population and Economic Growth: Perspectives from the Global South. Conference Proceedings and Recommendations, Center for the Study of the Global South, School of International Service, American University, Washington, D.C., March 1994.

Population and Quality of Life Independent Commission Newsletter [Paris] 3 (April–June 1994).

Putnam, Robert D. *Making Democracy Work: Civic Traditions in Modern Italy*. Princeton, N.J.: Princeton University Press, 1993.

Putting Gender on the Agenda: A Guide to Participating in UN World Conferences. New York: United Nations Development Fund for Women and United Nations Non-Governmental Liaison Service, 1995.

Rajavi, Maryam. Statement to the Beijing Conference, September 7, 1995. *World Wide Web*. http://www.igc.apc.org/womensnet/beijing/

Reid, T. R. "North Korean Silent at Rite for Father." *Washington Post*, July 21, 1995.

Report of the Commission on the Status of Women on its Thirty-Seventh Session. Vienna, March 17–26, 1993. New York: United Nations Economic and Social Council, 1993.

Report of Women Thinking Globally, Acting Locally: On the Road to Beijing and the 21st Century. Official U.S. Preparatory Meeting for the UN Fourth World Conference, April 22, 1994. Convened by Women's Bureau, U.S. Department of Labor, Region II; U.S. Department of State; New York and New Jersey Federal Executive Boards; Center for the Study of Women and Society, the Graduate School and University Center, City University of New York.

Rheingold, Howard. "PARC Is Back!" *Wired*, February 1994.

Rifkin, Glenn. "Mix and Match: A Shoe for Women, a Survivor's Tale." *New York Times*, July 3, 1991.

Roberts, Sam. "Hispanic Population Outnumbers Blacks in Four Major Cities as Demographics Shift." *New York Times*, October 9, 1994.

———. "Women's Work: What's New, What Isn't." *New York Times*, April 27, 1995.

Rodriguez, Richard. *Days of Obligation: An Argument with My Mexican Father*. New York: Viking, 1992.

Role of Women in Development. New York: United Nations Publications, 1989.

Role of Women in Rebuilding the Russian Economy. Women's Labor and Training Conference Final Report, Moscow. Washington, D.C.: Counterpart Foundation, Inc., 1994.

Rowen, Hobart. "Giving Population Planning a Boost, Despite the Vatican's Opposition." *Washington Post*, June 19, 1994.

———. "At Treasury, They're Banking on Women—Finally." *Washington Post*, July 18, 1994.

Russell, Cheryl. "Finding the Missing Men." *American Demographics*, May 1995.

Saffo, Paul. "It's the Context, Stupid." *Wired*, March 1994.

Scanning the Future: A Long-Term Scenario Study of the World Economy 1990–2015. Central Planning Bureau. The Hague: Sdu Publishers, 1992.

Schell, Orville. *Mandate of Heaven.* New York: Simon & Schuster, 1994.

Schiebinger, Londa. *Nature's Body: Gender in the Making of Modern Science.* Boston: Beacon Press, 1993.

Schmidt, William. "The Fertile Crescent Blooms Anew." *New York Times,* November 6, 1994.

Schwartz, Felice. "Management Women and the New Facts of Life." *Harvard Business Review,* January–February 1989.

———. "Women as a Business Imperative." *Harvard Business Review,* March–April 1992.

Schwartz, Peter. *The Art of the Long View: Planning for the Future in an Uncertain World.* New York: Doubleday, 1991.

———. "Shockwave (Anti)Warrior: An Interview with Alvin Toffler." *Wired,* November 1993.

———. "Interview with Peter Drucker." *Wired,* May 1994.

Science. Special Issue on Women, March 11, 1994.

Segal, David. "The Shell Game." *Washington Monthly,* July–August 1993.

Shapiro, Harvey. "After NAFTA." *Hemispheres,* March 1995.

Shaw, Bernard. "Our Attitude about Women." *Alfred M. Landon Lectures on Public Issues Series,* Kansas State University, Manhattan, Kansas, November 20, 1992.

Shearer, Rhonda Roland. "From Flatland to Fractaland: New Geometries in Relationship to Artistic and Scientific Revolutions." Symposium on the occasion of Benoit Mandelbrot's Seventieth Birthday, Boston, Mass., 1994.

———. *The Flatland Hypothesis: Geometric Structures of Artistic and Scientific Revolutions.* New York: Springer-Verlag, forthcoming.

Shiva, Vananda. *Staying Alive: Women, Ecology, and Development.* Atlantic Highlands, N.J.: Zed Books, 1989.

———, ed. *Close to Home: Women Reconnect Ecology, Health and Development Worldwide.* Philadelphia: New Society Publishers, 1994.

Sohoni, Neera. "Being Female Can Be Deadly." *San Francisco Chronicle*, January 31, 1994.

State of World Rural Poverty. International Fund for Agricultural Development. Rome: Arti Grafiche Fratelli Palombi, 1992.

Stephenson, Neal. "In the Kingdom of Mao Bell." *Wired*, February 1994.

Sterling, Bruce. "War Is Virtual Hell." *Wired*, premiere issue, 1993.

Stone, Merlin. *When God Was a Woman*. San Diego: Harvest/HBJ, 1976.

Strossen, Nadine. *Defending Pornography: Free Speech, Sex, and the Fight for Women's Rights*. New York: Scribner, 1995.

Swoboda, Frank. "The Case for Corporate Downsizing Goes Global." *Washington Post*, April 9, 1995.

Sullivan, Walter. "New Theory on Ice Sheet Catastrophe Is the Direst One Yet." *New York Times*, May 2, 1995.

Tannen, Deborah. *That's Not What I Meant!* New York: Ballantine Books, 1986.

———. *You Just Don't Understand*. New York: Ballantine Books, 1990.

Tax, Meredith. *The Power of the Word: Culture, Censorship and Voice*. New York: Women's World Organization for Rights, Literature and Development, 1995.

Thomas, Pierre. "Women in Charge at Justice Department." *Washington Post*, July 29, 1994.

"The Tiger Steps Out: A Survey of India." *Economist*, January 21, 1995.

Times-Mirror Center for the People and the Press. *Technology in the American Household*. May 1994.

Toffler, Alvin, and Heidi Toffler. *Creating a New Civilization: The Politics of the Third Wave*. Atlanta: Turner Publishing, 1995.

Tomasevski, Katarina. *Women and Human Rights*. Atlantic Highlands, N.J.: Zed Books, 1994.

Toward Gender Equality: The Role of Public Policy. Washington, D.C.: World Bank, 1995.

Tracy, William. "Mapping the Middle East in America." *Aramco News*, November–December 1994.

"Transforming Development for the 21st Century." *Unifem News* 3, no. 1 (March 1995).

Truong, Thanh-dam. *Sex, Money and Morality: Prostitution and Tourism in Southeast Asia*. Atlantic Highlands, N.J.: Zed Books, 1990.

Tuljapurkar, S., N. Li, and M. W. Feldman. "High Sex Ratios in China's Future." *Science*, February 10, 1995.

Turkle, Sherry. *Life on the Screen*. New York: Simon & Schuster, 1995.

"Two Muslim Prime Ministers Visit Scarred Bosnian Capital." *San Francisco Chronicle*, February 3, 1994.

Tyler, Patrick E. "At Women's Forum, Peru's Leader Defies Church." *New York Times*, September 13, 1995.

UNIFEM Annual Report, 1992. New York: United Nations Development Fund for Women, 1992.

U.S. Congress. House. Committee on Armed Services. *Defense for a New Era: Lessons of the Persian Gulf War*. 102nd Cong., 2d sess. Washington, D.C.: U.S. Government Printing Office, 1992.

U.S. Congress. House. Committee on Small Business. *New Economic Realities: The Rise of Women Entrepreneurs*. 100th Cong., 2d sess. Washington, D.C.: U.S. Government Printing Office, 1988.

U.S. Congress. Senate. Joint hearings before the Committee on Foreign Relations and the Committee on the Judiciary. *International Terrorism, Insurgency and Drug Trafficking: Present Trends in Terrorist Activity*. 99th Cong., 1st sess. Washington, D.C.: U.S. Government Printing Office, 1986.

U.S. Congress. Senate. Subcommittee on Terrorism, Narcotics and International Communications of the Committee on Foreign Relations. *Drugs, Law Enforcement and Foreign Policy: Panama*. 100th Cong. Parts 1, 2. Washington, D.C.: U.S. Government Printing Office, 1988.

U.S. Congress. Senate. Subcommittee on Terrorism, Narcotics and International Operations of the Committee on Foreign Relations. *Drugs, Law Enforcement and Foreign Policy: The Cartel, Haiti and Central America*. 100th Cong., 2d sess. Washington, D.C.: U.S. Government Printing Office, 1989.

U.S. Department of Labor, Federal Glass Ceiling Commission. *Good for Business: Making Full Use of the Nation's Human Capital*. Washington, D.C., March 1995.

U.S. Department of Labor, Women's Bureau. *Working Women Count: A Report to the Nation*. Washington, D.C.: U.S. Government Printing Office, 1994.

Vasilieva, Larissa. *Kremlin Wives*. New York: Arcade Publishing, 1992.

Wall, Steve. *Wisdom's Daughters: Conversations with Women Elders of Native America*. New York: HarperCollins, 1994.

Waring, Marilyn. *If Women Counted: A New Feminist Economics*. New York: Harper & Row, 1988.

Weinstein, Marsha. "Coalition of U.S. Women for CEDAW, the Convention on the Elimination of All Forms of Discrimination Against Women." *World Wide Web*. http://www.igc.apc.org/womensnet/beijing/

"Welcome to Cyberspace." Special Issue. *Time*, Spring 1995.

"When George Soros Meets Granny Smith." *Economist*, April 22, 1995.

"When Will Women Get to the Top?" *Fortune*, September 1992.

Whitney, Craig R. "Comfortable Germans, Slow to Change (Especially If It Means More Work)." *New York Times*, December 18, 1994.

Wikan, Unni. *Behind the Veil in Arabia: Women in Oman*. Chicago: University of Chicago Press, 1991.

Witt, Linda, Karen Paget, and Glenna Matthews. *Running as a Woman: Gender and Power in American Politics*. New York: The Free Press, 1994.

Wolf, Naomi. *Fire with Fire*. New York: Random House, 1993.

"Women Changing Travelers' Profile." *USA Today*, November 15, 1994.

"Work and Family." *Business Week*, June 28, 1993.

World Bank Annual Report 1993. Washington, D.C.: World Bank, 1993.

World Bank Atlas 1994. Washington, D.C.: World Bank, 1993.

World's Women 1970–1990: Trends and Statistics. Social Statistics and Indicators, Series K, No. 8. New York: United Nations, 1991.

Wulf, Dierdre. *Refugee Women and Reproductive Health Care: Reassessing Priorities*. New York: IRC Women's Commission for Refugee Women and Children, June 1994.

Yergin, Daniel, and Thane Gustafson. *Russia 2010*. New York: Random House, 1993.

Zia, Helen. "The Global Fund for Women: Money with a Mission." *Ms.*, July–August 1993.

Zuckerman, Harriet, Jonathan R. Cole, and John T. Bruer. *The Outer Circle: Women in the Scientific Community.* New Haven, Conn.: Yale University Press, 1992.

INDEX